E-WASTE MANAGEMENT

This book offers an extensive review of e-waste management in India, the world's third-largest producer of waste from electrical and electronic equipment. With a focus on the evolution of legal frameworks in India and the world, it presents impacts and outcomes; challenges and opportunities; and management strategies and practices to deal with e-waste. First of its kind, the book examines relevant concepts and issues from across 15 disciplines and six areas of policy making and will serve as a comprehensive knowledge base on electronic waste in India. It links key themes to the global context of Sustainable Development Goals and explores the convergence with technological, infrastructural, and social initiatives in e-waste management.

A range of topics are discussed, such as resource efficiency policies; circular economy; toxicity; technicalities and complexities of e-waste management including role of the informal sector and need for recognising social and human costs in policy making. The book deals with the role of statistics; legal trends and reforms; linkages with green Agenda 2030 and UN initiatives; implementation of Extended Producer Responsibility (EPR); environmental factors; business prospects; consequences on human health; Life Cycle Impact Assessment; the 'six Rs' (Responsible use, Repair, Refurbish, Recycle, Recover and Reuse); recycling practices and problems, material flow and informal sector in trade value chain; fostering partnership between formal-informal sectors; safe disposal; alternatives to landfilling; role of jurisprudence and regulatory bodies; and education and awareness. It also includes a survey of pan-India initiatives and trajectories of law-driven initiatives for effective e-waste management along with responses from industries and producers.

Timely and essential, this volume will be useful to scholars and researchers of environment studies, digital waste management, waste management, development studies, public policy, political ecology, sustainable development, technology and manufacturing, design and instrumentation, environmental and international law, taxation, commerce, electronic industry, economics, business management, metallurgy, and engineering, labour studies, as well as to policymakers, nongovernmental organisations, and interested general readers.

Varsha Bhagat-Ganguly is Professor at Institute of Law, Nirma University, Ahmedabad, India. She has been Professor at Centre for Rural Studies, Lal Bahadur Shastri National Academy of Administration, Mussoorie, and Fellow at Indian Institute of Advanced Study, Shimla. She has worked in the education and development sector as a development sociologist and has conducted research studies on various social and developmental issues. She focuses on linking field-based and academic research with its versatile applications, including ground-up public policy regime, strategic action plan for social change, and raising awareness and communication. Among her publications are 15 books and 22 research articles/book chapters. She has been an editor of three academic journals. Her areas of interest are research for development, land question, citizen's rights and collective actions, process of marginalisation and Gujarat.

E-WASTE MANAGEMENT

Challenges and Opportunities in India

Varsha Bhagat-Ganguly

LONDON AND NEW YORK

First published 2022
by Routledge
2 Park Square, Milton Park, Abingdon, Oxon OX14 4RN

and by Routledge
605 Third Avenue, New York, NY 10158

Routledge is an imprint of the Taylor & Francis Group, an informa business

© 2022 Varsha Bhagat-Ganguly

The right of Varsha Bhagat-Ganguly to be identified as author of this work has been asserted by her in accordance with sections 77 and 78 of the Copyright, Designs and Patents Act 1988.

All rights reserved. No part of this book may be reprinted or reproduced or utilised in any form or by any electronic, mechanical or other means, now known or hereafter invented, including photocopying and recording or in any information storage or retrieval system, without permission in writing from the publishers.

Trademark notice: Product or corporate names may be trademarks or registered trademarks, and are used only for identification and explanation without intent to infringe.

British Library Cataloguing-in-Publication Data
A catalogue record for this book is available from the British Library

Library of Congress Cataloging-in-Publication Data
A catalog record has been requested for this book

ISBN: 978-0-367-14724-2 (hbk)
ISBN: 978-0-367-24998-4 (pbk)
ISBN: 978-0-429-28542-4 (ebk)

DOI: 10.4324/9780429285424

Typeset in Bembo
by SPi Technologies India Pvt Ltd (Straive)

To Hirak and Isha

CONTENTS

List of illustrations viii
Preface x
Acknowledgements xv
List of abbreviations xviii

Chapter 1   Sustainable development and e-waste management   1

Chapter 2   Extended producer responsibility: a mainstay for e-waste management   49

Chapter 3   Toxicity and impacts on environment and human health   68

Chapter 4   Treating e-waste, resource efficiency, and circular economy   93

Chapter 5   E-waste management through legislations in India   108

Chapter 6   Strategies and initiatives for dealing with e-waste in India   133

Chapter 7   Moving towards horizons   165

Bibliography *183*
Index *199*

LIST OF ILLUSTRATIONS

Figures

1.1	Life cycle of an e-product	4
1.2	Hazardous and non-hazardous substances in e-products	5
1.3	Components of e-waste management	7
1.4	Tackling e-waste	31
1.5	E-waste generation in India (2005–2019)	36
1.6	Essentials of cohesive e-waste management thinking in India	38
1.7	E-waste flow and recycling scenario in India	40
3.1	Toxicity, environmental, and health impacts	69
3.2	Toxicity, EoL solution, and environmental concerns	71
3.3	Environmental mapping of a smart phone manufacturing	73
4.1	Recycling, resource efficiency, and circular economy	94
4.2	Linear economy model versus circular economy model	99
4.3	Recycling, circular economy, and improvement in environment	100
4.4	Number of recycling units in India (2010–2021)	104
6.1	Overview of pan-Indian initiatives for dealing with e-waste during 2000 and 2020	146
6.2	Policy issues for e-waste management before 2010	148
7.1	Way ahead for e-waste management in India	166

Tables

1.1	E-waste generation between 2013 and 2019 across the globe	3
1.2	E-waste quantities as per its categories – comparing 2016 and 2019	10
1.3	E-waste generation, collection, and recycling across regions – comparing 2016 and 2019 data	10

1.4	Environmental, health, and economic data from undocumented flows of e-waste (2019)	13
1.5	Countries having legislation or policy for e-waste management (2019)	17
1.6	Overview of RoHS 1,2,3	22
1.7	Multi-lateral environmental agreements signed by different regions	25
1.8	UN initiatives to tackle e-waste across different regions during 2004 and 2017	34
2.1	An overview of EPR implementation under legislation/policy in different countries	55
3.1	Emissions from primary production of metals used in a personal computer	72
3.2	Comparison of use of energy and water consumption in production of metals from e-waste and ores	72
3.3	Three tier treatment processes for recycling e-waste	76
3.4	Pollutants and their occurrence in WEEE, and impact on human health	82
4.1	Constituents of e-waste	96
4.2	Metal recovered from 1,000 kg of PCBs and perception value based on prevalent market rate (2009)	102
4.3	Comparative of recycling processes, recovery, and cost calculations	105
5.1	Overview of Indian regulations under which e-waste was managed	113
5.2	An overview of *E-waste (Management) Rules, 2016* and *Amendment Rules, 2018*	117
5.3	EPR as regulatory, enforcement, and awareness creation strategy under the *Rules, 2016*	120
5.4	State's initiatives for implementation of EPR for e-waste management	122
5.5	Recycling facility in India as on 24 March 2021	123
5.6	CAG reporting performance of CPCB for e-waste management (2015)	125

Boxes

1.1	SDGs and e-waste related targets and indicators	32
3.1	PCBs as a resource and as a hazardous object	76
3.2	Mapping health hazards of cell phones	81

PREFACE

The usual way of introducing the Indian electronic waste (e-waste) sector is through three highlights: extent of e-waste generation and India ranking fifth in 2017 (ranking third in 2020), the dominant presence of the informal sector across the value chain (collection, dismantling, recycling, and resale of the recovered materials) of e-waste, and rudimentary methods for recycling which are creating challenges of environment and health hazards, and legal provisions that have created opportunities for scientific recycling and operationalising e-waste management in a formal manner. There is a long way to go, as most Indians are not aware of the facts and the dangers the hazards that e-waste can create. As a development sociologist, I understood that the informal sector is inferred with its multiple connotations, including cash economy, the units engaged in collection and recycling are not registered and not covered under the existing law/s, consequently not complying on minimum wages, not providing safe working environment, employment of child labour would be rampant, unsafe way of recycling, and no accountability for throwing away the residues, cash transactions between different actors engaged in these operations, and so on. This means that the informal sector is either unaware of the consequences of adverse impact on health and environment, or that there exists a wide gap between the 'desirables' and the 'doings', on the counts of accountability, legal compliance, subsidising costs of labour, human health, and environment, etc. between the government and these informal operations. I started understanding the contrasts at every level, existing polarity in the discourse, i.e, dominant presence of informal economy across the value chain of e-waste, and compromising on environment protection, human health concerns versus the government's need and urge for regularisation of e-waste through regulations, and pushing it towards formal and circular economy without recognising human and social costs. In between these two poles, the following dimensions of e-waste are becoming linked sporadically, repeatedly, such as, need for spreading awareness across consumers and enforcement of 'E-waste

Management Rules', 2016; need for fostering informal and formal sector's partnerships; policy dialogues with the concerned authorities in each state, especially the regulatory bodies; understanding EPR and its non-effective implementation due to 'leakage' of e-waste, and how legal binding is counter-productive for e-waste management; and role of different stakeholders, and nitty-gritties of legal compliance.

While working with Urmul Trust as an ecosystem partner to the 'E-waste Management Program in India', launched by International Finance Corporation (IFC), and a producer responsibility organisation (PRO), Karo Sambhav Pvt. Ltd., in four states of western India for almost 20 months, I learnt about different macro-miso-micro aspects, dimensions, processes linked to e-waste management. My academic and catalytic mind promoting people-centric policy and initiatives motivated me to write about these experiences. Thus, this publication is a combination of academic, entrepreneurial and policy pursuits that signals ground realities, and captures and communicates comprehensive discourse on e-waste management, sharing technicalities and complexities of e-waste which require special attention in its management, and spreading awareness among users – students, academics, and researchers, policy makers at national and international levels, and conveying solidarity as a potential actor for the e-waste management.

Organising different aspects of e-waste has been a very challenging task, as it combines at least 15 academic disciplines across the globe, and each disciplines has created specific literature, they are: management; technology – instrumentation, complying with international standards, cost-effectiveness, and indigeneity; medicine; toxicity and bio-chemistry/medical; design of an electronic product (e-product); electronics/electronic engineering or computer engineering, that is, selection of components – hazardous, non-hazardous and their assembly; environment engineering; chemical engineering; metallurgy; law – national and international legislations/regulations, treaties, covenants, bi-lateral or multi-lateral agreements, etc; commerce – revenue and tax regime including advance fee, business models, producer's responsibilities and costs; public policy/administration; circular economy (CE) and resource efficiency (RE) cutting across many sectors; waste management; development studies; community development/labour studies/civil society engagement; statistics; and international relations. Each discipline has its specific knowledge pool and resources, which are overlapping and/or closely linked with other disciplines. Due to these characteristics of e-waste, several points are repetitively talked about, yet every person looks at from own academic discipline. For example, 'recycling' of e-waste is spread across ten disciplines, which include toxicity; chemical engineering; technology; high-cost recycling infrastructure; recycling standards and REs; resource recovery and resale of recovered materials across the world; legal provisions/bindings across the nation and the world for movement or sale of materials (especially metals – basic, precious, rare earths, etc.) for e-products; use of water, energy, fossils, etc. during the production of an e-product; impact on living being including humans, and environment; treatment for the health problems or health care required; and protection measures – adhering to landfilling standards (avoiding leaching), safety measures for the workers, and so on. Therefore, 'recycling' as an end-of-life (EoL) solution appears across every chapter, with specific reference to legal provisions, impact on health and environment, CE, technological innovations, etc.

As multiple disciplines are linked to the e-waste and its management, each discipline highlights its view on e-waste but linking different disciplines with other is challenging. I have consciously built bridges between different disciplines for evolving a picture of e-waste management thinking in India. For example, 'sustainable development' remains a common concern for e-waste management. Historically, environment protection has been a major concern for 'sustainable development,' which led to focus on 'Design for Environment' (DfE) aspects of e-waste, such as use of materials, assembly and dismantling of the materials, life span, potential for increasing life span through repair/refurbish, etc. as well as legal binding on movements of e-waste within a country or to the other countries. The *WEEE Directives* and *Basel Convention* are repeatedly referred to as part of e-waste management. GHG emissions while treating e-waste contributing to global warming; contamination of air, water and soil, etc; indiscriminate use of natural resources during production of e-products; etc. are major concerns expressed for safe environment. Along with legal/regulatory framework, Extended Producer Responsibility (EPR) is considered to be a core part of 'sustainable development,' with a reference to 'who bears the cost for environment protection?' and each country is expected to evolve tax regime for the producer and the users for collection to disposal of e-waste in environmentally sound manner. These are the reasons for the engagement of United Nations (UN) and its different agencies (StEP Initiative, UNEMG, UNU, UNU-ViE SCYCLE) in undertaking special programmes for e-waste management across different regions, including standardising methods for creating harmonised statistics on e-waste, Carbon emission, collection and recycling, and legal/regulatory framework across the world; entered partnership with other international agencies; capacity building measures; and linking e-waste to different Sustainable Development Goals (SDGs) as part of the Agenda 2030. Similarly, the concepts of CE and REs have become policy buzzwords and concepts for operationalisation across many sectors in the context of waste management in general, specifically applicable to e-waste, with inherent limitation of overlooking human and social costs.

With this overview of strategies, approaches for dealing with e-waste and key concepts/terms, an outline of the chapters is shared here. Every chapter covers one important aspect/theme of e-waste management, connecting aspects with other chapters; each chapter has India-specific details in the context of a topic under discussion and global scenario. Thus, the entire book comprehensively covers different aspects of e-waste management. Three chapters exclusively focus on India, they are: on pan-India initiatives; legislative framework; and way forward sharing how the law-driven initiatives have started rolling the ball, and has created several opportunities, and potential areas for further exploration for effective e-waste management.

The first chapter introduces the reader to the existing discourse on e-waste and its management with its development of definition in the world, statistics across the world, opportunities, and challenges that are articulated as part of legal/

regulatory framework, SDGs, CE, and LCIA (Life Cycle Impact Assessment) and MFA (Material Flow Analysis) followed by introducing Indian scenario. Chapter 2 comprehensively discusses EPR as a concept, a strategy, a regulatory framework for achieving specified goals across different countries; the Indian scenario is discussed in detail in this chapter. Chapter 3 focuses on toxicity and its impacts on environment and human health. The recycling chain, three-tier treatment processes for recycling e-waste, and technology are described to map recycling risks (release of different toxins, extent of toxicity), linking with hazardous impact of e-waste on human health described with types of pollutants and which pollutant affect which part of human body, in which form are described. Chapter 4 is brief, focusing on recycling-resource efficiency-CE themes in the context of resource use and sustainable development. Urban mining, informal sector operations and need for resource use policy, financial support for recycling infrastructure building, etc. are discussed in Indian context. Chapter 5 presents Indian policy regime and examines how – and to what extent – different aspects of e-waste management have been incorporated in the existing regulatory framework. After presenting historical deliberations on e-waste as hazardous waste and legal framework, it discusses the *E-waste Management Rules, 2016* and the *Amendment Rules 2018* in detail including assessing EPR as a strategy and its enforcement, and role and performance of regulatory body. There is a separate section on evolving jurisprudence on e-waste management, which is in very nascent state, and towards the end, the chapter briefly compares Indian legislation with international legislatures. Chapter 6 encompasses pan-Indian initiatives dealing with e-waste management in detail, ranging from building knowledge base through research and social action by different stakeholders to technological and legal advancements, and industrial initiatives. All these initiatives are organised on time scale, in a manner, to capture every initiative in its context with its evolutionary journey. Throughout the chapter, roles played by different Indian actors – government agencies, industry actors, non-government agencies, research institutions, and the judiciary – and how each one interacted with bi-lateral, multi-lateral and international actors/agencies on individual or collective basis are mapped out. The initiatives include measures awareness raising; educational initiatives; conducting research on various topics, such as, formal-informal partnership, gap analysis in e-waste management based on multi-stakeholder views, etc; preparing roadmap for the Agenda 2030; experimentation for REs and working out its economics as part of CE and bringing in standardisation; and launching academic courses on e-waste management. Chapter 7, being the last chapter, summarises the e-waste scenario, opportunities and challenges around four domains: legal and judicial domain; economic concerns; recycling culture/society; and environment concerns.

A few points on stylistics are shared here. As the existing vast, repetitive literature on e-waste covers different disciplines, bringing uniformity is necessary. First, in most literature, names of the metals are written with chemical names and in small letters; I have continued the same style here, by writing the name of the metal, followed by its chemical name in parenthesis if required, for example, silver (Ag). Second, sometimes, one report is cited in two ways, one with its author's name another with its publisher's name, for instance, 'StEP Green Paper 2015' and 'McCann and Wittmann 2015'. In such cases, name/s of the authors are preferred over the agency. Third, regarding references, original sources are cited rather using 'quoted in'; only in cases where the original source is not accessible, the phrase 'quoted in' is used. This is one of the reasons that some sources are of 1980s and 1990s, especially related chemical methods used in recycling and toxicity, resource recovery, etc. Use of such references also indicates that either the newer methods and results are not developed or there is a possibility of repetitive use references are in circulation, which is one of the characteristics of the literature related to e-waste. Fourth, most tables and illustrations are prepared based on more than one sources, and wherever it is based on one source, the material is revised or reorganised or compiled rather than reproduced. All the legislations are presented in italics, e.g., *E-waste Management Rules, 2016*, and *Environment Protection Act, 1986*.

By covering e-waste management in India in its totality, from multiple perspectives and academic disciplines, this book will serve as a guide to understanding e-waste management and benefit everyone.

ACKNOWLEDGEMENTS

Anshul Ojha and Pranshu Singhal are the first to be acknowledged, having introduced me to the e-waste sector and e-waste challenges in India. Both as e-waste sector practitioners, Anshul exposed me to the entire value chain and human interface at every stage, starting from the role of last mile collectors (LMCs) in e-waste collection to the repair, refurbishing, recycling, and final disposal. As Pranshu is a veteran practitioner of e-waste management, I could learn from and discuss industry perspective with him, providing exposure to possible solutions, and vast opportunities and potentials of e-waste management. This book was to be written with Pranshu, a founder of a PRO – Karo Sambhav Pvt. Ltd. ('Karo' henceforth); however, he could not continue his journey as a co-author because of the exponential growth of 'Karo' and adopting different ways of knowledge management. My sincere gratitude to Anshul and Pranshu for being co-travellers all these days.

As a partner of the ecosystem created by the IFC and Karo under the 'E-waste Program in India', I was exposed to several industry actors, practitioners, policy makers, and practitioners, senior bureaucrats, media persons, and others. Each one of them has been a co-traveller in knowledge-based advocacy, action, and policy pursuit, and has contributed to my learning about e-waste management across the globe and India-specific thinking and practices. Among them, I thank Mr Sanjit Rodrigues who provided me an opportunity and support for understanding e-waste scenario in Goa state, and for chalking out e-waste management plan. This exposure has helped me tremendously in reflecting ground reality, linking them to technical and technological solutions, and policy spaces. In the same spirit, I am thankful to team members, late Arvind Ojha, late Ravi Mishra, Sudheer Pillai, Vipin Upadhyay, Abhijit Sonavane, Shabbir and Dinesh Sharma for providing me exposure to ground reality through different operations across e-waste sector.

Very special thanks to Dr Satish Sinha, Toxics Link, Ms. Rachna Arora, GIZ, Mr Naresh Thakar, engineer (retired), Gujarat State Pollution Control Board and associated with Nisarg Community Science Centre, Gandhinagar; and Mr Devang Thakar, engineer in charge for e-waste management, Gujarat State Pollution Control Board for sharing their pioneering work experiences on e-waste management, provided necessary reading materials, discussed different policy points of e-waste management, and recent initiatives on standardisation in e-waste sector. Along with seeking information about e-waste sector from them, I could gain major insights, developed knowledge and policy pursuits and their operationalisations. Dr Satish Sinha went through the last chapter and abstracts of all the chapters at the last minute, and we could together scan the entire manuscript from human, institutional, and toxicity perspectives. The last-minute value additions could take place with this interaction, and we sincerely hope that such changes in e-waste sector can take place with this spirit. These interactions make me humbler and grateful to Satish Ji, Nareshbhai, Devangbhai, and all other who have contributed to the process of academic deliberations and policy pursuits for efficient e-waste sector.

I have interviewed important industrial actors including Dr S Parthasarathy, Managing Director of E-Parisaraa; Dr Sandip Chatterjee, Director, Ministry of Electronics Information Technology (MeitY), Government of India; Ms. Wilma Rodrigues, founder and member of SAAHAS Zero Waste; Ms. Smita Rajabali representing Swachh, Pune; Mr Nivit Kumar Yadav, *Down to Earth* magazine, Centre for Science and Environment, New Delhi; Ms Pallavi Joshi working with waste aggregators in Maharashtra state; and Mr Bablu, Rongjeng Technologies working for e-waste management in the north-eastern states of India. I am extremely thankful to all of them for their interactions with me, sparing time for the interviews, sharing their work experiences and chalking out policy points for dealing with e-waste efficiently in India. Interactions with them have helped in building up a complex jigsaw puzzle of e-waste sector and management in India, incorporating global perspectives, processes, and practices.

Ms. Rejitha Nair, a law teacher, my friend and former colleague at Nirma University, requires special thanks. She read the entire chapter on Indian legislative initiatives and gave feedback. Discussions with her from a legal perspective – on legal framework, jurisprudence, and linking legal provisions with the ground reality – have been meaningful in building up the discourse on legislative driven implementation for e-waste management in India. Special thanks to Ms. Reena Banerjee for her unconditional support in organising the manuscript, meticulous checking and verification and ensuring flawless lists and boxes, figures, and tables, abbreviations, and more than 250 references. Managing such academically important yet cumbersome, tedious tasks through a friend's help is highly valued and I express here my gratitude for the assistance received. Often, I used to feel overwhelmed with multiple, technical facets of e-waste and its management, and spent sleepless nights. I am grateful to many of my friends, relatives, and supporters for their cheers and encouragement at every stage of this book, among them, Nirav Mahadevia, Nupur, Rasila Kadia, and Shilpa Vasavada deserve special mention. The reviewer of the book deserves special mention and thanks; based on the reviewer's comments, I reorganised the entire manuscript – the chapters, content of every chapter, added special section presenting Indian scenario, and added comparisons between other countries vis-à-vis India in the contexts of legislations, and strategies and actions dealing with e-waste. I thank each and every one who has helped in completion of this book, whether named or not named.

I wish to thank Ms. Shoma Choudhury, Ms. Rimina Mohapatra, and the team of Routledge for their support for this book. Almost three years ago, when Shoma suggested to submit a proposal for writing this book, e-waste as a sector was not much explored by academics and policy makers. She could foresee the importance of this book, and has been supportive throughout, at every stage of the publication process.

I cannot thank enough Hirak, my son, and Isha, my daughter-in-law, who have supported me wholeheartedly in the completion of this book. It took almost 30 months to complete; more intensively during last 14 months (pandemic time). On one hand, the lockdown and no socialisation provided special opportunity to work on the book, but on the other hand, we as a family faced pandemic associated uncertainties, additional burden of house chores, sleepless nights, etc. Both ensured my intensive working on this book during this very challenging, testing time. Moreover, Hirak, as a practicing lawyer, helped me extensively in identifying, organising legal materials, and explaining every legal case on e-waste, difference between different courts, and bearing of the judgement/order of the respective Court on the e-waste management, and so on.

ABBREVIATIONS

Ag	Silver
Al	Aluminium
As	Arsenic
Au	Gold
ARF	Advanced Recycling Fee
Ba	Barium
BAT	Best available technologies
Be	Beryllium
Bi	Bismuth
BAN	Basel Action Network
BCRCSEA	Basel Convention Regional Centre for South-East Asia
BER	Brand Environmental Responsibility
BFR	Brominated flame retardants
BIS	Bureau for Indian Standards
BMZ	German Ministry of Economic Co-operation and Development
Br	Bromine
CAG	Comptroller and Auditor General
CAGR	Compound Annual Growth Rate
Cd	Cadmium
CD	Compact disc
CE	Circular Economy
C&F	Cooling and freezing
CFC	Chlorofluorocarbon
CII	Confederation of Indian Industries
Co	Cobalt
CO$_2$	Carbon dioxide
COP	Conference of the parties

CPCB	Central Pollution Control Board
CPR	Collective Producer Responsibility
CPU	Central Processing Unit
CRM	Critical Raw Material
CRS	Compulsory Registration Scheme
CRT	Cathode Ray Tube
CSO	Civil society organisation
Cu	Copper
DFE	Design for Environment
DGFT	Directorate General of Foreign Trade
DPCC	Delhi Pollution Control Committee
DRF	Deposit Refund Scheme
DRS	Deposit Refund Scheme
DVD	Digital Versatile Disc
ECHA	European Chemicals Agency
EEE	Electrical and electronic equipment
ELCINA	Electronic Industries Association of India
EMG	Environment Management Group
EMPA	Swiss Federal Laboratories for Materials Testing and Research / Swiss Federal Institute for Materials Science and Technology
ENVIS	Enrichment of Environmental Information System
EOL	End-of-life
EPA	Environment Protection Agency, USA
EPR	Extended Producer Responsibility
ESM	Environmentally sound management
ESDM	Electronics System Design and Manufacturing
EU	European Union
EUR	Euro
FDES	Framework for the Development of Environment Statistics
Fe	Iron
GEM	Global E-waste Monitor
GESP	Global E-waste Statistics Partnership
GHG	Greenhouse gas
GIZ	German International Co-operation
GOI	Government of India
GPS	Global positioning system
Hg	Mercury
HS CODE	Harmonised Trade System code
Ir	Iridium
IT	Information technology
JICA	Japan International Co-operation Agency
IC	Integrated Circuit
ICT	Information and Communication Technology
ILO	International Labour Organisation

In	Indium
IPR	Individual Producer Responsibility
Ir	Iridium
ISIC	International Standard Industrial Classification
ISWA	International Solid Waste Association
IT	Information Technology
ITU	International Telecommunication Union
Kg	Kilogram
Kg/inh	Kilogram per inhabitant
Kt	Kiloton
LCIA	Life Cycle Impact Assessment
LCD	Liquid Crystal Display
LED	Light Emitting Diode
LMC	Last mile collector
LOW	List of Wastes
MAIT	Manufacturers Association of Information Technology
MEITY	Ministry of Electronics and Information Technology
MEA	Multi-lateral environmental agreement
MFA	Material Flow Analysis
Mg	Magnesium
MJ	Megajoule
Mn	Manganese
MPCB	Maharashtra Pollution Control Board
MSTC	Metal Scrap Trading Corporation
MSW	Municipal Solid Waste
MT	Metric ton
Mt	Million Metric Tonne
NASSCOM	National Association of Software and Services Companies
NEP	National Environment Policy
NEAP	National Electronics Action Plan
NGO	Non-government organisation
Ni	Nickel
NITI AAYOG	National Institution for Transforming India
NSDC	National Skill Development Corporation
OECD	Organisation for Economic Co-operation and Development
OEM	Original equipment manufacturer
OSH	Occupational safety and health
PACE	Platform for Accelerating the Circular Economy
PAH	Polycyclic Aromatic Hydrocarbons
Pb	Lead
PBB	Polybrominated biphenyls
PBDE	Polybrominated diphenyl ethers
PC	Personal computer
PCB	Printed circuit boards

PCB	Polychlorinated biphenyls
PCC	Pollution Control Committee
Pd	Palladium
PGM	Platinum Group Metals
PIAP	Pan-India Awareness Programme
PIC	Prior informed consent
PICT	Pacific Island countries and territories
PIP	Person in the Port
POP	Persistent Organic Pollutant
PRO	Produce Responsibility Organisation
Pt	Platinum
PUM	Put on market
PVC	Poly vinyl chloride
PWB	Printed wiring board
RE	Resource Efficiency
REACH	Registration, Evaluation, Authorisation, and Restrictions of Chemical Substances
Rh	Rhodium
ROHS	Restriction of Hazardous Substance
Ru	Ruthenium
SAICM	Strategic Approach to International Chemicals Management
Sb	Antimony
SECO	Swiss State Secretariat for Economic Affairs
SCYCLE	Sustainable Cycles
SCP	Sustainable consumption and production
Se	Selenium
SEEA	System of Environmental-Economic Accounting
SCGJ	Skill Council for Green Jobs
SME	Small and Medium Enterprise
SNA	System of National Accounts
Si	Silicon
Sn	Tin
SO2	Sulphur dioxide
SR	Strontium
STEP	Solving the E-waste Problem
SVHC	Substances of Very High Concern
TBBPA	Tetrabromobisphenol A
Te	Tellurium
TGEW	Task Group on Measuring E-Waste
TV	Television
UK	United Kingdom
UNECE	United Nations Economic Commission for Europe
UNEMG	United Nations Environment Management Group
UNEP	United Nations Environment Programme

UNSD	United Nations Statistics Division
ULB	Urban Local Body
UNU	United Nations University
UPPCB	Uttar Pradesh State Pollution Control Board
US-EPA	United States Environment Protection Agency
USD	United States Dollar
VCSS	Voluntary consensus sustainability standards
WEEE	Waste Electrical and Electronic Equipment
WEF	World Economic Forum

1
SUSTAINABLE DEVELOPMENT AND E-WASTE MANAGEMENT

> Tackling particular e-waste issues often requires the consideration of a wide range of perspectives, including interactions with labour, health, environment, logistics, management practices, regulations, chemicals, consumer preferences and cultures etc... In considering these perspectives when tackling e-waste, the strengthening of collaboration and partnerships among UN entities and other stakeholders, may be an important step forwards in addition to the sharing of knowledge, data and information, expertise and monetary resources.
> United Nations Environment Management Group (2017: 42)

Importance of electrical and electronic equipment in a nation's development, and e-waste as toxic companion of digital era

A country's development or any modern society is often epitomised with the communication revolution of 1980s and the digital revolution since the 1990s. The communication revolution has brought enormous changes in the way we organise our lives, our economies, industries, and institutions. The revolution is observed in form of development, comfort, technological advancement and ever-increasing sale of these products. The digital technology facilitates transformation of information, communication, transportation, energy supply, health, and security systems, making a country more productive and developed. This technology is proliferated with different electrical and electronics equipment (EEE) or e-products, such as PCs, the Internet, Satellite TV, standardised containers, fibre-optic cables, electronic barcodes, and global supply chains, making human lives more convenient and work more efficient (Steger and Roy 2010; Parajuly et al. 2019). A broad range of goods is classified as EEE, which include large and small household appliances (consumer appliances) such as refrigerator, washing machine, air conditioner, microwave oven,

DOI: 10.4324/9780429285424-1

etc; information technology (IT) equipment including computers, computer games and peripherals; cellular telephones and other telecommunication equipment; portable electronic devices such as, video and audio equipment and their peripherals; and electrical tools.

E-waste (electronic waste) as the fastest growing waste stream is now recognised as 'tsunami' by the United Nations (UN). E-waste is also described as 'the toxic companion of digital era; one cannot escape it in the present gadget loving age' (Haldar 2020). The rapid growth of technology, upgradation of technical innovations, and a high rate of obsolescence in the electronics industry have led to one of the fastest growing waste streams in the world, which focuses on the Life Cycle Impact Assessment (LCIA) as well as end-of-life (EoL) solutions. In the waste management parlance, optimal and efficient use of natural resources, minimisation of wastes, development of cleaner products, environmentally sustainable recycling, and disposal in environmentally friendly manner of wastes are some of the issues which need to be addressed by all concerned while ensuring the economic growth and enhancing the quality of life (LARRDIS 2011: 2). In addition to this, it is hoped that better e-waste data eventually contributes to cohesive, effective e-waste management. Statistical database is looked upon as a useful tool in expanding discourse on e-waste management; along with toxicity, improvement in environment and human health, legislative and extended producer responsibility (EPR) related initiatives, statistics added newer dimensions of resource efficiency, circular economy, livelihood opportunities or job creation, right to repair and so on.

In *Global E-waste Monitors (GEM) 2017*, 44.7 Mt e-waste described as equivalent to 4,500 Eiffel Towers (Baldé et al. 2017: 4). The PACE and WEF report (2019: 9) describes that about 50 million tonnes of e-waste is produced every year, which is equivalent to the mass of 125,000 Jumbo Jet aircrafts. If London's Heathrow Airport has to clean this amount of e-waste, it would take up to six months to clear that many aircraft from its runways. If you find that difficult to envisage, then try the mass of Jets, jam them all in one space, side by side and they would cover an area the size of Manhattan city, USA (United States of America).

The latest, *GEM 2020*, informed that in 2019, the world generated 53.6 million metric tonnes[1] (Mt) (7.3 kg/inh[2]), of this, 17.4% was officially documented as properly collected and recycled. In 2016, the world generated 44.7 million metric tonnes (Mt) e-waste or an equivalent of 6.1 kilogram per inhabitant (kg/inh) annually; in 2014, 41.8 Mt/5.8 kg/inh e-waste was generated. As against total e-waste generation increased by 9.2 Mt, addition of 1.8 Mt in collection and recycled is observed since 2014. This indicates that the recycling activities are not keeping pace with the global growth of e-waste (Forti et al. 2020). Safe and sustainable disposal of e-product as e-waste in the context of generation and recycling is also a major concern, as 'only 35% of this waste is recycled, while the remaining 65% is exported, illegally recycled, or simply thrown into common landfills' (Pont et al. 2019: 2). 'Globally, volumes of e-waste are estimated to be increasing by approximately 3 to 5% annually since the 1990s and it continues to grow three times faster than municipal solid waste.' (Ledwaba and Sosibo 2017: 2) (Table 1.1)

TABLE 1.1 E-waste generation between 2013 and 2019 across the globe

No.	Year of e-waste data, source	Generated in Mt (kg/inh)	Formally treated[a] (%)	Intrinsic value of secondary materials estimated	No. of country having national legislation (% of world population covered)
1.	2013 (GEM 2014)	41.8 Mt (5.8 kg/inh)	6.5 Mt (15.5%)	Approx. 48 billion EUR	61 (44%)
2.	2016 (GEM 2017)	44.7 Mt (6.1 kg/inh)	8.9 Mt (approx. 20%)	Approx. 55 billion EUR	67 (66%)
3.	2019 (GEM 2020)	53.6 Mt (7.3 kg/inh)	9.3 Mt (17.4%)	Approx. 57 billion USD (48 billion EUR)	78 (71%)

Source: Baldé et al. (2015); Baldé et al. (2017); Forti et al. (2020). Compiled by the author.
[a]The 'formally' connotes activities usually fall under the requirements of national e-waste legislation/regulation/policy. E-waste is collected by designated organisations, producers and/or the government; e-waste is treated by designated/authorised recyclers.

It is important to know that the generation of e-waste and its 'distribution is uneven: richer countries produce more. Norway, for example, produces 28.5 kg per person per year, compared to an average of less than 2 kg in African countries' (Parajuly et al. 2019: 8). Also, that although the GEMs (2014, 2017, 2020) provide e-waste generation and estimate of intrinsic value of secondary materials recovered from the e-waste generated, they do not provide statistics on production of EEE and their contribution to nation's development or development index of a nation. This is the intrinsic limitation of the e-waste statistics.

I: Let's understand e-waste

Every electrical and electronic product (e-product) has stipulated life. Once any e-product reaches its end of its useful life, it becomes e-waste. Before any e-product reaches EoL or stops functioning or a new technology makes the e-product obsolete, however, the e-product could be repaired or refurbished. The lifespan of any e-product could be increased with repair and refurbishing,[3] and could be brought to reuse (Figure 1.1).

Among varied definitions of e-waste, the following are the most accepted: 'An e-product becomes EEE waste (e-waste) when its owner discards the whole product or its parts without an intention to reuse it' (Miliute-Plepiene and Youhanan 2019: 5); and 'anything with a plug, electric cord or battery (including EEE) that has reached the end of its life, as well as the components that make up these end-of-life

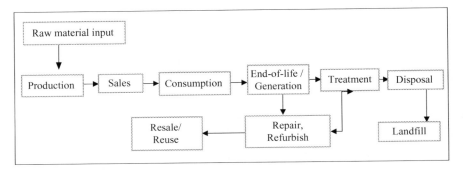

FIGURE 1.1 Life cycle of an e-product

products' (PACE and WEF 2019: 7). Broadly, e-waste means any EEE, whole or in part discarded as waste by the consumer or bulk consumer as well as rejects from manufacturing, refurbishment, and repair processes (Bhardwaj 2016: 1). Based on lifespan, usability of the product, and obsoleteness of the technology, the waste has been defined. International Labour Organisation (ILO) (2019a: 2) opined, 'the term "e-waste" itself can be misleading since it overlooks the inherent value of the discarded products'. The terms WEEE (waste EEE) and e-scrap are used interchangeably for e-waste in the existing literature including legal frameworks. E-waste is a casual name for electronic waste generated after helpful life of e-products.

WEEE is different from any other waste (solid, liquid, bio-medical, and construction waste) on two counts: first, e-waste contains hazardous waste, thus, is considered as a toxic waste stream. Toxicity of hazardous substance get leached to soil and water and contaminate,[4] which can cause serious environmental and health problems;[5] and improper management of e-waste contributes to global warming.[6] Second, WEEE is a complex waste flow in terms of variety of products, composed of different materials and components, contents in hazardous substances and growth pattern. Any e-product is a complex composition of different elements (valuable and hazardous); though the largest part of them by weight is represented by metals and plastics, the materials used in e-products can be classified into four main groups: metals, rare earth elements,[7] plastics and other petroleum-based materials, and minerals and non-metallic materials[8] (Miliute-Plepiene and Youhanan 2019: 7). Therefore, proper treatment of e-waste (mainly EoL solution / dismantling / recycling) and its discard are stressed upon, to prevent its adverse effects on the environment and human health on one hand while resource recovery and reuse on the other (Figure 1.2).

E-waste contains several toxic additives or hazardous substances, such as, hazardous (highly toxic), and non-hazardous; both types have potential negative environmental impacts. Hazardous substances are – Beryllium (Be), Cadmium (Cd), Chromium (Cr), Lead (Pb), Mercury (Hg), Brominated Flame Retardants (BFRs), Chlorofluorocarbon (CFCs), Hydro chlorofluorocarbon (HCFCs), PVC (PolyVinyl Chloride) and phosphorus compounds. Many organic pollutants such as polyaromatic hydrocarbons (PAHs), Poly Chlorinated Biphenyl, BFRs, Poly Brominated

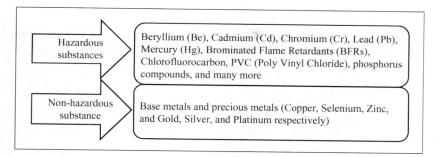

FIGURE 1.2 Hazardous and non-hazardous substances in e-products

Diphenyl Ethers (PBDEs), and polychlorinated dibenzo-p-dioxin furans (PCDD/Fs)) are released into the environment during improper e-waste processing (Awasthi et al. 2016: 259). A total of 50 tonne of mercury and 71 kt (kilo tonne) of BFR plastics are found in globally undocumented flows of e-waste annually, which is largely released into the environment and impacts the health of the exposed workers (Forti et al. 2020). Non-hazardous substances are base metals (Copper, Selenium, and Zinc) and precious metals (Gold, Silver and Platinum).

Safe environment and health concerns are closely linked to preventing contamination of air, soil and water, harming micro-organisms, disrupting ecosystems and entering food chains though complex bio-accumulation mechanisms. Thus, other than proper disposal by the users, treatment, and management of WEEE in environmentally sound manner (ESM) is stressed upon. The ESM refers to scientific methods for resource recovery, doing away from largely prevalent rudimentary methods of recycling of e-waste, such as, acid bath, open burning of wires and cables, etc. and manual scrapping/dismantling to certain extent. Different care aspects against improper recycling and disposal processes used for treating e-waste pose serious threats to human health (failure of organs, diseases, and adverse impact on skin and other parts of human body), and environment in order to prevent health hazards are critical.

Every government aims at optimal and efficient use of natural resources, minimisation of waste, development of products having longer life and lesser use of hazardous substances, and environmentally sustainable recycling, and disposal system of waste are some of the issues which need to be addressed by all concerned while ensuring the economic growth and enhancing the quality of life, as part of e-waste management (LARRDIS 2011). Usually, the municipal solid waste (MSW) management considers the framework of 3Rs – reduce, reuse, recycle; its recycling is associated with energy generation and other by-products related benefits. E-waste requires additional considerations in this existing framework of waste management, mainly because of presence of hazardous substances, metals, glass, plastics and other elements.

Deriving from other wastes management strategy ('waste management hierarchy'),[9] e-waste management has started recognising need for adding three more Rs (repair, refurbish, resource recovery) to the existing 3Rs framework (reuse, recycling, and recovery) for waste management, making 6R framework for e-waste management. Pont et al. (2019: 18) has suggested another model focusing on e-product users/consumers, by adding 3Rs, that is, release (spread the information, awareness), realise (know the importance of e-waste management), and responsibility (assume your role in 3Rs framework plus recycling and resource recovery). The components of recycling and resource recovery in e-waste management are seen as a process of 'problem to resources', bringing circular economy (CE) and resource efficiency (RE) to centre-stage along with safe environment and human health. The CE and RE are associated with social and economic benefits including job creation, investment in technology development and infrastructure building.

E-waste management thinking across the globe

The ILO (2019a: 2) sets the tone by narrating approaches to e-waste, as follow:

> Since the 1990s, discussion of e-waste has focused on actual and potential environmental damage; on major risks to human health, workers and communities; and on the flows of e-waste from developed to developing countries. Past policy recommendations have focused overwhelmingly on the introduction of environmental legislation and regulation. However, there is growing recognition that enterprises, employers, workers, cooperatives and other social and solidarity organizations, as well as ministries of labour or employment, and labour market policies all have a key role to play in advancing decent work in the management of e-waste.

In the existing literature, mostly, the need for 'e-waste management' arises referring to its regulation and treatment, along with e-waste definition, classification, generation, and its flow with a policy/regulatory framework/legislation is the general trend. Until 2010, e-waste was closely associated with safe environment and human health through legislation or its management under the EPR as a strategy, adopting waste management framework. In the last five years or so, this thinking has added two more aspects: first, the consumer is the purchaser of electronics as well as the generator of e-waste; and second, in the digital era, e-products are epitome of development, efficiency, and comfort and transforming entire production and market system of various products as well as activities in various sectors, such as, education, healthcare, entertainment and so on. Therefore, consumption of electronic gadgets is likely to increase multiple folds, and in turn increase in e-waste generation. Higher rates of e-waste generation are caused by shorter life cycles of e-products, and fewer repair options. Thus, introducing resource recovery, REs and CE link with recycling/treating e-waste. Spreading awareness among users of e-products, user roles in minimising e-waste, and contribution to tax regime/fees for recycling also have become the agenda of e-waste management.

The dominant discourse on governance of e-waste includes increasing e-waste collection and recycling; generating and harmonising statistics on e-waste across the world; existing regulatory/legislative framework, expansion of legal net and legal

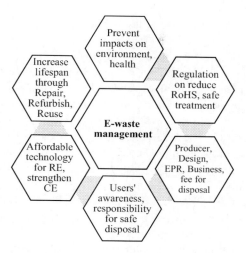

FIGURE 1.3 Components of e-waste management

compliance; urban mining; economic potentials − resource recovery and reducing use of virgin materials; and protecting health of workers exposed to hazardous e-waste in improper working conditions; adhering environmental concerns. Different components of e-waste management thinking are presented in Figure 1.3. To be more accommodative and able to incorporate the evolving ideas and practices regarding e-waste, the term is used, 'e-waste management thinking'.

Evolution of legal definitions of e-waste

Until 2007, there was no globally accepted standard definition of e-waste, though a few countries had developed their own definitions, interpretations and usage of the term "e-waste/WEEE". With evolution of legal frameworks, e-waste has been defined based on its characteristics, such as use of hazardous elements, chemicals, and organic persistent pollution; and therefore, transboundary movements of e-waste have been under vigil through regulations.

Internationally, three sets of legislation/regulatory frameworks exist mainly for management of e-waste: (i) EU (European Union) legislations applicable to EU countries, such as *Restriction on Hazardous Substances (RoHS) Directive*[10] and *WEEE Directive*[11] − and a regulation on *Registration, Evaluation, Authorisation and Restriction of Chemicals (REACH)* (Registration, Evaluation, and Authorisation of Chemical Substances);[12] (ii) multi-lateral environmental agreements including *The Basel Convention on the Control of Transboundary Movements of Hazardous Wastes and their Disposal*[13] (henceforth *Basel Convention*), *Rotterdam Convention on the Prior Informed Consent Procedure for Certain Hazardous Chemicals and Pesticides in International Trade* (1998), and *Stockholm Convention on Persistent Organic Pollutants* (2001); and (iii) Strategic Approach to International Chemicals Management (SAICM). Of these, *WEEE Directives*, *RoHS Directive* and the *Basel Convention* are frequently referred regulatory frameworks. As names of the regulations suggest, they aim to regulate hazardous substances, chemicals and transboundary movements of the e-waste.

At first, definition of WEEE has been described as per the *WEEE Directives* and the *Basel Convention* as mentioned by *Inventory Assessment Manual* by UNEP (2007: 12). The Manual describes definition under the *WEEE Directive* along with ten categories of WEEE and items covered under the categories as follow:

> *(2002/96/EC)* The definition of e-waste as per the **WEEE Directive**
> "Electrical or electronic equipment which is waste including all components, subassemblies and consumables, which are part of the product at the time of discarding."
> The Directive 75/442/EEC, Article 1(a) defines "waste" as "any substance or object which the holder disposes of or is required to dispose of pursuant to the provisions of national law in force."
> (a) 'electrical and electronic equipment' or 'EEE' means equipment which is dependent on electrical currents or electromagnetic fields in order to work properly and equipment for the generation, transfer and measurement of such current and fields falling under the categories set out in Annex IA to Directive 2002/96/EC (WEEE) and designed for use with a voltage rating not exceeding 1,000 volts for alternating current and 1,500 volts for direct current.
> (UNEP 2007: 13)

The *Basel Convention* covers all discarded/disposed materials that possess hazardous characteristics as well as all wastes considered hazardous on a national basis. The Annex VIII refers to e-waste, which is considered hazardous under Art. 1, para. 1(a) of the Convention (UNEP 2007: 21). The Article 2 ("Definitions") of the *Basel Convention*, defines waste as "substances or objects, which are disposed of or are intended to be disposed of or are required to be disposed of by the provision of national law" (quoted in Forti et al. 2020: 17). The waste '…includes all components, subassemblies and consumables, which are part of the product at the time of discarding.' It further clarifies that 'national provisions concerning the definition of waste may differ, and the same material that is regarded as waste in one country may be non-waste in another country.' (*op. cit.*)

The Solving the E-waste Problem (StEP) initiative[14] in its White Paper (UNU/StEP 2014: 4) establishes importance of definition of e-waste, mentioning that

> There is global inconsistency in the understanding and application of the term "e-waste" in both legislation and everyday use. This has resulted in many definitions contained within e-waste regulations, policies and guidelines…To provide a foundation to support the definition of e-waste, it is necessary to first define electrical and electronic equipment (EEE). The StEP definition of EEE is: "Any household or business item with circuitry or electrical components with power or battery supply…" The term "e-waste" itself is self-explanatory, in the sense that it is an abbreviation of "electronic waste."

A key part of the definition is the word "waste" and what it logically implies – that the item has no further use and is rejected as useless or excess to the owner in its current condition.

The definition of e-waste that has been agreed by StEP is:

'E-Waste is a term used to cover items of all types of electrical and electronic equipment (EEE) and its parts that have been discarded by the owner as waste without the intention of reuse.'

Three terms are explained as part of the definition in StEP White Paper (2014: 5):

As there is no room for regional variance or preference in a global definition; the fact that the item in question meets the definition "with circuitry or electrical components with power or battery supply" qualifies it for inclusion. The inclusion of "parts" within the definition refers to parts that have been removed from EEE by disassembly and are electrical or electronic in nature… The use of the term "discarded" meaning to throw away or get rid of as useless. The term implies that the item in question is considered excess or waste by the owner. It is the critical point at which the potential nature of the item changes from a useful product to that of waste.

The StEP Paper (2014: 6–7) defines reuse,[15] preparation for reuse,[16] recycle,[17] and disposal;[18] also continue to explain perception of e-waste by the owner and subjectivity in the definition, 'the point at which EEE becomes e-waste: when it is discarded as waste by the owner without the intention of reuse.' This is the most elaborated, inclusive definition of e-waste, developed by StEP in 2014.

The concept of e-waste or e-scrap has evolved from different types of devices and their classification as per the *WEEE Directive*[19] (enforced in the EU states), and the *recast of the WEEE Directive* from 15 August 2018. The recast of the *WEEE Directive* comprise of six categories of e-waste were evolved; at present these categories are followed in the *GEMs – 2014, 2017 and 2020*. They are: (i) temperature exchange equipment; (ii) screens and monitors; (iii) lamps; (iv) large equipment; (v) small equipment; and (vi) small IT and telecommunication equipment (Forti et al. 2020: 14–15).

II: E-waste statistics: quantities, collection and recycling

The *GEM* published by the UNU (United Nations University) in 2014, 2017 and 2020 are the most important documents that capture e-waste statistics from all the countries across the world since 2009 and considered to be the only authentic source for quantity of e-waste.[20] At present, 54 EEE product categories are grouped into six general categories that correspond closely to their waste management categories (Forti et al. 2020: 18–19).[21] Based on these categories, e-waste generation,

10 Sustainable development

collection, recycling, intrinsic value, number of countries having e-waste legislations, etc. statistics are generated and harmonised across the world.

E-waste categories and harmonising statistics

In 2016, global e-waste volume was collected from 190 countries, and in 2019, from 193 countries. The Table 1.2 provides and overview on e-waste quantities, recycling and flow in each region, also describing the trends and characteristics of each region in dealing with e-waste.

The highest amount of e-waste comprises small equipment followed by large equipment, temperature exchange equipment. The lamps are the smallest portion among the e-waste.

Table 1.3 presents data on e-waste generated (in Mt and in kg/inh) and formally collected and recycled, comparing across five regions in 2016 and 2019.

TABLE 1.2 E-waste quantities as per its categories – comparing 2016 and 2019

E-waste category	Amount of e-waste (in Mt) 2016	Amount of e-waste (in Mt) 2019	Quantity change (%)
Small equipment	16.8	17.4	+4
Large equipment	9.1	13.1	+4
Temperature exchange equipment	7.6	10.8	+7
Screens and monitors	6.6	6.7	−1
Lamps	0.7	0.9	+4
Small IT and telecommunication equipment	3.9	4.7	+2
Total	**44.7**	**53.6**	

Source: Baldé et al. (2017), Forti et al. (2020). Compiled by the author.

TABLE 1.3 E-waste generation, collection and recycling across regions – comparing 2016 and 2019 data

Continent / region	No. of countries	Total e-waste generated (in Mt) 2016	Total e-waste generated (in Mt) 2019	Total e-waste generated kg/inh 2016	Total e-waste generated kg/inh 2019	Documented e-waste – to be collected, recycled (in Mt) (in %) 2016 (in %)	Documented e-waste – to be collected, recycled (in Mt) (in %) 2019 (in %)
Africa	53	2.2	2.9	1.9	2.5	0.004 (0.0)	0.03 (0.9)
Americas	34	11.3	13.1	11.6	13.3	1.9 (17.0)	1.2 (9.4)
Asia	46	18.2	24.9	4.2	5.6	2.7 (15.0)	2.9 (11.7)
Europe	39	12.3	12	16.6	16.2	4.3 (35.0)	5.1 (42.5)
Oceania	12	0.7	0.7	17.3	16.1	0.04 (6.0)	0.06 (8.8)
Total	**184**	**44.7**	**53.6**			**8.944 (73.0)**	**9.29 (83.3)**

Source: Baldé et al. (2017), Forti et al. (2020: 25). Compiled by the author.

The comparison between the data of 2016 and 2019 across the regions reveals the following: there is an increase in e-waste generation across in Africa, Americas, and Asia regions while Europe reported minor drop, and Oceania reported *status quo* (reduction in per capita e-waste). As against e-waste generation, Americas and Asia observed drop in formal collection and recycling. The significant increase in Asia matches with China producing maximum 10,129 kt (10.2 Mt) e-waste. Based on these statistics, Europe's performance is better compared to the others – drop in e-waste generation along with per capita and increase (7.5%) in formal recycling. As against e-waste generated, collection rate is much lower; absence of legislation and influential presence of informal sector are two reasons given repeatedly by various observers.

The *GEM 2020* reported that despite the relatively high environmental awareness in the EU), e-waste is still disposed of in residual waste, and the small e-waste ends up in residual waste bins. This comprises approximately 0.6 Mt of the EU's e-waste (Forti et al. 2020: 77). Central Asia reported most e-waste being landfills or illegal dumping sites. PACE and WEF (2019: 9) shared, 'Of this total amount, 40 million tonnes of e-waste are discarded in landfill, 21 burned or illegally traded and treated in a substandard way every year.'

The difference of e-waste generated in developed versus developing countries is quite large. The richest country in the world in 2016 generated an average of 19.6 kg/inhabitant, whereas the poorest generated only 0.6 kg/inhabitant (MeitY & NITI Aayog 2019: 29).

Africa region

Total 2.9 Mt e-waste was generated in Africa in 2019, which is 5% of total e-waste generated in the world. This data is collected from 53 countries with 1.2 billion population: among them, Egypt (0.58 Mt), Nigeria (0.46 Mt) and South Africa (0.41 Mt). The highest e-waste generation per inhabitant is Southern African countries with 6.9 kg/inh. South Africa, Morocco, Egypt, Namibia and Rwanda have some facilities in place for e-waste recycling, but those co-exist with the existence of a large informal sector. Nigeria, Ghana and Kenya are reliant on informal recycling. Of 53 countries, 13 countries have a national legislation, regulation or policy in place (Forti et al. 2020: 71).

Americas (north and south) region

In Americas, total e-waste generation was 13.1 Mt in 2019, which is almost 25% of total e-waste generated in the world. Of this, almost half of it is generated by America (6.9 Mt), 20.9 kg/inh in North America followed by Brazil (2.1 Mt); Jamaica is the least e-waste generating country with 18 kt. A total of 1.2 Mt is documented to be collected and recycled, mostly coming from North America. The geographical distribution and e-waste management characteristics are very different across the continent. Of 34 countries, 10 countries have a national legislation/regulation/policy in place.

Asia region

In Asia, the total e-waste generation was 24.9 Mt (5.6 kg/inh) from 46 countries with 4.45 billion population in 2019, its proportion is almost 40% of the e-waste generated in the world. Three countries generating the highest e-waste in Asia are: China (10.1 Mt), India (3.2 Mt, Japan (2.6 Mt), and Indonesia (1.6 Mt) while Kyrgyzstan produces the least (10 kt). Western Asia generates 2.6 Mt (9.6 kg/inh) e-waste. Of 46 countries, 17 countries have a national legislation, regulation or policy in place.

The sub-region includes both high-income countries, such as, Qatar and Kuwait while 6% of e-waste is reported to be collected and recycled, mainly by Turkey, negligible from Cyprus and Israel (Baldé et al. 2017: 70).

The *Regional E-waste Monitor: East and Southeast Asia* provided country profiles, which throws lights on extent of e-waste generated:

> e-waste arising found in Hong Kong of 21.7 kg/capita in 2015, followed by Singapore (19.95 kg/capita) and Taiwan, Province of China (19.13 kg/capita). Of the countries studied for this report, Cambodia (1.10 kg/capita), Vietnam (1.34 kg/capita) and the Philippines (1.35 kg/capita) had the lowest e-waste arising per capita in 2015.
>
> (Honda et al. 2016: 59)

Europe region

In Europe, the total e-waste generation was 12.0 Mt from 39 countries with 0.74 billion population in 2019, its proportion is little more than one-fourth of the total e-waste generated in the world. Total 5.1 Mt (42.5%) documented to be collected and recycled e-waste. Germany generated 1.6 Mt the highest quantity of e-waste in Europe, followed by Great Britain (1.6 Mt), and Italy (1.0 Mt). Europe, Switzerland, Norway and Sweden show the most advanced e-waste management practices across the globe. However, other countries are still catching up with Northern Europe, whose collection rate is 59% and western Europe with 54%, are the highest in the world. Of 39 countries, 37 countries have a national legislation, regulation or policy in place (Forti et al. 2020: 76).

Oceania region

In Oceania, the total e-waste generation was 0.7 Mt from 13 countries with population of 0.042 billion in 2019. The collection rate is 6%; consequently 0.06 Mt was documented to collected and recycled. The top country with the highest e-waste generation in absolute quantities is Australia (0.55 Mt, 21.3 kg/inh) followed by New Zealand with 96 kt. Of 12 countries, one country has a national legislation, regulation or policy in place (Forti et al. 2020: 78).

The Australian government implemented its National Television and Computer Recycling Scheme in 2011. Official data shows that only 7.5% of the e-waste generated in Australia is documented to be collected and recycled while in New Zealand and the rest of Oceania, the official collection rate is nil. The e-waste is now mostly landfilled. Across the Pacific Island countries, e-waste management practices are predominantly informal. The Pacific Island sub-region, consisting of 22 countries and territories (PICTs) faces unique challenges due to their geographical spread regarding e-waste collection and recycling (Baldé et al. 2017: 76).

The *GEM 2020* provided environmental and health concerns/data from undocumented flows of e-waste (e.g. potential release of GHG emission, amount mercury, and amount of BFRs), and economic concern / data (e.g. value of raw materials in e-waste). Table 1.4 presents these details across different regions.[22]

The data from undocumented flows of e-wastes revealed substantial emission of CO_2 and BFRs, and deposition of mercury. The link between emission of CO_2 and global warming leading to climate change is well-established. Mercury is persistent and bio-accumulative in the environment and retained in organisms. Most of the mercury found in the environment is inorganic mercury, primarily entering the environment through emissions to the air from several sources.

The *GEM 2020* has presented a list of suggestion, which are purely curative waste management aspects (collection and recycling), such as, implementation of EPR, strengthen monitoring for legal compliance, creating favourable investment conditions for recyclers, incentivising informal sector to give away e-waste to formal recyclers, evolving financing models (upfront fee by the producers, making consumers responsible for disposal of e-waste, and adopting market share approach for financing operational costs), and so on.

TABLE 1.4 Environmental, health, and economic data from undocumented flows of e-waste (2019)

Continent / region	Potential release of GHG emissions (in Mt CO_2)	Amount of mercury (in kt)	Amount of BFR (in kt)	Value of raw materials (in billion USD)
Africa	9.4	0.01	5.6	3.2
Americas	26.3	0.01	18.0	14.2
Asia	60.8	0.04	35.3	26.4
Europe	12.7	0.01	11.4	12.9
Oceania	1.0	0.001	1.1	0.7
Total	110.2	0.091	71.4	57.4

Columns 2–4: *Environment concerns/data from undocumented flows of e-waste*. Column 5: *Economic concern/data from undocumented flows of e-waste*.

Source: Forti et al. (2020: 70–76). Compiled by the author.

The occupational health and conditions of workers, especially children that are getting exposed to hazards of e-waste have been reported by the *GEM 2020*. The associations between exposure to informal e-waste recycling and health problems, such as, adverse birth outcomes (stillbirth, premature birth, lower gestational age, lower birth weight and length, and lower APGAR scores), increased or decreased growth, altered neurodevelopment, adverse learning and behavioural outcomes, immune system function, lung function and DNA damage, changes in gene expression, cardiovascular regulatory changes, rapid onset of blood coagulation, hearing loss, and olfactory memory are reported (Forti et al. 2020: 65).

GHG emissions, contribution of e-waste to global warming, contamination of air, water and soil are major concerns expressed for safe environment. The prevalent scenario has become a part of discourse on e-waste management across the globe.

E-waste flow and data on transboundary movements

Transboundary movement is considered to be a way of dumping waste / e-waste from one country to another. Lundgren (2012) has provided examples to show substantial internal and regional trade; e-waste is shipped from developed to developing countries is not always true. For example, in 2001, Africa exported most of its e-waste to Korea and Spain, and since 2006, the growth in global trade overall has been primarily in two areas: in internal markets, and in Asia becoming the dominant recipient of global exports. 'E-waste recycling operations have been identified in several locations in China and India. Less-investigated locations are in the Philippines, Nigeria (in the city of Lagos), Pakistan (Karachi) and Ghana (Accra)' (Lundgren 2012: 14). The issue of transboundary movement is closely linked with shipping of e-waste to developing countries where rudimentary techniques are often used to extract materials and components. 'Global trading of electronics and substandard recycling in developing countries has led to environmental catastrophes in places like Guiyu, China and Agbogbloshie, Ghana, to name two examples' (Baldé et al. 2015: 4).

The following statistics show gradual decrease in transboundary movement of e-waste, for ten years; that is, 2002 to 2012. During the period 2004 to 2006, over 10 million tonnes of export per year was reported, with an increase of 15% in 2006 compared with 2004. This is mainly due to changes in wastes defined as hazardous wastes according to Article 1.1.b of the *Basel Convention*. Transboundary movements of hazardous wastes as defined under Article 1.1.a of the Convention show an increase of only 4% in the same period. Transboundary movements of 'other wastes' are decreasing (Wielenga 2010: 12).

Based on a case study of 'person-in-the port' project in Nigeria in 2015–2016, Baldé et al. (2017: 45) provides data on transboundary movements:

> Around 71,000 tonnes of WEEE were imported annually into Nigeria through the two main ports in Lagos. WEEE imported in containers, with and without vehicles, contributed around 18,300 tonnes of WEEE per year

with 52% imported in containers with vehicles. In total, most imported WEEE originated from ports in Germany (around 20%) followed by the UK (around 19.5%), and Belgium (around 9.4%). The Netherlands (8.2%) and Spain (7.35%), followed by China and the USA (7.33% each), are next in the ranking of main exporters, followed by Ireland (6.2%). Overall, these eight countries account for around 85% of WEEE imports into Nigeria. EU member states were the origin of around 77% of WEEE imported into Nigeria.

In 2012, EU exported 0.09 Mt was exported for reuse out of 1.5 Mt e-waste of screens; 0.03 Mt was exported for reuse out of approximately 1.4 Mt of e-waste cooling and freezing equipment (Baldé et al. 2016: 10).[23]

In 2010 in USA, approximately 258.2 million units (equivalent to approximately 1.6 Mt) of used electronics (computers, monitors, TVs and mobile phones) were generated; of which 171.4 million units (0.9 million tonnes) were collected, and 14.4 million units (0.027 million tonnes) used electronic products were exported to the developed and developing countries) (Duan et al. 2013: 10–11). Mobile phones dominate generation, collection and export on a unit basis, but TVs and monitors dominate on a weight basis. Regarding flow, Latin America and the Caribbean is a common destination for products, along with North America. Asia represents the next largest destination. Africa is the least common destination (Duan et al. 2013: 12–13).

The ILO report (Lundgren 2012: 14–17) has described important observations about transboundary movements of e-waste; wherein four aspects or phenomena are described: (i) illegal trade which has intensified corporate, or 'white collar' crime; (ii) use of 'second hand goods' label – to disguise mislabel containers and mix waste with legitimate consignment, and lack of reliable data on illegal waste activity; (iii) recent emergent field of 'green criminology' – e-waste trade as an example, which poses environmental risk and expected to be compliant to regulatory norms, though not criminalised as such; and (iv) security implications – more research is needed in order to find out more about the networks behind the illegal export that is taking place.

Creating and updating statistics, datasets: opportunities and challenges

An overview of the existing statistics reveals that macro level data have begun to emerge and throw light on different aspects and trends of e-waste management, namely, standard definition of e-waste, quantity of e-waste generated and treated, methodology, flow of e-waste including transboundary movements, and initiatives towards achieving 2030 Development Agenda.

Three GEMs (2014, 2017 and 2020) at the regular interval of three years is considered to be trendsetting and promising initiative for statistics and exploring existing e-waste scenario. Advantages and disadvantages of every method are elaborated, challenges of creating and updating data are also articulated – gaps are identified, processes that lead to misinformation or wrong labelling and misleading data (especially on transboundary movements) are identified – are avenues to improve upon.

The *GEM 2020* has begun build up to data on three important aspects of e-waste management – CE, toxicity and impact on children and workers. More information on different aspects of environment and human health could be built up further, either through national registry or micro studies, for example, on extent of toxicity, types of toxicity, every aspect of environment (energy in LCIA approach to e-waste, fossil use, carbon prints, contamination of air, soil and water). As more countries are adopting e-waste legislation/regulatory policy, it is important to provide data that facilitate the complexities of decision-making, for example, whether to treat e-waste domestically or through export, issues that are of environmental, political, economic and ethical nature and how to address them by legal framework.

III: An overview on status of e-waste related legislation across the globe

Most legislative instruments aim at resource recovery through recycling and focus on countermeasures against environmental pollution, and adverse impacts on human health, at the EoL of products. The reduction of e-waste volumes and substantive repair and reuse of EEE has been limited so far (Forti et al. 2020: 52).

The laws and policies concerning the proper management of electronic devices are continuing to evolve in different parts of the globe. The legislation does not imply complete legal compliance, as in many countries, policies are non-legally binding strategies, but only programmatic ones (Forti et al. 2020). The legislation largely focusses on regulating guidelines for collection, reuse and recycling of e-waste, except New York city of USA which has introduced landfill bans of scrap. Other initiatives include setting up take-back channel, initiating programmes for collection and recycling and appointing private companies for recycling (Baldé et al. 2017: 60), or regulating e-waste through a directive or administrative regulation. The following table presents law related information in different regions of the world (Table 1.5).

In 2014, 61 countries were covered by legislation/ regulation/policy with 44% of world's population; in 2017, 67 countries were covered by legislation/policy/regulation with 66% of world's population; and in 2019, 78 countries were covered by legislation/policy/regulation with 71% of the world's population (Forti et al. 2020: 26). Less than half of the countries (78 out of 193) in the world covered by e-waste legislation, regulation or policy framework; this is an increase by 5% from 66% in 2017. This also means that 11 countries (including the state of Alabama in the USA, Argentina, Cameroon, Nigeria, South Africa, Sri Lanka, Zambia) enacted legislation or introduced policy/regulation on e-waste in last three years; and more countries may be in the process of enacting legislation or policy to tackle e-waste.

EPR is a common feature in these legislations in most countries; much more responsibility is put on producers to deal more effectively with the e-waste and e-products they produce. Chapter 2 discusses EPR in detail. Producers are tasked

Sustainable development 17

TABLE 1.5 Countries having legislation or policy for e-waste management (2019)

Continent / region	Name of country where the legislation in existence, year	Legislation underway / absent	% of population covered by legislation per sub-region
Africa	Madagascar (2015), Kenya (2016), Ghana (2016), Uganda, Rwanda, Cameroon, Nigeria, South Africa, Zambia,		Eastern 33 Middle 7 Western 33 Northern 21 Southern 6
North America	United States Environment Protection Agency has taken some generic measures – Electronics Action Plan in 2005; Sustainable Materials Management (SMM); managing domestic e-waste through the Resource Conservation and Recovery Act; regulations for recycling CRTs; and the National Strategy for Electronics Stewardship framework. USA, state & provincial laws Puerto Rico and DC (consumer take-back law); New York City has banned landfill. Alabama	USA – Ohio, and Massachusetts Canada – states have local regulation except the Yukon and Nunavut	North 39 (including Caribbean) Central 18
South America	South / Latin America – Argentina, Bolivia, Chile, Colombia, Costa Rica, Ecuador, Mexico and Peru. California, Massachusetts, Maine and Minnesota states have imposed regulation on design, manufacture, reuse, recovery, disposal of e-waste	Brazil, Panama and Uruguay	Approx. 43
Asia	China (2007), India (2011 onward), Japan, South Korea, Vietnam (2015), Cambodia (2016), Singapore, Taiwan, Sri Lanka		Eastern 36 Central 0.7 South-eastern 15 Southern 42 Western 6
Europe	The EU enacted RoHS and WEEE Directive (2003), REACH (2007). Balkan sub-region – Albania, Bulgaria, Bosnia and Herzegovina, Montenegro, Macedonia, Serbia, and Slovenia are covered. UK national law has adopted WEEE Directive in 2006	Moldova	Eastern 39 Northern 14 Southern 21 Western 26
Oceania	Australia (2011)	New Zealand	Australia, New Zealand – 75 Melanesia, Micronesia & Polynesia – 25

Source: This table is compiled by the author based on data available from Baldé et al. (2017: 48); LARRDIS (2011: 87–90); Ram Mohan et al. (2019: 176–181); Patil and Ramakrishna (2020: 6–8); and Forti et al. (2020: 105–116).

with extensive reporting and monitoring procedures to demonstrate compliance with the regulation. The waste hierarchy has been extended and prioritised as prevention, reuse, recycle, recovery and, as a last resort, disposal of waste.

Of 78 countries having legislation to regulate e-waste management, more than half reported dominant presence of the informal sector; i.e. from collection to recycling of e-waste. In many countries, government control of e-waste sector is minimal, and infrastructure for recycling is non-existent or grossly mixed; overall the informal sector is dominant in collection, refurbishing and repairing e-waste.

Regarding recycling and legislation, Patil and Ramakrishna (2020: 2–5) observed that, as there is no uniformity in e-waste legislation across all the countries, it is difficult to monitor e-waste recycling on a global scale. Eastern European countries (Russia, Ukraine, and Moldova) are not as advanced as EU countries; in Poland, Czech Republic, Hungary and Bulgaria, e-waste collection and recycling are mainly led by the private sector. In North America, e-waste is well managed by the government. The California Electronic Waste Recycling Act, 2003 shifts financial burden of recycling on consumer since 2005. Asian continent represents a mix of countries at different stages of economic development. The economic condition of the countries influences their domestic e-waste production and management. In East-Asia, the official collection rate is close to 25% but in Central and South Asia, it is still nil (informal sector). China levies penalty on non-compliance of the administration of e-waste. Overall, not many countries reported more than 25% of e-waste collection and recycling across the world.

In the case of Africa, particularly western Africa (e.g. Ghana and Nigeria) as a dumping yard destination for e-waste from various regions of the world is discussed in the context of legal framework, and two concerns are highlighted: first, illegal import of e-waste, and second, recycling activities carried out in informal basis and the residues are landfilled, impacting the health of recycling workers and local environment. If both practices are properly regulated and managed, recycling e-waste can help to develop local economies and reduce poverty (Baldé et al. 2015: 38).

Relevance of international legislative frameworks across the globe: trends and challenges

Internationally, mainly three sets of legislation/regulatory frameworks exist for management of e-waste: (i) EU) legislations applicable to EU countries; (ii) multilateral environmental agreements; and (iii) SAICM.

(i) *EU legislations applicable to EU countries*

The legislations / treaties founded by the EU are applicable to EU and its member states. The European Parliament is the only body in the EU to which EU citizens directly elect members to represent them. The Parliament has a term of office for five years; with the Council of the European Union, both are the main legislators of the EU. The treaties instruct domestic courts that priority is given to EU law over national law, which means that member state legislators have to modify domestic laws to align with EU laws if there is a conflict between the two secondary sources of EU law transposed from the treaties consist of regulations and directives. A regulation is binding and is directly incorporated into member state law without that member state having to use national legislation to incorporate them into law, whereas a directive sets out the requirements that the legislation should achieve; and a directive then leaves it to the member state to implement as it sees fit to meet the requirements. The directive will provide for a set period of time within which implementation has to be achieved via nation state legislative processes (Stewart 2012: 20).

The regulatory framework of EU, especially *WEEE Directives*, have followed the terminology of

> product life cycle thinking by encouraging producers to prevent waste generation in the first instance...By following this principle, the member states are expected to adhere the following: prevention of waste, preparation of waste for reuse, recycle waste, other recovery (e.g. energy), and disposal.

Every item is defined under the Directive, such as 'waste,'[24] 'waste management,'[25] 'prevention,'[26] 'recovery,'[27] and 'recycling,'[28] (*op. cit.*: 25–26) which is similar to 3Rs framework for waste – reuse, recycling, recovery.

EU legislation includes the following regulatory frameworks – (i) *RoHS Directive* (2002/95/EC – RoHS1) by EU) in 2003 and subsequent amendments in 2011 (2011/65/EU – RoHS2), 2017 (amending Annex II of RoHS2), and Directive (EU) 2015/863 – RoHS3;[29] (ii) *WEEE Directive* (2002/96/EC), 2003 and WEEE 2 (Directive 2012/19/EU), 2014; and (iii) The regulation on *REACH* (Registration, Evaluation, Authorisation, and Restrictions of Chemical Substances) (EC 1907/2006).

WEEE directives

The WEEE directive is set out over 19 articles, among them the important ones are: scope (Article 2–10 categories of WEEE), definitions (Article 3), product design (Article 4), separate collection (Article 5), treatment (Article 6), recovery (Article 7). The other Articles provide details on responsibilities of different stakeholders include registration and reporting to national authorities on volumes of EEE placed on their market; organising and/or financing the collection, treatment, recycling, and recovery of WEEE and providing specific information to recycling companies; and labelling products with the crossed-out wheelie bin symbol to allow for correct disposal by end-users.

The *WEEE Directive*[30] sets out the financial responsibilities; and mandates the treatment, recovery, and recycling of EEE by every producer; and encourages the design of electronic products that ensures environmentally safe recycling and recovery. All applicable products in the EU market after 13 August 2006 must pass WEEE compliance and carry the wheelie bin sticker. The *WEEE Directive* covers collection and recycling of waste from a broad range of EEE at their EoL solutions.

The *WEEE directive* tackles WEEE and complement EU measures for preventing landfill and incineration of e-waste, overall reduction of e-waste and adopting environmentally sound disposal methods. Five areas of e-waste management are addressed under the EPR, namely: (i) production, including improved product design; (ii) distribution; (iii) consumption (by domestic and business consumers) and separate collection of e-waste with targets specified for recovery, reuse, and recycling of different classes of WEEE (creating take-back channel by the producer); (iv) e-waste handling – reuse, recycling, and recovery; and (v) e-waste treatment and disposal including specifications for exporting e-waste for treatment. The *WEEE Directive* has covered aspects of financing and electronics user awareness (Ledwaba and Sosibo 2017; GIZ and MESTI 2019).

> In 2012, a recast version of the *WEEE Directive*[31] includes new, ambitious targets. These targets are no longer based on a collection target per inhabitant, but instead on a percentage of the amount of EEE placed on market or the amount of WEEE generated.
>
> (Ffact et al. 2013: 5)

The *WEEE Directive* (2002) was assessed by three independent consultants in 2007. All three of the reports highlighted the vast differences in practices between member states in a few key areas and questioned whether some member states were actually complying with the directive at all. These reports also made a few suggestions for tackling the problems. The WEEE Directive was recast based on these three reports (Stewart 2012).

RoHS directives

This EU legislations (RoHS 1,2,3)[32] restrict the use of hazardous substances in EEE, promoting the collection and recycling and/or reuse of EEE, and consumers returning their used WEEE free of charge.

> The Directive on the RoHS (2002/95/EC) is companion legislation to the WEEE Directive. Unlike the WEEE Directive, the RoHS Directive is enacted by Article 95 of the Treaty establishing the European Community (Treaty Amsterdam 1997), which has much less flexibility that those enacted by article 175 such as the WEEE Directive.
>
> (Stewart 2012: 38)

The *RoHS Directive* is set out in ten articles and an associated annex and should be read in tandem with its sister legislation – the *WEEE Directive*.

The *RoHS1* required that any product in scope should not contain any of the six restricted substances (Lead, Mercury, Cadmium, Hexavalent Chromium and

Flame Retardants – Poly Brominated Biphenyls (PBB) or PBDE) and its weight; the company (manufacturer, importer, or distributor) placing the product on the EU market should maintain records to show compliance; and these restricted substances need to be substituted by safer alternatives. The *RoHS2* requires additional compliance, that is, recordkeeping from everyone in the supply chain at least for ten years (including a conformity assessment, CE marking, maintenance of compliance throughout production, and self-reporting of non-compliance). The *RoHS3*, or the *Directive 2015/863*, adds four additional restricted substances (phthalates[33]) to the original list of six substances, as cited under the *REACH* regulation; and adds Category 11 products (https://ec.europa.eu/environment/waste/rohs; www.rohs-guide.com). Table 1.6 presents an overview of RoHS 1,2,3.

REACH (registration, evaluation, authorisation and restriction of chemicals)

The REACH regulation was released in 2006 and entered into force on June 1, 2007. This is a regulation of the EU, adopted to improve the protection of human health and the environment through the better and earlier identification of the intrinsic properties of chemical substances, deals with 197 Substances of Very High Concern (SVHC).

> The regulations were published in 2006 along with amendments to its sister legislation the *Dangerous Substances Directive* (*Directive 67/548/EEC*). The Regulation is set out in 141 articles and 17 annexes, spanning 849 pages, so this section simply attempts to give an overview of the main highlights.
> (Stewart 2012: 44)

The regulation impacts almost every product made in or imported into the European Economic Area (EEA).[34] This is done by the four processes of REACH, namely the registration, evaluation, authorisation and restriction of chemicals and places the burden of proof on companies. This regulation affects the use and sale of a vast array of items, ranging from industrial goods to cleaning products, clothing, furniture and appliances; e-waste specific matters are presented here. REACH places responsibility on the manufacturer/producer for ensuring that any chemicals they put on the market are properly assessed and managed in terms of their risks. Public authorities are tasked with ensuring the industry meets this obligation.

REACH also aims to enhance innovation and competitiveness of the EU chemicals industry. The manufacturers and importers of EEE are required to gather information on the properties of their chemical substances, which will allow their safe handling, and to register the information in a central database in the European Chemicals Agency (ECHA) in Helsinki. Thus, REACH manages the databases necessary to operate the system, co-ordinates the in-depth evaluation of suspicious chemicals and is building up a public database in which consumers and professionals can find hazard information.[35]

TABLE 1.6 Overview of RoHS 1,2,3

RoHS details	ROHS1 (27 January 2002)	ROHS2 (8 June 2011)	ROHS3 (31 March 2015)
ROHS details, its objectives	Directive 2002/95 / EC of the European Parliament and of the Council applicable until 8 June 2011 Restricting the use of certain hazardous substances in electrical and electronic equipment	Directive 2011/65 / EU of the European Parliament and of the Council applicable until 22 July 2019 Restricting the use of certain hazardous substances in electrical and electronic equipment	Commission delegated Directive (EU) 2015/863 of 31 March 2015 amending Annex II to Directive 2011/65 / EU of the European Parliament and of the Council applicable until 22 July 2021 A list of substances subject to restrictions
Device categories covered by this policy (i) Home appliances; (ii) Small household appliances; (iii) IT and telecommunications equipment; (iv) Consumer electronics; (v) Lighting fixture; (vi) Electrical and electronic tools (except stationary large industrial tools); (vii) Toys and sports and leisure equipment; (viii) Medical devices (with the exception of all implanted and infected products); (ix) Monitoring and control instruments; and (x) Automatic output devices	All applicable (i to x)	All applicable (i to x) + (xi) Other electrical and electronic equipment	All applicable (i to x) + (xi) Other EEE
Other EEE	—	Newly introduced restrictions regarding Phthalates	Newly introduced

| Substances which are subject to restrictions, as referred to in Article 4(1), and maximum concentrations in homogeneous materials by weight | Lead (0.1%) Mercury (0.1%) Cadmium (0.01%) Hexavalent chromium (0.1%) Polybrominated biphenyls (PBB) (0.1%) PBDE (0.1%) | Lead (0.1%) Mercury (0.1%) Cadmium (0.01%) Hexavalent chromium (0.1%) Polybrominated biphenyls (PBB) (0.1%) PBDE (0.1%) | Lead (0.1%) Mercury (0.1%) Cadmium (0.01%) Hexavalent chromium (0.1%) Polybrominated biphenyls (PBB) (0.1%) PBDE (0.1%) Added Di (2-ethylhexyl) phthalate (DEHP) (0.1%) Butyl Benzyl phthalate (BBP) (0.1%) Dibutyl phthalate (DBP) (0.1%) Di-isobutyl phthalate (DIBP) (0.1%) |

Source: www.sna.de – adapted by the author.

Link between RoHS, WEEE and REACH

These are three key pieces of legislation relating to EEE and WEEE. All three frameworks lay out results that must be achieved by the European countries, but each country is free to choose the means of achieving those results when transposing European rules into national laws. WEEE and RoHS Directives deal with complex sets of WEEE (both apply to the same range of products with some differences); these legislations work in complementarity. RoHS regulates the hazardous substances (wiring, components, circuit boards, displays, subassemblies, cabling) used in the manufacture of EEE while WEEE regulates the disposal of this same equipment; REACH controls all chemicals (enclosures, brackets, coatings, paints, solvents, etc.) and that might be used to manufacture EEE. All the RoHS restricted substances (identified as being carcinogenic, mutagenic,[36] reprotoxic,[37] bio-accumulative and toxic, or as endocrine disruptors) are also on the REACH restricted list. RoHS compliance unites into WEEE by reducing the amount of hazardous chemicals used in electronics manufacture (https://www.rohsguide.com/rohs-faq.htm).

EPR is a common feature/framework in these legislations; much more responsibility is put on producers to deal more effectively with the e-waste and e-products they produce. Producers are tasked with extensive reporting and monitoring procedures to demonstrate compliance with the regulation. The waste hierarchy has been extended and prioritised as prevention, reuse, recycle, recovery and, as a last resort, disposal of waste. EPR is dealt in detail in the following section of this chapter.

Many of the points mentioned in the evaluative study of the *WEEE Directive* are important and relevant even after thirteen years of its completion. The estimate regarding e-waste generation, need for higher rate of collection and better treatment for resource recovery, role of awareness in e-waste management and implementation of such regulatory measures, and recycling of old and newer EEE like CRT and LCD/LED TVs.

(ii) Multi-lateral environmental agreements (MEA)

There are three important international conventions seeking to control the shipping of waste; after these, various regional conventions have been signed to regulate hazardous waste movements. They are: (i) *Basel Convention on the Control of Transboundary Movements of Hazardous Wastes and their Disposal* (1989); (ii) *Rotterdam Convention on the Prior Informed Consent Procedure for Certain Hazardous Chemicals and Pesticides in International Trade* (1998);[38] (iii) *Stockholm Convention on Persistent Organic Pollutants* (2001).[39]

Article 11 of the *Basel Convention* allows Parties to enter bilateral, multi-lateral or regional agreements regarding transboundary movements of hazardous waste. Thus, three regions – Africa, the EU and the South Pacific – have instituted agreements concerning such movements of waste and, in particular, e-waste. Relevant agreements have also taken shape and come into force in Latin America. The following table summarises MEA signed by different regions and countries (Table 1.7).

TABLE 1.7 Multi-lateral environmental agreements signed by different regions

No.	Country/region	Convention/declaration	Details
1.	Africa	*Bamako convention* – signed in Bamako, Mali, in January 1991 and entered into force in 1998	⇨ Ban of the import into Africa and the control of transboundary movement and management of hazardous wastes within Africa, especially from non-contracting parties. ⇨ According to the African Union, in 2010, 24 of the 52 countries which form the African Union have ratified the Bamako Convention. ⇨ Enforcement remains a challenge because of the lack of adequate and predictable resources. ⇨ Ghana had not signed this convention until 2017, now under process.
		Durban Declaration – was developed from COP8 of the Basel Convention on e-Waste Management in Africa in 2008	⇨ It calls for the establishment of an African regional platform and/or an e-waste forum in cooperation with established African networks and international bodies. ⇨ It requires countries to review existing legislation, improve compliance with existing legislation and amend existing waste management legislation to allow for regulation of e-waste management. ⇨ Policies centring on banning or regulating imports or practices such as open burning have so far been weakly enforced.
		Libreville Declaration	⇨ Health and Environment in Africa recognises that there is a need for further research and policies to increase understanding of the vulnerability of humans to environmental risk factors, particularly in Africa. Risk factors identified in relation to e-waste are chemicals, poor waste management practices and new toxic substances.

(*Continued*)

TABLE 1.7 (Continued)

No.	Country/region	Convention/declaration	Details
2.	European Union	*Aarhus Convention* – entered into force in 2001	⇨ It grants rights to the public and imposes on Parties and public authorities' obligations regarding access to information, public participation and justice. ⇨ Under the Convention, the Aarhus Protocol on Heavy Metals was one of eight protocols intended to address air quality issues within the EU.
		The WEEE Directive – entered into force in 2003	⇨ It is based on the principle of producer responsibility and promotes the green design and production of electronic products. ⇨ It includes separate collection of e-waste, and the use of best available treatment, recovery and recycling techniques and makes producers responsible for financing the take-back and management of e-waste; to better control the illegal trade of e-waste. ⇨ Despite extensive legislation targeting the e-waste problem, experience in the first few years of implementation of the WEEE Directive has shown that it is facing difficulties – less than half of the collected e-waste is currently treated and reported.
		RoHS Directive – entered into force in 2003 *REACH* – entered into force in 2007 *The EU Waste Framework Directive*, 2008	⇨ Aims to restrict the use of hazardous substances in EEE and contribute to the protection of human health and the environmentally sound recovery and disposal of e-waste.

3.	Latin America	Mercosur Policy Agreement of 2006 mandates its member states, Argentina, Paraguay, Uruguay and Brazil, to take national actions to ensure post-consumer responsibility by producers and importers	⇨ Most countries need to evolve legal framework. ⇨ Costa Rica, the first country in the region to develop specific, national e-waste legislation. ⇨ An attempt to introduce the concept of EPR as an environmental policy principle. ⇨ Central American Integration System is developing a model waste law discussing possible common hazardous wastes rules for Central America, possibly including e-waste.
4.	South Pacific	*Waigani Convention* – signed in 1995 and entered into force in 2001. As of June 2008, there were 13 Parties to the Convention.	⇨ Bans the importation of hazardous and radioactive waste and controls the transboundary movements and management of hazardous waste within the South Pacific region ⇨ Although there is no specific reference made to e-waste; Annex A does include waste having constituents such as cadmium and lead compounds.
5.	Ghana	National legislation – Electronic Waste (Disposal and Recycling) Regulations	⇨ To control the importation of e-waste. Non-compliance is subject to a fine, with the revenue invested in an e-waste recycling trust fund. Other measures include the designation of disposal assembly points and a code of conduct for the safe disposal of e-waste.

Source: Lundgren (2012: 35–38); and Baldé et al. (2017: 48). Compiled by the author.

The Basel Convention

The *Basel Convention* is considered to be one of the initial initiatives for dealing with e-waste – its transboundary movement and regulations to prevent adverse impact on environment and human health. The *Basel Convention* is an initiative of UNEP, which focuses on controlling transboundary movements of hazardous wastes and its disposal. It was first adopted on 22 March 1989 by the Conference of Plenipotentiaries in Basel, Switzerland, in response to public outcry following the discovery about toxic waste flowing to Africa and other parts of developing world, in the 1980s. The Convention came into force in May 1992, and started working on e-waste in 2002, with later addendums in 2006 (*Nairobi Declaration*) and 2011 (*Cartagena Decisions*). In 2006, the EU transposed the *Basel Convention* and the OECD Council Decision into European regulation with the European Waste Shipment Regulation (WSR). The WSR implements the international obligations of the two regulations and includes the internationally agreed upon objective that wastes shall be disposed of in an environmentally sound manner (Baldé et al. 2016: 5). The regulatory system under the *Basel Convention* includes prior informed consent for export and import; and the intended movement is possible only after receiving written consent from both the concerned state authorities.

The *Basel Convention* is also considered to be one of the most significant MEA in relation to tackling the issues surrounding e-waste and its management – its transboundary movement and regulations to prevent adverse impact on environment and human health. There are four important aims of the Convention related to e-waste, as follow:

> (i) prevention – to reduce hazardous waste generation at its source; (ii) reduction – to promote and ensure the environmentally sound management of hazardous waste; (iii) resource recovery – to promote the proximity principle, advocating disposal as close to the source as possible; and (iv) final disposal – to regulate and monitor the remaining transboundary movements of hazardous waste.
>
> (Lundgren 2012: 33)

> Under Article 6 of the Convention, the hazardous waste shipment must undergo the prior informed consent (PIC) procedure – this system requires exporters to notify the destination country, any intermediary countries, of its intent to conduct trade in hazardous waste, through a notification of consent prior to the transboundary movement.
>
> (*op. cit.*)

In order to combat illegal traffic of e-waste, the Convention provides for the development of tools and training activities through the Green Customs Initiative (GCI). The *Basel Convention* started to address e-waste issues in 2002 through the adoption of The *Mobile Phone Partnership Initiative* (MPPI).[40] After which the *Nairobi Declaration*[41] (during COP8[42]) was adopted which gave a mandate to the Secretariat to implement the environmentally sound management of e-waste (Chaudhary

2018: 3). These initiatives provided the mandate for a roadmap for future strategic action on e-waste. In October 2011, during COP10, all 178 Parties agreed to allow an early entry into force of the BAN Amendment, a major breakthrough decision. As of October 2018, 186 states and the EU are parties to the Convention; Australia, Canada, Japan, South Korea, and USA have not ratified this Convention (Lundgren 2012: 34; www.archive.basel.int).

The importance of the *Basel Convention* is that if it properly implemented and enforced, negative impacts of treating waste at the importing state could be prevented. The procedures for legal cross-border movements have set up mechanisms for avoiding ecological disasters and maintaining a high level of protection of workers and the public. The shipment can only take place if the state of transit and the state of import give their written consent. Moreover, a confirmation is required of a contract between the exporter and the disposer specifying ESM (Levinson et al. 2019: 163).

The synergies among the *Basel, Rotterdam,* and *Stockholm conventions* are: promote a life cycle approach to chemicals management as each convention targets different stages of a chemical's life cycle; and developing programmatic cooperation and support for the implementation of the three conventions in areas of common concern, such as e-waste (Lundgren 2012).

(iii) The strategic approach to international chemicals management

SAICM is an international policy framework to promote chemical safety, adopted by the First International Conference on Chemicals Management (ICCM1) at Dubai, on 6 February 2006, with the overall objective of achieving sound management of chemicals throughout their life cycle. The second international conference on chemicals management, ICCM2, agreed to initiate a project on chemicals in e-products with a multi-stakeholder and multi-sectoral character and emphasises chemical safety as a sustainability issue. This approach aims at minimising the way chemicals are produced and used in ways which by 2020, in order to minimise significant adverse impacts on environment and human health. Its objectives are grouped under five themes: risk reduction, knowledge and information, governance, capacity building, technical cooperation, and illegal international traffic (www.saicm.org; Lundgren 2012: 35).

This policy framework is closely linked to three regulatory frameworks, they are: (i) *London Guidelines for the Exchange of Information on Chemicals in International Trade* (1989) (henceforth 'London Guidelines');[43] (ii) *Montreal Protocol*;[44] and (iii) *The Minamata Convention on Mercury*, 2013.[45]

Complementing international and regional conventions, international organisations also have an important role to play, for example, in monitoring the transport of toxic substances and running programmes to reduce the impact of e-waste on human health and the environment.

An analysis of the legislations/regulations, such as, the *Basel Convention, WEEE Directives,* MEA and national legislative framework, shows that the *WEEE Directives* seemed to be most comprehensive in nature since they have defined e-waste and introduced EPR. Cumulatively, these regulatory frameworks have impacted three strategic points of e-waste management in India – first, acceptance and implementation of EPR; second, recover resources and enhancing CE; and third, improvement in environment and human health. The existing regulatory frameworks have promoted institutional mechanism, guidelines for implementation of legal provisions, widening net of stakeholders and defining their responsibilities, and spreading awareness about use of chemicals (hazardous and non-hazardous) and their impact on environment and human health.

Increasing thrust on circular economy

The CE approach intends for restorative economy and to create a regenerative system of handling e-waste by handling them in closed loops through which optimal reuse, renovation, remanufacturing, and recycling of products and efficient recovery of materials could be ensured. For efficient resource recovery, it focuses on product design, e-waste collection and disposal practices and mechanism, recycling technology, reuse, etc., and closing resource loops by employing reverse supply chain and the reverse logistics[46] strategies/frameworks. By improving e-waste collection and recycling practices worldwide, a considerable amount of secondary raw materials – precious, critical and non-critical – could be made readily available to re-enter the manufacturing process while reducing the continuous extraction of new materials (Forti et al. 2020: 59). This entire loop including proper EoL services, and reuse of EoL products, facilitated by specific government's regulations, has generated new economic markets, and new entrepreneurial activities, which has great economic potentials across the world. This way, CE is gaining greater relevance in academic research and policy making agenda. In this context, reverse logistic processes of collection, recycling and reuse of e-waste plays a critical role for different reasons; also, can be regarded as a business strategy in which recovery activities are imposed for the purpose of increasing sustainability (Isernia et al. 2019: 2–4).

The CE as a concept employs REs, resource recovery and re-using resources; making suitable shift to 6Rs framework (repair, reuse, refurbish, responsibly disposed, recycle and resource recovery) from the existing 3Rs framework (reduce, recycle and reuse – applicable to other wastes), making management of secondary materials an integral part of e-waste management. The RE considerations are now being advocated in the design products and increase in productivity other than electrical and electronic sector, especially in the communications, construction and engineering sectors. The CE and RE are stressed upon in the context of dominant presence of informal sector in several countries, from e-waste collection to recycling, and final disposal.

As presented in Table 1.3, the quantum of e-waste generation is increasing, while the percentage of formally collected and recycled e-waste shows undulating movement – from 15.5% in 2013 to 20% in 2016, and 17.4% in 2019. Yet, the value of selected raw materials/intrinsic value of e-waste indicates (approx. 48–55 billion EUR) potential of resource recovery. For example, *GEM 2020* has presented an example of how demand of iron, aluminium, and copper can be met if the current

E-waste to be regulated for safe environment, human health Extended Producer Responsibility for end-of-life solution

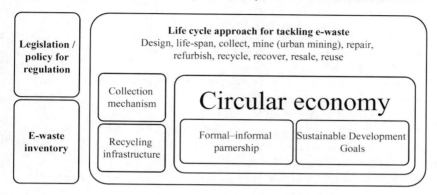

FIGURE 1.4 Tackling e-waste

recycling rate (17.4%) is increased. At this rate, a potential raw material value of 10 billion USD can be recovered, along with 4 Mt of secondary material would become available for recycling. Detailed discussion on recycling is covered linking it with toxicity in Chapter 3 and with REs and CE in Chapter 4.

The Figure 1.4 represents e-waste management thinking/tackling e-waste at global level. India has developed e-waste management parlance following global way of tackling e-waste.

IV: UN initiatives for e-waste management: creating partnerships and achieving Agenda 2030

By recognising e-waste as a tsunami, the UN has undertaken various initiatives at international and regional levels, especially the collaborative efforts. A number of global agencies have formed 'Global E-waste Statistics Partnership' (GESP) in 2017 to address e-waste challenges by improving e-waste data.

As part of a range of initiatives have undertaken by the UN e-waste management, forming a group or an agency, initiating a programme or intervention is noteworthy. For example, co-ordinating with the Environment Management Group (EMG);[47] the 'Solving the E-waste Problem' (StEP) initiative; the Sustainable Cycles (SCYCLE) programme;[48] and UNU-ViE SCYCLE.[49] Each programme or agency contributes to e-waste management in a specified manner. The partnership has achieved the result by publishing the second edition of the *GEM 2017* and building a website (www.globalewaste.org) to publicly visualise the most relevant e-waste indicators. Other initiatives include training of people from 60 countries for internationally adopted methodology for building statistics (Forti et al. 2020).

BOX 1.1: SDGS AND E-WASTE RELATED TARGETS AND INDICATORS

Target 3.9:
Use of hazardous chemicals and its impact on human health.
Target 8.3 and 8.8:
Decent job creation and access to financial services, and safe working environment and protecting labour rights.
Target 11.6 and its indicator 11.6.1:
Percentage of urban solid waste regularly collected and with adequate final discharge with regard to the total waste generated by the city.
Target 12.4 and indicator 12.4.2:
Treatment of waste, generation of hazardous waste and hazardous waste management, by type of treatment.
Target 12.5 and indicator 12.5.1:
National recycling rate and tonnes of material recycled.

Sources: Author unless otherwise specified.

In the context of Agenda 2030/SDGs, more specific targets and their sub-indicator have been recognised for monitoring growth of e-waste, taking cognisance of its potential hazardousness, and its high residual value. The SDG's targets include 3.9[50] (use of hazardous chemicals and its impact on human health), 8.3 (decent job creation and access to financial services), 8.8 (safe working environment and protecting labour rights), 11.6 (preventing adverse environmental impacts through wastes management), 12.4 (reduction in use of hazardous substance and their disposal) and 12.5 (substantially reduce waste generation through prevention, reduction, repair, recycling and reuse). The details are presented in the following box. As every country collects and updates data on each SDGs, its targets and indicators to keep track on Agenda 2030, the existing database could be used for each country's e-waste management quotient (Box 1.1).

SDGs are considered a roadmap for sustainable development by every country, and therefore, every country has started documentation of progress on each SDG, its targets and indicators, and its publication on regular basis/annually. Thus, SDGs have become a platform which provides country based updated data, a check point for progress and sustainability, and a future roadmap of every SDG. Given the high raw material demand for the production of EEE, e-waste is closely linked to the SDG indicators on the material footprint (SDGs 8.4.1 and 12.1.1) and the SDGs on the domestic material consumption (SDGs 8.4.2 and 12.2.2). GESP and the Partnership Measuring ICT for Development has developed methodology for SDG indicators, specifically for the SDG 12.5.1 – National recycling rate and tonnes of material recycled (e-waste sub-indicator), and SDG indicator 12.4.2 on hazardous waste.

The e-waste sub-indicator in SDG 12.5.1 has been defined as follow:

$$\text{SDG 12.5.1 sub-indicator on the e-waste} = \frac{\textbf{Total e-waste recycled}}{\textbf{Total e-waste generated}}$$

where the 'Total e-waste recycled' is equivalent to the 'e-waste formally collected' is divided by the 'e-waste generated'[51] (Forti et al. 2020: 31). This method could be employed to examine extent of hazardous waste created in each country every year.

Sustainability and CE are two sides of a coin. The depletion of mineral deposits, declining metal recoveries and grades, the concentration of strategic minerals in politically unstable regions and general risks associated with primary mining (Ledwaba and Sosibo 2017: 2). Mining and the extraction of raw materials[52] are important links and sources of environmental and human health problems associated with the lifecycle of e-products. Reduction in mining may lead to less destruction to the environment and local ecosystems of the mining regions.

The UNEMG report (2017) has documented UN systems' response 154 initiatives[53] covering ten focus areas, and 12 types of interventions, and their focuses, types and performance across different regions; along with various partnerships and collaborative efforts put in by the UN systems in 14 years (between 2004 to 2017) by the 23 entities associated with UN systems.[54] However, those most active UN agencies including UNU and the UNU-led StEP initiative, UNIDO, UN Environment, DFS and UNICEF; the secretariat of the Basel Convention, ITU, and the GEF (Global Environment Facility) are left absent due to their focus on internal corporate e-waste management rather than the provision of direct support to member states on e-waste matters (UNEMG 2017: 23) (Table 1.8).

Taking cognisance of the existing informal e-waste system in different countries, of 154 initiatives by UN, 63 related to recycling and ESM of e-waste, and 12 initiatives are Education/Employment/Health related, which indicate need for addressing problems of recycling, health and environment. Of a total of 63 initiatives, (i) three are related to acquisition of raw materials; (ii) four are linked to design; (iii) five each for production, transportation/delivery, repair; (iv) seven each for consumer use and reuse; and (v) 12 each for EoL treatment, and final disposal. The foremost concern is to work on the life cycle principle; that is, to understand different stages of the life cycle of EEE in the e-waste initiatives.

The types of initiatives undertaken by the UN are: (i) one for standardisation; (ii) two for policies; (iii) three for programmes; (iv) six for working groups and workshops; (v) seven each for glossaries and compilations, and trainings and learnings; (vi) 11 for partnerships; (vii) 13 for networks and consortiums; (viii) quantitative assessments; (ix) 23 are studies and reports related; (x) 28 for projects; and (xii) 30 for preparing manuals and guidelines.

Total 139 collaborations and partnerships by UN provide an idea of various aspects of e-waste management and need for addressing requirements on different counts. The characteristics of existing collaborations for e-waste management are: 68 (49%) collaborations are UN and public; 50 (36%) collaborations are UN and private; and 21 (15%) collaborations are UN-only.[55]

TABLE 1.8 UN initiatives to tackle e-waste across different regions during 2004 and 2017

Region	Focus of the initiative		Total number
North America	Shipment of e-waste	01	01
South America	Knowledge sharing	01	13
	E-waste management and disposal	06	
	Chemicals	03	
	Others	03	
Europe	Legal/regulation/patents	04	19
	E-waste management and disposal	06	
	Education/Employment/Health	02	
	Knowledge sharing	01	
	Shipment of e-waste	03	
	Material/Design	01	
	Others	02	
Africa & Sub-Sahara	Knowledge sharing	01	25
	ICTs	02	
	Chemicals	06	
	E-waste management and disposal	12	
	Legal/regulation/patents	03	
	Other	01	
Asia & Oceania	Shipment of e-waste	02	34
	Knowledge sharing	03	
	ICTs	01	
	Chemicals	07	
	E-waste management and disposal	17	
	EPR	01	
	Education/Employment/Health	02	
	Legal/regulation/patents	01	
Total			92

Source: UNEMG (2017: 34–39). Compiled by the author.

V: Indian scenario: e-waste generation, collection and recycling

India ranks third in the world with waste generation of 3,230 kt or 3.2 Mt in 2019 (2.0 Mt in 2016), 2.4 kg/inh followed by China (10,129 kt or 10.1 Mt, 7.2 kg/inh), and USA (6,918 kt or 6.9 Mt, 21 kg/inh). India moved up to third rank (in 2019) in three years from fifth in 2016, leaving Japan (2.1 Mt in 2016) and Germany (1.9 Mt in 2016) behind in 2019. At present, there are ten countries producing more than 1,000 kt e-waste annually. At present, officially documented global e-waste collection and recycling rate is 17.4%.

India collected and recycled 30 kt (0.030 Mt) in 2019 (Forti et al. 2020: 109), which is less than 0.036 Mt of its e-waste in 2016–2017 (Baldé et al. 2017: 68). This reveals that the e-waste generation in India is almost 60% higher in three years, as against its recycling capacity. As of today, some 95% of e-waste is managed by the informal sector in India including collection, transportation, dismantling, recycling, and selling of secondary/recovered materials in the market. The informal sector[56] broadly refers to existence, material and financial flows – it characterises an informal existence and setup (it may not be registered as a dismantling or recycling unit) and follow a disorganised way of functioning, with an informal economy including cash transactions, inadequate tools and safety measures, inadequate wages to labour, and often employing semi-skilled labourers or even children,[57] lack of social security for labour, etc; informal channels for e-waste collection, transportation and informal way (rudimentary techniques) of treating e-waste; insufficient resource recovery; getting rid of e-waste residues; and remaining out of legal frameworks in some ways. In the absence of a database, the number of jobs, levels of remuneration, and conditions of employment in e-waste management remain largely unknown (ILO 2014).

E-waste in India is majorly processed using inefficient technologies, inadequate infrastructures, and improper and unhealthy eco-system (Toxics Link 2019b: 2). Despite being highly effective in collecting WEEE, its recycling techniques yield low extraction rates and result in large scale environmental pollution, which negatively affects the physical wellbeing of thousands of people (GIZ 2017: 4). In 2017, over 200 manufacturers of electronic goods, including some e-giants, were served notices by the Central Pollution Control Board (CPCB) for not complying with e-waste procurement norms (Henam 2018).

Historical, domestic e-waste in India: generation and composition

One of the first studies was carried out by GTZ and BIRD in 2007. This study calculated 'the total annual e-waste generated in India in the year 2007 is 382,979 metric tonnes (MT),[58] including 50,000 MT of imports in India...the amount available for recycling was 144,143 MT but due to the presence of considerable refurbishment market only 19,000 MT of e-waste has been recycled in the year 2007' (Khattar et al. 2007: 9).

The CPCB estimated 146,800 MT of e-waste was generated in India in 2005; at that time, an estimate was projected – 800,000 MT by 2012, and 16.4 lakh [1.64 million] MT by 2014 (Committee on subordinate legislation 2016: 34). The main sources of e-waste in India are the government, public and private industrial sectors, which account for almost 70% of total e-Waste generation.

> An Indian Market Research Bureau (IMRB) survey of 'e-waste generation at source' in 2009 found that out of the total e-waste volume in India, televisions and desktops including servers comprised 68% and 27% respectively. Imports and mobile phones comprised of 2% and 1% respectively (LARRDIS 2011: 5). As such, large household appliances like washing machines and refrigerators

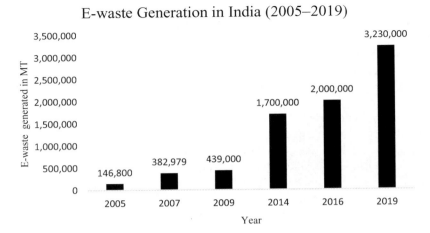

FIGURE 1.5 E-waste generation in India (2005–2019)

in the overall e-waste stream composition is not that significant but not disposing them (more than 50% stored quantities) reflect disposal behaviours of consumers in India (Figure 1.5).

(Dwivedy and Mittal 2010b)

Of a total of 2.0 Mt e-waste generated in India in 2016, 1.58 Mt (79% of the total) from unorganised manner while 0.42 (21% of the total) Mt was from organised sector. Of the e-waste collected, computers accounted for almost 70% of e-waste, followed by telecommunication equipment-phones (12%), electrical equipment (8%) and medical equipment (7%) with the remainder consisting of household e-waste (ASSOCHAM-cKinetics 2017).

A survey by ASSOCHAM-NEC in 2018b revealed that ten states in India contribute the most to e-waste generation. Maharashtra tops with 19.8% of the total e-waste generated (including 120,000 MT from Mumbai and 25,000 metric tonnes from Pune), followed by Tamil Nadu (13% including 67,000 metric tonnes from Chennai), Andhra Pradesh (12.8% including 32,000 metric tonnes from Hyderabad), Uttar Pradesh (10.1%), West Bengal (9.8% including 55,000 metric tonnes from Kolkata), Delhi (9.5% including 98,000 MT from Delhi-NCR), Karnataka (8.9% including 92,000 metric tonnes from Bangalore), Gujarat (8.8% including 36,000 metric tonnes from Ahmedabad), Madhya Pradesh (6.6%), and Punjab (ASSOCHAM-NEC 2018b: 43).

Imported e-waste in India

Skinner et al. (2010: 9) mentioned in 2010 that e-waste is often shipped via third world countries; it is unrealistic to expect these statistics to be exact. They further mentioned that of the e-waste imported by India, it is estimated that approximately 80% originates from the USA, while the remaining 20% is predominantly imported from the EU. As such, the import of e-waste is regulated with recent legislation in India, but until 2016 its import was illegal.

The main global sources of e-waste are the United States, the EU, Australia, Japan and the Republic of Korea, and the main recipients of e-waste are China and India, followed by Mexico, Brazil, the Eastern European countries, and African countries, including Egypt, Ghana and Nigeria, among others.
(Lundgren 2012: 64)

The *E-waste Management Rules, 2016* tasks the state pollution control boards (SPCB) to make the estimates of imported e-waste based on inventory prepared, but no SPCB has done that yet (Kaur 2018).

Futuristic projections for e-waste in India

By 2020, the demand for e-products in India is expected to reach nearly $400 billion with a CAGR (Compound Annual Growth Rate) of 41% during 2016–2020 (MeitY and NITI Aayog, 2019: 14). As a result, e-waste is likely to be increased by 30% during 2018–2020. Out of the 67.8 billion tonnes of global material use, India's share was about 7.1% amounting to 4.83 billion tonnes. With rising population and at the current high growth rates, India's material use is expected to triple by 2030. According to *GEM 2017*, the estimated value of raw materials which can be mined from e-waste stood at €55 billion, of which mobile phones alone constituted €9.5 billion (*op. cit.*: 16–17).

Essentials of e-waste cohesive management thinking in India

India has largely focused on a regulatory framework, employing EPR as management and enforcement strategy for various aspects of e-waste management along with increasing thrust on RE and CE. Under the existing legal framework, i.e. the *E-waste Management Rules, 2016* (henceforth 'Rules, 2016') and *E-waste Management (Amendment) Rules, 2018* (henceforth 'Amended Rules, 2018'), effective implementation of EPR occupies centre stage. The producers or the producer responsibility organisation (PRO) is expected to establish collection channel, segregation, safe transportation and ensure recycling of e-waste. The e-waste items are specified in the rules, and proportion of e-waste collection and recycling is also specified for every consecutive year after 2016. The responsibilities of consumer and 'bulk consumers'[59] are also specified in the rules. Chapter 5 focuses exclusively on e-waste management through legislation in India.

The MeitY (Ministry of Electronics and Information Technology) and NITI Aayog (National Institution for Transforming India), Government of India has launched a document, titled, *Strategy on REs in EEE sector* in January 2019. The strategy paper presents that RE would lead to CE, a key element to sustainable development as well as the solutions to possible conflicts which can arise from socio-economic, socio-political and politico-economic inter-relationships which are caused due to the scarcity of resources. It also envisages linking of three missions – Make in India, Digital India, and Clean India (Swachh Bharat) for effective e-waste management.

When essentials of e-waste management in India are thought of and enlisted, the need for material flow analysis (MFA) is identified, which elaborates a list of essentials for cohesive e-waste management thinking in India, as presented in the following chart (Figure 1.6).

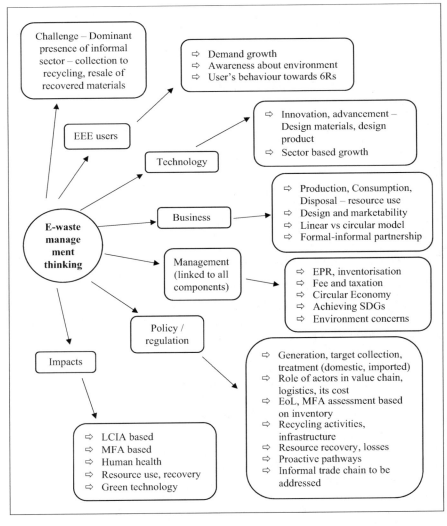

FIGURE 1.6 Essentials of cohesive e-waste management thinking in India

The management incorporates user's behaviour; technology (design product and sector-based growth); business; inventorisation (e-waste generation, target collection and treatment to e-waste, shipment (if applicable – transboundary movements), stages from collection to recycling including role of actors in value chain, and logistics and its cost, EoL solutions, resource recovery and losses); and implementation of policies. The impacts include environmental concerns – toxicity and pollutants (harmful chemicals), and pollution of soil, water, and air; energy use during e-product production, consumption and disposal; human health hazard due to exposure to e-waste containing toxins, natural resource (water, land, energy) use and recovery; and clean and green technological solutions.

The MFA[60] for e-waste management works as a tool for comprehensive understanding on why, how, where, and what of e-waste (the flow of matter – compounds, chemical elements, materials, or commodities) at different levels / with a certain categorisation (e.g. national-level assessment, regional-level assessment, product-level assessment, element-level assessment). The MFA helps in what supports a material balancing, conservation flow that brings in multiple axes – e-waste generation estimation, material flow and stock estimation, potential material recovery, socio-technical structure of WEEE management, economic sustainability of e-waste management system, product substitution effects due to technology transition, product and element characterisation, etc. (Islam and Huda 2019).

Informal e-waste trade chain in India

As per the rules of 2016, the EEE manufacturers and users (consumers, bulk consumers) are the generators of domestic e-waste; the inflow of imported e-waste is observed, though legally banned. This is the first layer in this sequence of e-waste disposal and collection. The individual consumers are disposing e-waste – either give away for reuse to individuals and institutions or sell it to the *kabaadiwala*. The bulk consumers either auctioned off, sold to scrap dealers, or given away to PROs. The manufacturers dispose of e-scrap to scrap dealers, and the imported e-waste is directly entering the trade by dealing with scrap dealers. The second level – e-waste collection introduces three actors – first level of *kabaadiwala*, scrap dealer/scrap trader/ government agency (MSTC) that trades in metal scrap/PRO, and scrap dealer/scrap trader who may or may not refurbish the e-waste. In the third layer of dealing with e-waste, mainly the local *kabaadiwala* sell the e-scrap to city level waste aggregators. Before the e-waste steps to large-scale aggregators in the fourth layer, most e-waste is reported to be sorted, dismantled and/or cannibalised. The last layer is of large-scale waste aggregators who may be informal recyclers; if not, they sell off e-waste to the formal and informal recyclers. The e-scrap dealer/trader sells e-waste to the formal/informal recyclers while the PROs pass on the e-waste to the formal/authorised recyclers for legal compliance. In this layer, leakage of e-waste is reported, and thus, the e-waste (sorted, dismantled, cannibalised) come back to the market for resale. The last layer is of sale of secondary material in the market for reuse/in the supply chain (Figure 1.7).

40 Sustainable development

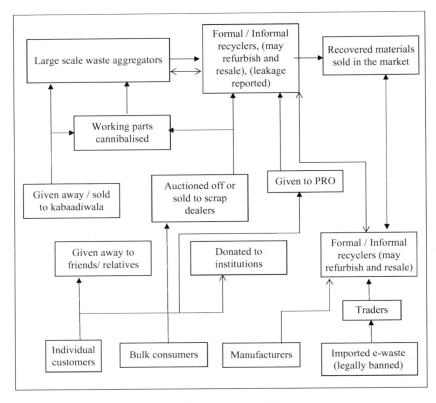

FIGURE 1.7 E-waste flow and recycling scenario in India

In this trade value chain, the collection to recycling trade provides livelihoods to a significant number of urban poor. Moreover, recovery of materials from this waste and ploughing them back into the supply chain process are some of the advantages of the sector. The flipside of the recycling sector is the hazardous practices and processes (Basu 2019; Sinha 2019a). In this context, building up partnership of formal-informal players has been considered as a strategic action for larger legal compliance and cohesive e-waste management.

Other aspects of cohesive e-waste management thinking, such as CE, recycling, RE, impacts on environment and human health are dealt with in detail in Chapter 3; users perspectives, business and technological concerns are dealt with in Chapter 6.

Opportunities and challenges of e-waste management in India

Among the opportunities of e-waste, REs tops,[61] followed by infrastructure developed for collection and treatment of WEEE, and achieving improved environment and human health by dealing with toxicity of e-waste. Mainly three opportunities are seen in e-waste – very high value material, especially gold, silver and platinum group metals; harvesting e-waste would lead to produce lesser CO_2 emission compared to mining in earth's crust, and in turn reduce global warming; and extending the life of products (revised product design, repair, refurbish) and re-using components brings even larger economic benefits.

Opportunities

As per one estimate, e-waste is worth at least $62.5 billion annually, which is more than the gross domestic product (GDP) of most countries (PACE and World Economic Forum 2019: 5). Some metals recovered per year globally is as follow: copper (4,500,000 tonnes), tin (90,000 tonnes), antimony (65,000 tonnes), cobalt (11,000 tonnes), and silver (6,000 tonnes). Proper separation of different elements from WEEE, recovering of the elements of economic value, and prevention of environmental pollution of hazardous components depend on dismantling and recycling technologies (Toxics Link 2019b: 5). For India, the FICCI CE Report, 2017 estimated,

> the business opportunity for extracting gold from e-waste is to the tune of $0.7–$1 billion (approx. 70–75 crore INR). Furthermore, one ton of ore has an extractable reserve of about 1.4 grams of gold while a ton of mobile phone PCBs can produce about 1.5 kg.
>
> (Quoted in MeitY and NITI Aayog, 2019: 20)

> Environmental impacts are now shifting from 'use' to the 'production' and 'material extraction' stages... lifecycle impact of bulk metals per unit is smaller than that of special metals (e.g. gold, palladium and cobalt). The mining of critical resources often requires more effort than for bulk metals.
>
> (Quoted in Parajuly et al. 2019: 13)

and, it may lead to conflicts.

Contributing to methods for collecting data and creating reliable database is looked upon as an opportunity. Better e-waste data will eventually contribute to minimising e-waste generation, prevent illegal dumping and improper treatment of e-waste, promote recycling, and create jobs in the refurbishment and recycling sector (Baldé et al. 2017: 2). The GoI considers creating awareness about e-waste management among users, which would in turn help in effective implementation of existing legal framework and producers' of EEE and their pro-activeness for operationalising EPR are also seen as opportunities.

With the introduction and implementation of the rules in 2016, a few noteworthy opportunities were created, such as the possibility of creating database statistics, the use of data for effective enforcement (monitoring and evaluation of achieving targets and compliance) and legal compliance, and movement towards formal economy could begin (dealing with informal sector with competitive spirit and business activities) for domestic e-waste. With this shift towards formal economy, more jobs would be created. Specific data on imports of e-waste would be useful in identifying transboundary movement of e-waste and take necessary action for proper treatment of e-waste, may that be repaired and reused or recycled in ESM and EoL.

Challenges

The set of opportunities are challenges too for e-waste management. Imagine about 3.0 Mt untreated e-waste is discarded for landfill or burnt or illegally traded or treated in a substandard way every year, and the threat it creates to the environment, sustainable development, economy, human health and surrounding ecosystems.

Practitioners of e-waste management have shared challenges, such as, establishing logistics and transportation cost for collection of e-waste; recycling technology, economics and viability of recycling ventures; dealing with informal sector and informal economy and how make a shift to formal economy through e-waste management; and role of citizens and producers of EEE in effective implementation of the legal framework and EPR respectively (Turaga and Bhaskar 2019). The leakage of e-waste and resale of leaked e-waste being resold – from one vendor to another vendor or recycler and returning to the market again, is a major problem reported. Such circulation of e-waste, without getting treated, may show as 'treated e-waste' on paper for legal compliance is reported as a challenge. This is a challenge for effective enforcement of the existing regulatory framework (Singhal 2019a). Further, regarding technology, innovation and advancement including design of the product (planned obsolescence, inability to repair, or software compatibility issues) and materials used, and sector-based growth are closely linked; these aspects have remained peripheral issues, least talked about, least enforced under the broad canopy of EPR.

In order to comply with the *WEEE Directive*, industrialised countries have made convenient use of the word 'recycling;' they justify the free trading of hazardous waste materials to the developing countries of Asia, where labour is cheap and health and environmental restrictions are negligent. For emerging economies, these materials offer a business opportunity, and entire new economic sectors revolve around trading, repairing, and regaining materials from surplus electronic devices (Babu et al. 2007: 311). On the other hand, the semi-formal or informal sector actors employ rudimentary techniques for recovery of materials, which are risky and earning lower income compared to advance technology of recycling. Thus, as against the opportunity of creating of jobs or livelihood for the workers, the informal sector in India creates challenges for e-waste management.

The report of MeitY and NITI Aayog (2019: 28, 45) articulated challenges of e-waste management in India, which are presently guided by complex dynamics. They are: (i) producers have been tasked with ensuring collection of EoL material, and parallelly the informal sector has been handling WEEE (from collection to recycling) through its wide network for the last few decades; (ii) EEE is diverse and complex with respect to the materials and components used and, waste streams from the manufacturing and recycling processes; (iii) characteristics of e-waste is of paramount importance for developing a resource efficient, economically viable and environmentally sound recycling system – high cost of setting up recycling facility and making it sustainable; (iv) accurate and updated data on e-waste generation, flow, collection and treatment, and trends are also difficult to ascertain; (v) mapping of documentation of the entire value chain is difficult, as there are several human actors involves, each with different set of functions and responsibilities; (vi) establishing linkage amongst stakeholders and preparing them with win–win situations through various incentives, awareness measures, penalties, etc. is a challenge in itself; (vi) little awareness amongst different sectors about the rules of 2016; and (vii) strong implementation of legislation across the whole country, wherein exist. The gap between business concerns (resource availability, recovery and management of secondary materials, marketability of an e-product, etc.) versus linear thinking (model, concepts, and concerns) of the existing policy/Rules, 2016, pressing for enforcement through EPR, fee and taxation and facing penalties in cases of non-compliance. In this gap, morale and intent of producers and PROs for achievement under EPR, lack of motivation and incentives for all the stakeholders, and economic viability of recycling infrastructure are critical.

Notes

1 1 million metric tonnes = 1,000,000,000 kg.
2 'kg/inh' represents kilogram per inhabitant.
3 Refurbishing is a process to make devices functional in a way that they work according to new standards vis-à-vis obsolete technology. For example, old parts are replaced by new ones, new software could be installed.
4 The samples of soil and water collected from acid processing/leaching facility in Delhi in 2005, heavy metals (Lead, Cadmium, Mercury, Tin) were detected in high levels in the final spent acid wastes (e.g. 68 mg/L antimony, 240 mg/L copper, 20 mg/L lead, 478 mg/L nickel, 340 mg/L tin and 2,710 mg/L zinc) (Greenpeace 2005: 5). Residues of phthalate esters and chlorophenols were also detectable in these acid wastes. Toxic substances like mercury and lead are commonly used in e-products, which contaminate the land, water, and air.
5 The toxins are different types, such as, carcinogenic (having potential to cause cancer), neurotoxic (can cause damage to nervous systems), reprotoxic (toxic effect on reproduction processes), bio-accumulative, mutagenic (Mutagen is a physical or chemical agent that changes genetic material. In genetics, a material that can alter genetic material, for example, DNA is mutagenic), etc.
6 98 Mt of CO_2-equivalents were released into the atmosphere from discarded fridges and air-conditioners that were not managed in an environmentally sound manner (Forti et al. 2020: 15).
7 There are 17 rare earth elements – Cerium (Ce), Dysprosium (Dy), Erbium (Er), Europium (Eu), Gadolinium (Gd), Holmium (Ho), Lanthanum (La), Lutetium (Lu), Neodymium (Nd), Praseodymium (Pr), Promethium (Pm), Samarium (Sm), Scandium (Sc), Terbium (Tb), Thulium (Tm), Ytterbium (Yb), and Yttrium (Y) (Buchert et al. 2012: 1).

8 Silicone and its derivatives are the main substrate material in the production of microchips and semiconductors. Other non-metal or semimetal materials are antimony, bismuth, cobalt, fluorite, garnet, magnesium and talc. Other materials like ceramics are also used for its insulation characteristics. Certain clays, glasses, calcium and carbon (in various forms) are also often used.
9 The waste management hierarchy is as a strategy or guiding principle for manufacturers, governmental organizations, consumers, and other actors in society on how to prioritize waste management approaches to decrease its environmental impacts and increase circularity. In this hierarchy, waste prevention and minimisation, reuse, recycling, energy recovery and landfilling are the stages (Miliute-Plepiene and Youhanan 2019: 25–26).
10 RoHS is for the restriction of the use of certain hazardous substance in the EEE, and to promote greener products. It came into force with effect from 1 July 2006' (LARRDIS 2011: 84).
11 Directive 2002/96/EC of the European Parliament and Council of 27 January 2003, as amended by Directive 2003/108/EC of the restriction of the European Parliament and Council of 8 December 2003 on WEEE (OJ [Official Journal] L37/24, 13.02.2003) (quoted in Levinson et al. 2019: 151).
12 REACH regulation came into force on 1 June 2007. It asked for approximately 30,000 existing substances to undergo a registration procedure during 2007–2018. This regulation moves burden from the authorities to the industries (Ram Mohan et al. 2019: 170, 175–176).
13 The *Basel Convention* is an initiative of UNEP, which focuses on 'controlling transboundary movements of hazardous wastes and its disposal'. Started in 1989 and came into force in 1992, the convention started working on e-waste in 2002. This Convention has been ratified by 187 countries.
14 The StEP is an initiative of the United Nations (UN). It is a global network of more than 55 member organisations for holistic e-waste management. For further details visit http://www.step-initiative.org.
15 'Reuse' of EEE or its components is
   to continue the use of it (for the same purpose for which it was conceived) beyond the point at which its specifications fail to meet the requirements of the current owner and the owner has ceased use of the product.
   Products could be donated or traded before or in this phase.
16 'Preparation for reuse' comprises any operation performed to bring used EEE or its components into a condition to meet the requirements of a next potential owner.
17 Recycling:
   The phase of the product lifecycle where due to lack of functionality, cosmetic condition or age the product is broken down into component materials and recycled into raw material for use in the manufacture of new EEE or other products.
18 Disposal:
   Material that cannot be recycled into raw material for use in manufacture of new EEE or other products would need to be disposed of using other methods, such as energy recovery or landfill. Items that are disposed of in household bins may move directly to this phase avoiding any opportunity of reuse or recycling.
19 The first WEEE Directive listed 10 categories for which data was collected. Those were: (i) Large household appliances; (ii) Small household appliances; (iii) IT and telecommunications equipment; (iv) Consumer equipment; (v) Lighting equipment; (vi) Electrical and electronic tools (with the exception of large-scale stationary industrial tools); (vii) Toys, leisure, and sports equipment; (viii) Medical devices (with the exception of all implanted

and infected products); (ix) Monitoring and control instruments; and (x) Automatic dispensers (Forti et al. 2018: 14–15).
20 For details, refer McCann and Wittmann. 2015 (StEP Green Paper Series), p. 10. Data also available from Baldé, C.P., Wang, F., Kuehr, R., Huisman, J. (2015), The global e-waste monitor – 2014, United Nations University, IAS – SCYCLE, Bonn, Germany.
21 Category 1 for temperature exchange equipment including cooling and freezing equipment. Category 2 for screens and monitors includes televisions, monitors, laptops, notebooks, and tablets. Category 3 covers lamps. Category 4 for large equipment incorporating washing machines, clothes dryers, dishwashing machines, electric stoves, large printing machines, copying equipment, and photovoltaic panels. Category 5 small equipment includes vacuum cleaners, microwaves, ventilation equipment, toasters, electric kettles, electric shavers, scales, calculators, radio sets, video cameras, electrical and electronic toys, small electrical and electronic tools, small medical devices, small monitoring, and control instruments. Category 6 for IT (information technology) and telecommunication equipment includes mobile phones, Global Positioning System (GPS) devices, pocket calculators, routers, personal computers, printers, and telephones.
22 No details are provided in *GEM 2020*, for example, about method for deriving these figures, equivalent details, or its impact on environment. In absence of such details, it is assumed that these figures are projections, based on informal way of treating e-waste and emission of CO_2 and BFRs, and deposition of mercury.
23 For region-wise information of type of e-waste across transboundaries, refer Baldé et al. 2016.
24 Any substance or object which the holder discards or intends or is required to discard.
25 The collection, transport, recovery and disposal of waste, including the supervision of such operations and the aftercare of disposal sites, and including actions taken as a dealer or broker.
26 Measures taken before a substance, material or product has become waste.
27 Any operation the principal result of which is waste serving a useful purpose.
28 Any recovery operation by which waste materials are reprocessed into products, materials or substances whether for the original or other purposes.
29 There has been difference of opinion regarding ROHS3. The website rohsguide.com considers as (EU) 2015/863 is considered as ROHS3 by (https://help.assentcompliance.com/hc/en-us/articles/360001203047-What-is-EU-RoHS-3-). However, Valeire Kruntz contested this by saying, 'There is a common misconception that Directive (EU) 2015/863 which amends Directive 2011/65/EU (also referred to as "RoHS 2") can be referred to as "RoHS 3"' (Kruntz 2020).
30 For more details visit https://ec.europa.eu/environment/waste/weee/index_en.htm
31 Directive 2012/19/EG of the European Parliament and of the Council of 4 July 2012 concerning waste of electrical and electronic equipment (revised).
32 For more details visit https://ec.europa.eu/environment/waste/rohs_eee/index_en.htm
33 Phthalates are manmade compounds, used as additives, for softness and flexibility of the product, such as, plastics, food package, cosmetics, and medical devices.
34 EEA includes all European Union member states, in addition to Iceland, Liechtenstein, Norway and Croatia.
35 For more information, visit websites – https://echa.europa.eu/regulations/reach/understanding-reach; https://ec.europa.eu/environment/chemicals/reach/reach_en.htm; and https://echa.europa.eu/regulations/reach/understanding-reach
36 Mutagen is a physical or chemical agent that changes genetic material. In genetics, a material that can alter genetic material, for example, DNA is mutagenic.

46 Sustainable development

37 Reprotoxic represents reproductive toxicity. This is associated with some chemical substances which can interfere with normal reproductive functions.
38 This Convention was adopted on 10 September 1998 and entered into force on 24 February 2004. It promotes shared responsibility between exporting and importing countries in protecting human health and the environment and provides for the exchange of information about potentially hazardous chemicals that may be exported and imported; and creates legally binding obligations for the implementation of the PIC procedure (www.pic.int).
39 This Convention on Persistent Organic Pollutants (POP) was adopted in 2001 and came into force in 2004. E-waste contains many chemicals classified as POPs. The Convention requires Parties to take measures to eliminate or reduce the release of POPs into the environment, aiming at protection of human health and the environment from POPs. To date, 176 countries are Parties to the Convention (www.pops.int; Lundgren 2012).
40 The Mobile Phone Partnership Initiative (MPPI) was adopted by the sixth meeting of the Conference of the Parties to the Basel Convention in 2002. For more information, visit: http://www.basel.int/Implementation/TechnicalAssistance/Partnerships/MPPI/Overview/tabid/3268/Default.aspx
41 The Nairobi Declaration on the Environmentally Sound Management of Electrical and Electronic Waste. It was adopted in Eighth meeting of the Conference of the Parties to the Basel Convention on the Control of Transboundary Movements of Hazardous Wastes and their Disposal in Nairobi in 2006. For more information, visit: http://www.basel.int/portals/4/basel%20convention/docs/meetings/cop/cop8/nairobideclaration.pdf
42 Eighth Conference of the Parties.
43 The *London Guidelines* (1989) aim to assist governments in the process of increasing chemical safety in all countries through the exchange of information on chemicals in international trade. They aim to enhance the sound management of chemicals through the exchange of scientific, technical, economic and legal information, and assist states in the process of developing future instruments. The *Code of Ethics on the International Trade in Chemicals* (1994) complements the *London Guidelines*. It addresses industry and other private sector parties in all countries with the aim of setting out the principles, guidance and governing standards of conduct for the promotion of ESM of chemicals in international trade. Through the implementation of this code, the private sector parties are expected to enter into voluntary commitment (Lundgren 2012: 35).
44 The Protocol on Substances that Deplete the Ozone Layer entered into force in 1987 with the objective of protecting the ozone layer from chemicals destroying it. 96 chemicals are currently controlled by the *Montreal Protocol*. These chemicals are commonly found in articles such as old fridges (ibid.).
45 This Convention on Mercury is a global treaty to protect environment and human health from the adverse effects of Mercury. This Convention entered into force on 16 August 2017. Major highlights of the *Minamata Convention* include a ban on new Mercury mines, the phase-out of existing ones, the phase out and phase down of Mercury use in a number of products and processes, control measures on emissions to air and on releases to land and water, and the regulation of the informal sector of artisanal and small-scale gold mining. The Convention also addresses interim storage of mercury and its disposal once it becomes waste, sites contaminated by mercury as well as health issues (www.mercuryconvention.org).
46 Broadly, 'reverse logistics' refers to logistics activities carried out in source reduction, recycling, substitution, reuse of materials and disposal. This is a process of planning, implementing, and controlling the efficient, cost-effective flow of raw materials, in-process

inventory, finished goods, and related information from the point of consumption to the point of origin for the purpose of recapturing value or proper disposal. For different definitions of 'reverse logistics', see Isernia et al. (2019: 4).
47 The EMG is a UN System-wide coordination body on environment and human settlements. It was established in 2001 pursuant to the General Assembly resolution 53/242 in July 1999.
48 Sustainable Cycles (SCYCLE) is a programme hosted by UNU-ViE based in Bonn, Germany succeeding, the former UNU-IAS (Institute for the Advanced Study of Sustainability) SCYCLE. Its activities are focused on the development of sustainable production, consumption/usage, and disposal of ubiquitous goods with a special focus on EEE and advances sustainable e-waste management strategies based on life cycle thinking.
49 UNU-ViE SCYCLE was formed for conducting research; developing inter-disciplinary and multi-stakeholder public-private partnerships; assisting governments in developing e-waste legislation and standards; etc. (https://ehs.unu.edu/vice-rectorate/sustainable-cycles-scycle#overview).
50 By 2030, substantially reduce the number of deaths and illnesses from hazardous chemicals and air, water and soil pollution and contamination.
51 'E-waste formally collected' is defined as the amount of e-waste that is collected as such by the formal collection system, and 'e-waste generated' is defined as the amount of discarded e-products (e-waste) due to consumption within a national territory in a given reporting year, prior to any collection, reuse, treatment, or export.
52 The extraction of one kg of raw copper generates 310 kg of mining waste, while the extraction of one gm of gold generates 1–5 tonnes of mining waste. Additionally, 1–4 tonnes of waste could be produced during the processing of gold to make it ready for application in the electronics industry (Miliute-Plepiene and Youhanan 2019: 17).
53 Total 154 initiatives are classified as 10 focus areas, and 12 types. Since the figures are neither presented region-wise or inter-linking the focus and type of initiatives in the report, they are described here separately, with respective numbers. The focus of the initiatives is: (i) three initiatives are Statistics/Assessment related; (ii) three initiatives are EPR related; (iii) seven for Materials / Design; (iv) ten initiatives for Legal/Regulation/Patents; (v) 11 initiatives are EEE and ICTs related; (vi) 12 initiatives are Education/Employment/Health related; (vii) 13 initiatives are Knowledge sharing related; (viii) 15 initiatives are Chemicals related; (ix) 17 initiatives are for e-waste management; and (x) 63 for Recycling and ESM of e-waste related.
54 UN associated entities include (i) WHO (World Health Organisation) and UNICEF (United Nations Children's Fund) for Health and sanitation matters; (ii) UNDP (United Nations Development Program), UNCTAD (United Nations Conference on Trade and Development), World Bank, OECD (Organisation for Economic Cooperation and Development), UNIDO (United Nations Industrial Development Organisation), and ITU (International Telecommunication Unio) dealing with Development related issues; (iii) FAO (Food and Agriculture Organisation) and ILO for Agriculture and Labour related matters; and (iv) IMO (International Maritime Organisation), UN ESCAP (United Nations Economic and Social Commission for Asia and the Pacific), UN Environment for issues related to environment, energy, and transport.
55 For more details, see UNEMG report, 2017.
56 The informal sector in India is characterised with unorganised and irregular (as and when required) way of functioning of economic enterprises, mostly unregistered entities

that are engaged in production, and/or distribution of goods, and/or services meant for the purpose of sale, operate under ownership category of proprietary or partnership. For business, these enterprises employ workers on a daily basis or as casual–contractual worker. They operate in such a way that they do maintain records of their accounts, activities; and thus, they are not covered under legal and financial net.

57 In India, about 500,000 child labours between the age group of 10–14 are observed to be engaged in various e-waste activities, without adequate protection and safeguards in various yards and recycling workshops (ASSOCHAM-cKinetics 2017).

58 Of total 382,979 MT e-waste, 50,000 MT was imported, 56,324 MT was of computers, 27,5000 MT was of TVs, and 1,655 MT of mobile phones. Of total 144,143 MT e-waste available for recycling, 50,000 MT was imported, 24,000 MT was of computers, 70,000 MT was of TVs, and 143 MT was of mobile phones. Of total 19,000 MT e-waste recycled, 12,000 MT was of computers and 7,000 MT was of TVs.

59 As per the Rules 2016, a 'bulk consumer' includes central government or state government institutions, financial institutions (Banks), educational institutions (schools, colleges, universities, etc.), hospitals and other health care facilities (having turnover of more than one crore or have more than 20 employees), multinational organisations, international agencies, hotels, partnership and public or private companies registered under the Factories Act 1948, and companies Act 2013.

60 MFA is one of the most widely accepted and utilised tools in the industrial-ecology discipline, that measures the input-output materials and examines the pathways and flux of each material flow within the whole system is a systematic assessment of the flows and stocks of materials within a system defined in space and time.

61 As per recycling technologies available in India, metals like Copper, Aluminum, Ferrous metals, lead, Indium ingot, Tin, Silver, Gold, and Palladium; transparent glass and plastic scrap are recovered from CRTs, LCD panels, PCBs, and mobile phones. Among them, as neodymium (vital for magnets in motors), indium (used in flat panel TVs) and cobalt (for batteries) are the most precious metals (Toxics Link 2019b: 6,8).

2
EXTENDED PRODUCER RESPONSIBILITY

A mainstay for e-waste management

> *EPR is usually conceived as a comprehensive policy package, combining various instruments to simultaneously achieve three distinct objectives: Improved waste management and resource recovery: to establish effective collection of end-of-life (EoL) products from consumers, promote environmentally-sound treatment and efficient recycling, and reduce the amount of wastes for final disposal; Integrating environmental externalities into production and consumption: to transfer the financial burden for waste management from the public sector to the manufacturers; Design for the environment: to provide economic incentives for producers to incorporate product design that enables easier reuse and recycling of products.*
>
> Institute for Global Environmental Strategies (2012)

The evolution of EPR and wider acceptance suggests that it is multi-dimensional – a concept, a strategy, a legislative tool/policy instrument, a programme for legal compliance, and a path to business opportunities. EPR is the most highlighted legislative tool with which several goals could be attained; it is applied across several domains across the world, such as, different types of waste management, textile sector, carpets, and mattresses, pharmaceuticals, mercury lights, etc.

There exists vast literature on EPR, which covers varied perspectives, frameworks, and stakeholder's concerns. These aspects help in identifying complexities, and how to deal with them in attaining the goals of EPR in each domain. Different analytical frameworks are applied in order to understand life of a product and implementation of EPR, for example, product flows, financial flows, system management (institutions, city, local governments), and stakeholder roles, and perspectives. Heterogeneity in perspectives, and multi-centric nature of EPR, such as,

DOI: 10.4324/9780429285424-2

environmental policy, operation management guidelines, industrial ecology, conflicting needs and perspective of each stakeholder, and prevalent conditions, and socio-cultural aspects influencing implementation of EPR have stressed the need for adopting EPR for each sector with its particularity.

The chapter begins by describing evolution of concept of EPR and describes how it was evolved for waste management and now extended for e-waste management including its goals, implementation, and challenges. It then provides comprehensive overview on the EPR being implemented for e-waste management under the existing regulatory frameworks in different countries, and discusses three important aspects, i.e., role of PRO (producer responsibility organisation) prescribed in the existing regulatory framework, considerations for successful implementation of EPR, and challenges in implementing EPR for e-waste management. towards end, the chapter provides brief description of EPR and e-waste management in India, as EPR is covered in detail in Chapter 5.

Evolution of concept of 'extended producer responsibility'

The evolution of EPR has taken place in the broader context of sustainable development, which largely focuses on healthy and safe environment. Most developmental concerns, principles have been articulated from the perspectives of safe environment and sustainability. For example, the EU started discussing issues of environmental protection policy circles since early 1970s; considering a few fundamental principles of sustainable development, such as, the 'precautionary principle', the principle of 'prevention', and the 'polluter pays' principle. The necessity for the introduction of EPR comes from the growing awareness that other environmental policy measures might not be sufficient to reach the environmental goals of society (ISWA 2014).

The concept of EPR was first introduced by Thomas Lindhqvist, professor at the Lund University in Sweden in 1990 (ibid.); he has discussed policy principle to promote environment improvements of production systems in detail in his doctoral dissertation in 2000. During the 1990s, several European countries were preparing and commencing the implementation of various policy instruments to improve the management of EoL products, largely based on the preventive environmental strategies as promoted by UNEP in the 'Cleaner Production Programme'. The concept implies that responsibilities, which were traditionally assigned to consumers and authorities responsible for waste management, are to be shifted to product producers.

After introducing formal (primary) definition of EPR in 1992, Thomas revised the definition as a concept as a policy principle in 2000.

> EPR is a policy principle to promote total life cycle environmental improvements of product systems by extending the responsibilities of the manufacturer of the product to various parts of the entire life cycle of the product, and especially to the takeback, recycling, and final disposal of the product.
>
> (Lindhqvist 2000: v)

He presented a model of EPR where 'ownership' of a product is linked with four dimensions: liability,[1] economic responsibility,[2] physical responsibility,[3] and informative responsibility[4] (Lindhqvist 2000: iii–iv). This brings EPR principle in consistency with the 'polluter pays' principle, and a necessary condition for reflecting the essential life cycle costs in the price of the product. This revised definition stresses on 'life cycle perspective' as an important aspect for implementation of all policies; thus, the EPR principle and the implementation of policy instruments need to be viewed as a strategic attempt to reach sustainable solutions.

Davis Gary in 1994 defined 'Producer Responsibility Principle' as a policy principle, which is as follows:

> Concept that manufacturers and importers of products bear a degree of responsibility for the environmental impacts of their products throughout the products' life cycles, including upstream impacts inherent in the selection of materials for the products, impacts from manufacturers' production process itself, and downstream impacts form the use and disposal of the products. Producers accept their responsibility when they design their products to minimise the lifecycle environmental impacts and when they accept legal, physical or economic responsibility for the environmental impacts that cannot be eliminated by design.
>
> (quoted in Sander et al. 2007: I)

Thus, EPR as environmental strategy has been attempting to link the following dimensions: (i) area of products (implying that product system improvement including product material, design, expected life, etc.); (ii) design for environment/sustainable development (preventive environmental policy making) or Design for Disassembly (DfD) activities leading to overall life cycle environmental improvements of products and product systems; and (iii) public policy framework (which can ensure product will protect environment along with administrative, economic and informative instruments), which includes well-organised collection with high collection results, increased recycling, and costs connected to waste collection, recycling, or final disposal, etc.

> The practical development of EPR can be traced back to the enactment of the *German Ordinance on the Avoidance of Packaging Waste* in 1991. The success of the Ordinance that saw the consumption of packaging decoupled from the economic growth in Germany encouraged policy diffusion.
>
> (Manomaivibool and Hong 2014: 203)

In 1994, the European Commission developed a *Packaging Waste Directive* aimed to reduce packaging waste generation by 50% throughout Europe by 2001 (Mahesh 2007: 4–5).

EPR applied for waste management and extended for e-waste management

The EPR has been propagated as a mainstream paradigm in waste management since beginning of the 2000s by the OECD (Organization for Economic Co-operation and Development) countries, it was applied for 'packaging waste, electronic, and electrical equipment, batteries, bottles, paint cans, automobiles, waste oil, tyres and refrigerators' (UN ESCAP 2012: 1). The OECD defined EPR in 2001, as an environmental policy approach in which a producer's responsibility for a product is extended to the post-consumer stage of a product's life cycle. According to the OECD (2001: 18), 'EPR aims at reaching two goals: (i) shifting the responsibility away from the municipality and general taxpayer towards the producer; and (ii) provide incentives to producers to incorporate environmental considerations in the design of their products'. After 15 years, the OECD redefined EPR, based on the experience that EPR as an environment policy approach sought to shift the burden of managing certain EoL products from municipalities and taxpayers to producers, and ultimately to consumers. There is a need to redefine responsibilities; that is, the incentives provided to producers to redesign products and packaging, which would reduce the share of waste destined for final disposal, and thus increase recycling. Also, 'EPR policy alone does not aim to achieve a full internalization of environmental costs; the task of establishing an environmental price for a wide range of environmentally diverse waste streams makes this impractical' (OECD 2016: 21).

In the evolved EPR framework for e-waste management by OECD in 2016, the EPR embodies the notion that 'extending the producer's responsibility' describes producer's physical and/or financial responsibilities and covers all stages – from environmentally compatible product design and meeting material management goals through recycling to the post-consumer stage of a product life cycle. The producers typically pay towards the costs of e-waste processing, such as, collection, recycling, and disposal. The OECD (2016) has mentioned four broad categories of EPR instruments/responsibilities: (i) product take-back; (ii) economic and market-based instruments; (iii) regulations and performance standards; and (iv) information-based instruments.

The product take-back is considered a strategy, and therefore often becomes a voluntary initiative by the producers, by establishing collection and recycling targets for a product. The economic and market-based instruments provide financial incentives in form of deposit refund[5], advanced disposal fee[6], material tax, upstream combination tax/subsidy. These fees may be assessed by weight or per unit of product sold. After useful life of any e-product, physical responsibility (regulations and performance standards) of a producer encompasses take-back of the products from the consumers, which may enforce collection rate targets, and undertake recycling (processing for recovery). Information-based instrument/responsibility of a product mandates providing information on the attributes of the products, such as toxicity, safe disposal, recyclability, and including such requirements as product labelling, as well as related information on its website (Walls 2003; Patil and Ramakrishna 2020). In short, in a mandated EPR, 'producer bear cost of the entire reverse supply chain, including the cost of awareness, access-to-waste, collection, aggregation, transport, depollution, disposal, recycling, recovery and monitoring and regulating the system' (Khetriwal 2019: 143).

EPR: goals, implementation, and challenges for e-waste management

Goals

ISWA (2014) stressed that EPR need not be a stand-alone policy measure; it should always be incorporated in a mix of environmental policy measures.

EPR is usually conceived as a comprehensive policy package, combining various instruments to simultaneously achieve the following goals: (i) create a sustainable production, consumption, and waste management policy;[7] (ii) incentives for eco-design;[8] (iii) reduce landfilling and develop recycling and recovery channels; (iv) full internalisation of environmental costs, other instruments need to be introduced/ employed[9] (IGES 2012: 2; ISWA 2014: 5).

EPR can lead to the following:

> overall waste prevention; use of non-toxic materials and processes; development of closed material cycles; development of more durable products; development of more reusable and recyclable products; increased reuse, recycling and recovery; and transfer of waste management costs for used products onto producers consistent with the Polluters Pay Principle.
>
> (Mahesh 2007: 3)

Policy instruments

The EPR instruments have been implemented in a heterogenous or selective manner, mainly because of differences in framing of laws and implementing them as per the requirements of a country (Patil and Ramakrishna 2020). Among various 'regulatory instruments' mandatory take-back; energy efficiency standards; minimum recycled content standards; secondary material utilisation rate requirements; disposal bans and restrictions; material ban and restrictions; and product bans and restrictions. Among different 'economic instruments,' advance disposal fees; deposit/refund; material taxes; etc. are known. The 'information instruments' include seal-of-approval types of environmental information labelling – product environmental profiles for the whole life cycle of materials, product hazard warnings and product durability labelling (Mahesh 2007).

EPR implemented for e-waste management under the existing regulatory frameworks in different countries

The GEM 2017 recognises that:

> Most legislation and policies currently refer to the principle of EPR, which emerged in academic circles in the early 1990s. It is generally seen as a policy principle that requires manufacturers to accept responsibility for all stages in a product's lifecycle, including EoL management.

There are three primary objectives of the EPR principle:

- Manufacturers shall be incentivised to improve the environmental design of their products and the environmental performance of supplying those products.
- Products should achieve a high utilisation rate.
- Materials should be preserved through effective and environmentally-sound collection, treatment, reuse, and recycling.

The key principle behind the reasoning that producers or manufacturers should be primarily responsible for this post-consumer phase is that most of the environmental impacts are predetermined in the design phase (Baldé et al. 2017: 49).

The principle of EPR has been introduced in multiple countries and for a variety of waste streams. There is also a broad variety in the policy measures to implement EPR, the goals, and achievements. There is no one-size-fits-all approach of EPR, and its effectiveness will always depend on national circumstances, conditions, priorities, and waste streams. EPR implementation is a complex topic bringing many potential challenges; therefore, more 'practical' or 'operational' aspects to be considered for successful EPR implementation (ISWA 2014: 8).

Process of implementation

The process to implement the EPR concept typically involves the following three stages: (i) an appropriate policy instrument that embodies the EPR principles is identified and a legislative framework is developed; (ii) the legislation is translated into an EPR programme, involving design of a set of detailed operational rules, such as, specific mechanisms to finance the operations of the programme, to monitor, and evaluate the legal compliance of each entity involved, within the parameters of the legislation, etc; and (iii) execution of the EPR programme into a working system in practice (Gui et al. 2013: 2).

Due to the multi-agent nature of an EPR programme, efficiency of its implementation is greatly influenced by the heterogeneity in its perspectives. A mandated EPR programme can give rise to economic opportunities for businesses involved in e-waste collection and recycling. This may lead to competing interests between producers and informal sector, especially on collection to recycling mechanisms, on resource recovery, and management of secondary materials. However, establishing collection and recycling mechanism may increase economic burden of producers; location of these facilities also matters vis-à-vis transportation and storage cost or broadly, value of entire reverse supply chain. For legal compliance, cost of collection and recycling mechanisms and operations often result in a gap between the EPR system in practice and what is intended by the EPR principle and/or EPR legislation (ibid.).

EPR is implemented in different ways in different countries; varied models are developed in different countries. Table 4.8 presents an overview of EPR implementation in different countries – through legislation/policy, and through different combinations of institutions (Table 2.1).

TABLE 2.1 An overview of EPR implementation under legislation/policy in different countries

Country, region	E-waste legislation/policy and EPR implementation
European countries	
Belgium	The manufacturers and importers of EEE have founded Recupel[a] as a non-profit organisation with the support of the Belgian regional governments in 2001, which is responsible for collection, sorting, processing, and recycling of WEEE
Estonia	Every PRO offers its own containers to the inhabitants
Germany	A common container is accessed by the inhabitants and the collected waste is split between various PROs, prior to being sorted. Producers are required to finance the provision of the containers and collection, treatment, and recycling when assigned a pick-up by the Elektro-Altgeraete Register
Ireland	WEEE Ireland is the main EPR organisation responsible for the collection and treatment of e-waste on behalf of the producers since 2005
Italy	Producers can join one of several compliance schemes. The collection scheme provides pick-up of e-waste from all collection centres connected to the scheme, both municipal and retail collection points
Lithuania	The collection systems work without a strong involvement of coordinating bodies/government authorities. It determines the amount of historical WEEE that producers need to be collected and recycled based on the new EEE put on the market each year
Spain	Ecotic is the organisation responsible for the financing and management of e-waste. There are three types of collection points: recycling points and other municipal points; distribution company warehouses where waste is stored; Load Grouping Centres fitted out by Ecotic
Sweden	El-Kretsen is the EPR organisation responsible for financing of the take-back system, collaborating with municipalities, and recyclers. Consumer products are collected through the municipal collection system. Since 2015 retailers (online and physical stores) of EEE are obliged to accept e-waste
United Kingdom, partly Poland	No link between industry and municipalities
Asian countries	
China	Rules on the *Administration of the Recovery and Disposal of Discarded Electronic and Electrical Products* – was promulgated in 2009 and became effective in 2011. This consists of general rules, tax administration, subsidy utilisation, supervision, legal liability, and supplemental rules, and are applied to domestic EEE producers who are taxed by the State Administration of Taxation of China. EEE importers who are taxed by the customs
India	*E-waste Management Rules, 2016.* EPR is a mainstay of this regulation. Producers are mandated to manage collection to recycling of e-waste, its reporting, and filing annual return.
Indonesia	Specific article on EPR under *Solid Waste Management Act 2008*

(*Continued*)

TABLE 2.1 (Continued)

Country, region	E-waste legislation/policy and EPR implementation
Japan	WEEE management regulation to recycle and treat four major electrical equipment wastes specifically air-conditioners, televisions, laundry machines, and refrigerators (including freezers) under the *Home Appliance Recycling Law* in April 2001. The producers are responsible for recycling the collected waste, the retailers are responsible for the collection of e-waste, and consumers pay a fee to partially cover the costs of recycling and transportation. The *Law for the Promotion of Effective Utilization of Resources* covers EPR, by specifying administrative procedures for waste management businesses and standard procedures for managing different types of waste
Malaysia	Specific article on take-back and deposit refund under *Solid Waste and Public Cleansing Management Act 2007* and Draft Regulation on Recycling and Disposal of EEE
Philippines	Ecological solid waste management act of 2000, under which Consumer electronics, and white goods as e-waste required separate handling from other residential and commercial wastes
Singapore	The Ministry of the Environment and Water Resources has taken up initiatives to introduce a separate legislation for e-waste management that includes the EPR principle. A programme (National Voluntary Partnership Programme) started by the National Environment Agency has set up for the e-waste recycling under which awareness among the public is created
South Korea	EPR in Recycling Law, 2003. Mandatory take-back, with the flexibility to choose either individual collection or PRO, with clear targets on recycling rates for regulated industries. Violation of the recycling rate targets can cost penalties up to 130% of standard recycling costs. The consumer is also obligated to pay a volume-based fee at the time of e-waste disposal
Taiwan	Waste disposal act which was amended in 1998. Waste home appliances, and waste IT products as due recycled waste. Producers shall submit recycling-clearance disposal fees to the recycling management bodies
Thailand	A form of EPR regulation under its National Integrated Strategy for the Management of WEEE. This regulation requires producers to pay a fixed up-front product fee with the revenues from the fee used to fund a buy back program that pays a subsidy to the consumers who return their EoL electronic products to collection centres
Vietnam	Draft Regulations on the reclamation and treatment processes for disposal products was released in 2015

Source: Cao et al. (2016), IGES (2012), Chatterjee (2016: 217), Mahesh (2007: 13–14), EXPRA (2013: 4), Manomaivibool and Hong (2014), Miliute-Plepiene and Youhanan (2019: 32–37), Ogushi and Kandlikar (2007), Patil and Ramakrishna (2020), Sander et al. (2007: XI–XVI). Compiled by the author.

[a] Manufacturers and importers that belong to Recupel pay the recycling contribution to Recupel for each appliance put on the market. At the time of purchasing a new e-product, the end user contributes a fixed amount to the costs, which is determined by the type of appliance, and it corresponds to the actual cost of recycling.

European countries

In EU countries, EPR is implemented following the *WEEE Directives*. Broadly, four models are observed: (i) Producers create one common non-profit entity that collects the necessary funding, cooperates with local authorities and ensures recycling in the most cost-efficient and environmental way;[10] (ii) 'Dual model' adopted – shared responsibilities between the producers and local authorities (municipalities). A separate collection system assigned to local authorities and the producers have full operational and financial responsibility over collection, sorting and recycling;[11] (iii) 'Shared model' – between industry and the local authorities based on common agreements regarding collection;[12] and (iv) Every PRO signed up with as many municipalities as needed to fulfil targets according to market shares.[13]

Asian countries

A few developing Asian countries have formulated their own EPR regulations; namely China, India, Japan, South Korea, Vietnam, Cambodia, and Singapore.

In a circular economy, preserving resources and creating jobs in the areas of equipment maintenance, component refurbishment, and remanufacturing, were two major concerns in some countries, based on which a need had emerged for collection and processing of e-waste through direct regulation or by providing necessary incentives. Thus, the 'take-back system' as part of EPR was developed under e-waste laws in Asian countries following the *WEEE Directives* (McCann and Wittmann 2015: 13).

Role of a PRO prescribed in regulatory framework

Under the EPR, a producer can implement EPR either on their own (termed as Individual Producer Responsibility – IPR), or by collaborating with their peers and working as a collective group (termed as Collective Producer Responsibility – CPR). Every producer should be able to choose to meet their responsibilities on an individual basis (for example, appointing a PRO) or setting up authorised collection centres) or through a collective compliance mechanism, where producers may authorise common collection centres independently or by joining a consortium as a member.

A PRO is envisaged as an organisation that takes on the EPR mandate of a single producer/collective group of producers to fulfil the EoL waste related legal obligations on their behalf. In this conception, a PROs plays a centre-stage role, in thorough implementation of the EPR on behalf of a producer, such as, meeting targets of collection, recovery, and recycling obligations, etc. A PRO works with a range of stakeholders, and expected to create systems that bring transparency, and accountability in achieving goals defined/legal compliance for producers. The scope of PRO functioning expands to establishment of take-back channel, sorting, recycling target compliance, waste prevention, eco-design promotion, and communication material, verification of data and its reporting to the producer as well as the government/national authorities. They should guarantee that the collected e-waste is treated properly. For this, PROs need to have a solid financial basis. Governments must establish a strict authorisation process so that only reliable organisations with secure finances can receive a licence. Transparency is an important feature of PROs (EXPRA 2013: 3).

Some PROs have a public service mission, and operate in a not-for-profit or profit-not-for-distribution basis while others seek profit. PROs are expected to maximise environmental, economic, and social benefits along with their operational implementation.

Until 2016, 30 countries[14] in Europe have implemented EPR in their legislation and the industry has set up PROs.

Considerations for successful implementation of EPR

ISWA (2014: 6–7) has listed eight key considerations for successful implementation of EPR; of them, seven are relevant to e-waste management. ISWA mentions that effective policy design on EPR will depend on national circumstances, conditions, and priorities. The key considerations include: (i) involvement of stakeholders in the development of EPR; (ii) clear allocation of responsibilities among all stakeholders; (iii) producer's choice for IPR or CPR; (iv) transparency of EPR; (v) governmental support, monitoring, evaluation and control need to be accompanied by an effective and efficient legal framework; (vi) ambitious and clever policy targets are a necessity; and (vii) compensation of reasonable costs for the use of municipal infrastructure is necessary.

1. **Stakeholder involvement** in the development of EPR, which creates a basis for the EPR policy and improves the acceptability and effectiveness.
2. **Clear allocation of responsibilities among all stakeholders** involved is an important requirement for a legislation, which would avoid conflicts of interest between different stakeholders involved. While producers have the primary responsibility, all other actors in the product chain (producers, importers, wholesalers, retailers and consumers), as well as all the waste management actors (waste management collectors, recyclers) must be allocated specific responsibilities. This allocation should be made in view of the policy objectives and product characteristics along with clear mechanism for implementation.
3. Regarding **role of PROs**, it is necessary for the government to consider that producers cannot gain an unfair advantage over their competitors or avoid their responsibilities by choosing one or the other of different mechanisms. And, if national legislation allows multiple PROs to compete for the same waste stream, it should be ensured that they operate effectively together and without jeopardising the achievement of policy targets. This point has emerged from five models – combination of systems and financing model – applied for design incentives under the WEEE Directive.[15]
4. **Transparency of EPR**, which is a primary requirement in its implementation, as EPR is strongly linked to a public service; in this manner, both, producers,

and consumers can make informed choices. This should be ensured by using different ways to comply with the legislation, for example, reporting by producers or PROs, and regular audits by the government.

5. **Governmental support, monitoring, evaluation, and control** needs to be accompanied by an effective and efficient legal framework. Governments should enforce this legal framework to close loopholes and trace free riders. The legal framework required to include control mechanisms including monitoring, and actions vis-à-vis producers, in case of not achieving goals and targets. Information related compliance by producers should be reviewed in terms of the value of the information in relation to product, its disposal, burden to provide such data and information; in case, a PRO is implementing on behalf a producer, an accreditation process for PRO is also required. The implementation of EPR should also be periodically evaluated by governments and, if necessary, targets be adjusted.
6. **Ambitious, and clever policy targets are a necessity.** As a fundamental goal of EPR is to increase the collection and recycling of waste, clear targets on e-waste (generation, collection, recycling) should be specified. The targets could be qualitative and/or quantitative and could be set for a group of products or for individual product categories.
7. **Compensation of reasonable costs** for the use of municipal infrastructure is necessary. The local and regional authorities should not have any obligation to hand over collected waste falling under EPR if their reasonable costs are not covered by producers.

Challenges in implementation of EPR for e-waste management

Some strengths and challenges with EPR have been identified, largely based on experiences of the European countries. A pre-condition and a challenge – for the application of the full-scale EPR, it is necessary that a country has institutional capacity to operate a supportive scheme, such as waste-sorting system (UN ESCAP 2012). A pre-condition identified by the OECD countries is that clear roles and responsibilities of different actors / stakeholders, including the relationship between public bodies and PROs shall be defined; and to assign specific functions to each stakeholder while avoiding any possible overlap, loophole, and conflict of interest. Unclear and overlapping roles and responsibilities constitute the main challenges for governance and administration of EPR systems. Moreover, a close, mutual trust-based partnership between local authorities and industry-owned EPR organisation is a must (EXPRA 2013: 6).

Among strengths, EPR has potentials for improving resource efficiency by saving virgin material inputs and energy consumption as well as reducing e-waste to be land-filled, which lead to environmental benefits. This approach spurs innovation for more efficient production and packaging and creates business opportunities for recycling industry (UN ESCAP 2012).

Although EPR has been adopted by the most countries due to its promising potentials for effective e-waste management, it has been scrutinised on the following counts: legal provisions and lacuna; governance/enforcement related challenges including institutional mechanism for carrying out various functions, monitoring, and evaluation, etc; linking EPR with new business models/economic opportunities created; and other aspects, such as, socio-cultural difficulties in a given country, and whether methods, and standardisation processes are duly addressed.

Legal provisions related challenges

This set of challenges includes ambiguity in definitions, leaving it open to varied interpretations of each provision.

One of the first legal concerns is, clear definition of a 'producer' (its definition for avoiding ambiguities). A clear distinction is required with regard to the definition of a producer. A producer can be a producer of an e-product/large multinational original equipment manufacturers (OEM), or a manufacturer who assembles an electronic product using technology, or the one who earned by selling e-product to a consumer, or the one who produce some parts and materials which gets sourced in production of an e-product. If a 'producer' is not defined properly, the EPR related goals and functions remain ambiguous, creating loopholes in implementation.

Governance/enforcement related challenges

As the EPR as a concept is to be translated into a programme, the perspective of governance typically focus on the following aspects: (i) proper guidelines for every stakeholder covered under the legislation for legal enforcement, and compliance; (ii) proper institutional mechanism available/ developed; (iii) whether every producer's EPR plan is being examined, e.g. e-waste collection from whom, by whom, how, its cost, compliance process, etc. are mentioned in the guidelines; (iv) whether risks of compliance are identified; and (v) whether proper monitoring and evaluation guidelines are provided – process, mechanism, and standardization are well-defined, and are functioning as planned. In addition, Bhaskar and Turaga (2017: 10) mentioned two more challenges: political will and clarity in the enforcement of EPR, and careful attention to policy instruments – their choice as well as design – within the broad EPR framework.

Collection and recycling related challenges

E-waste collection is considered to be a great challenge as part of management. Though the 'take-back system' encourages users for recycling and resource conservation, and protection of environment, and human health, it has created a few challenges as part of the EPR.

> A takeback system is a complex interrelated structure that has four key components: (a) the rules that govern the system; (b) the operational areas of

collection and processing; (c) financing of the system; and (d) how to control the flow of e-waste into and out of a jurisdiction.

(McCann and Wittmann 2015: 14)

The collection centre related challenges are establishing and operationalising collection centres required budgetary provisions, which one producer may find burdensome; whether recycler would bear the cost of transportation or the producer that also has become a debatable point as part of budgetary concern. Collection of e-waste and its quality cannot be ensured through the collection centres.

As the recycling cost is considerably high with little infrastructure in developing countries, the government needs to provide clear guidelines – whether all EEE to be recycled or a specified subset of e-products need to be recycled; 'cherry picking' of e-waste items for recycling is a problem and a challenge. This decision depends on whether the material is critical to be recovered or it has severe impact on environment or infrastructure is available in the country. If e-products are not specified under the law, producers must pay a heavy price for this system; the cost-benefit ratio is skewed in this circumstance. Moreover, if a list of specified products is prepared, large part of e-waste may remain untreated, and remain a threat to environment and human health. For example, recycling CRT monitors, or and lamps are not accepted by recyclers because of their negative value fractions. With change in product design, reduction in use of hazardous substances, and metals is observed. Miniaturisation, technological developments, and changing material composition has an impact on the intrinsic material value and thereby on the economics of recycling is a challenge that needs to be recognised. If the efficiency of final recovery technology has physical limits, the overall efficiency of a take-back and recycling system is determined by the weakest link in the chain (Khetriwal 2019: 143).

According to the environmental economics literature, a mandated producer take-back policy may not be able to motivate manufacturers to adopt product designs that are more environmentally friendly (Walls 2003). However, Nokia's example is considered to be an exception to the set of challenges mentioned here. Nokia twice conducted a campaign for take-back of any mobile phone, first in 2009, and then again in 2012. In 2009, 1,400 specially designed secure bins at all its Care Centres and Branded Retail Stores (known as Nokia Priority Dealers) were set up in four cities of India; during 45 days of campaign, Nokia could collected 160 tonnes of e-waste (mobile phones). In 2012, Nokia collected 65 tonnes of mobile phones for recycling. As promised, it planted one tree for each mobile phone received as e-waste (Singhal 2010; Singhal 2012; Sohail 2015). Singhal (2012) proposed 'Ecosystem Approach' that the businesses can take to accomplish their brand environmental responsibility under EPR.

Risks of compliance and adverse consequences

For compliance, if detailed guidelines and standards are not provided for collection and recycling, the goals of resource recovery may suffer. The detailed guidelines related to legal compliance include the following: whether adequate awareness exists about different stakeholders and their requirements for compliance; whether periodic monitoring takes place, and process and mechanism for compliance are in place; in absence of monitoring and evaluation, paper trading[16] in the name of compliance may increase, and as a result, leakage of e-waste may continue on a large scale.

'When a policy instrument targets only one of the primary stakeholders with a potential to play a pivotal role across the product lifecycle, it poses a compliance risk' (Sharma 2019: 158). Therefore, 'recycling subsidies, advance disposal fees, and command and control standards and point out the impact of certain externalities in determining the efficiency of these policy instruments. Fair cost allocation and collective efficiency, volume uncertainty, long-term contract, local economic development, education and outreach' (*op. cit.*) etc. play critical roles in legal compliance by producers under EPR. Producers are expected to pay costs for collection, aggregation, transportation, storage, and recycling; if these costs are not shared by municipalities or any government agency for collection, recycling cost by the recyclers, etc., and when producers are not incentivised in any manner, motivation for compliance is found to be lesser, especially in the developing countries, wherein collection to recycling related operations are carried out by informal sector efficiently.

The concerns of product design, investment optimisation, resource recovery, management of secondary materials, etc. involve specific technicalities regarding value creation. Complementarity of formal and informal actors on such counts is a critical factor. If these are ensured, and monitoring is carried out on regular basis, they altogether reduce risks of compliance.

For producers, economically, coordination among different entities is difficult for compliance; for example, to establish collection centres/channels, and ensure adequate (required quantity to meet the target) e-waste collection; whether collection takes place through a PRO or a third party organisation; whether a consumer is financially incentivise; budget allocation for such incentives; reimbursing collectors and processors of equipment once work has been carried out; setting and enforcing treatment standards; approving processors and collectors to take part in the system, etc. This way, collection may not be economically viable, and can lead to additional layers of administration.

> 'From large multinational (OEMs) to small importers of EEE, companies are focused on keeping compliance costs for e-waste management at the minimum possible, and willing to cut corners where possible'; producers with such mind-set are 'lobbying to have volumes that are collected above the minimum collection target for 2018, count towards the collection target for the next year.'
>
> (Khetriwal 2019: 142)

Challenges faced by PROs

PROs, on behalf of producers, are expected implement mandated EPR through a range of activities (setting up e-waste management systems across entire value chain, compliance management), and working with different stakeholders. The selection process and its criteria set up by producers of a PRO is usually a challenge in itself; a PRO is selected usually for a year or two – that prevents

> PROs from making long-term and deep-rooted systemic transformation efforts…The success of PROs is dependent on the success of EPR implementation and the maturity of the e-waste sector. Producers will need to have a long-term vision and play an enabling role in the development of collection channels and recycling infrastructure.
>
> (Sinha 2019b: 151)

The concept of PROs is not yet mainstreamed in many developing countries; because of this, performance of PROs is usually affected, especially in terms of collection of e-waste. Leakage of e-waste from or to informal sector is a very common phenomenon in a country where informal sector is dominant. PRO being sandwiched between producers, and the government is identified with such malpractices and get discredited in the larger context of transparency and accountability.[17]

Some scholars (Skinner et al. 2010; Manomaivibool 2011) argue that the difficulty in identifying producers; illegal imports of e-waste; the existence of a large informal sector; and weak regulatory capacity pose major challenges to EPR regulations in developing countries.

Impact of EPR

This is one of the least explored areas; there are a very few studies that has captured impact of EPR. For example, while in many countries, informal sector is dominant, which pays for different scraps, including e-waste items. Such dimensions have created challenges in implementation of EPR.

Regarding the impact of EPR, research conducted by the European Commission on 36 case studies of EPR on different waste streams in the EU revealed that in most of the benchmark cases, the net operational costs for collection, transportation, and treatment of separately collected waste are covered by the EPR system. The extent to which net operational costs are assumed by producers is highly variable and depends notably on the share of organisational and financial responsibilities of the various stakeholders, as well as on the national framework for EPR (ISWA 2014: 7).

A study by Bhaskar and Turaga (2017) examining impact of *E-waste Management Rules, 2011* on e-waste management practices, they observed that:

> the EPR regulation forced the producers to take action on a few relatively inexpensive aspects of the rules, the collection and recycling system has not

been made convenient for the consumers to deposit e-waste in formal collection and recycling centers.

EPR and e-waste management in India

EPR in India was first introduced through the *E-waste Management Rules, 2011*, and the responsibilities for producers were defined, such as collection of e-waste generated during manufacturing of EEE and channelisation to the registered dismantler or recyclers; setting up collection centres or take-back system either individually or collectively; financing and organising a system to meet the cost involved in ESM of e-waste generated from the EoL. However, no target, neither collection nor the recycling amount of e-waste (in weight, item-wise) was specified under the EPR.

Experiences of EPR and take-back campaign by Nokia in 2009 and 2012

Between formal and informal operations for collection to recycling, the Nokia mobile company's example is often quoted among the industry actors, in the broader context of EPR and take-back systems, which could be more effective when 'brand environmental responsibility' (BER) adopts 'ecosystem approach' reasoned Singhal (2010). Nokia organised take-back campaigns for mobile phones in 2009 and 2012, in different phases. Nokia had promised that the company would plant a tree for every mobile handset collected, and all old phones and accessories would be recycled; over 50 tonnes of mobiles were collected and 60,000 trees were planted. The campaign became popular as '*Planet ke Rakhwaale*' (protectors of the planet); through this community platform, Nokia could bring and engage like-minded people together, who were willing to take steps for environment protection, starting from old phone recycling (Singhal 2010).

Along with a take-back campaign, Nokia conducted a survey covering 6,500 respondents from 13 countries about consumer attitudes towards and behaviours regarding recycling of mobile phones. The survey highlighted a contradiction that 74% didn't think about recycling their phones, while 72% thought that recycling makes a difference to the environment. Among 13 countries, 84% of Indians did not consider the need for recycling of unwanted devices; 83% did not know how mobiles are recycled, and whether or not recycled materials from them could be reused for making new products. In this context, Singhal (2010) has identified key factor that play crucial role in the development of a recycling ecosystem and shaping up of consumers' behaviour towards responsible recycling, which are valid even after a decade. These findings also have influenced the government for enacting a legislation. They include existence of possibilities, ease of acting, and incentive for consumers in a pro-environmental way; presence of information systems for consumers on why to act, how to act, when to act, and the benefits of the action for environment and society at large; existing environmental awareness amongst the consumers, and momentum in the society for environmental protection; presence of adequate recycling infrastructure; and a regulatory framework for e-waste management.

Effectiveness of EPR post-rules, 2011 in India: roles and responsibilities of producers

The Toxics Link (2014, 2015) attempted to evaluate and analyse the roles and responsibilities of the regulatory agencies and the producers and their assigned responsibilities, in the consecutive years – in 2014 and 2015, after two years of the implementation of the *Rules, 2011*. Total 50 Brands were evaluated on the basis of the decided criteria[18] (action taken by producers towards fulfilling their responsibility under the Rules) and given score.[19] The research of 2014 was conducted on 50 producers based on secondary data (accessing their website and contacting the helplines or customer care numbers) while the study of 2015 collected primary data (direct responses/interview method) and used secondary data (websites, information booklets, use of social media, print, visuals, etc. used by the producers for creating awareness).

Major findings of these reports are briefly shared here: in 2014, 17 companies earned 'bad performance'; 15 companies 'not so good'; 11 companies 'fair performance' and seven companies 'good performance.' Among them, the biggest defaulters are the cell phone companies; 17 out of 11 companies belong to 'bad performance' (Toxics Link 2014b). In 2015, 18 companies earned 'bad performance'; 15 companies 'not so good'; 15 companies 'fair performance' and three companies 'good performance'. Like 2014, many cell phone companies fared badly. RoHS compliance has helped companies scoring good points, though 15 companies remained on the 'not so good' slab. Of the seven companies in 'good performance' in 2014, three of them (Lenovo, Microsoft and Ricoh) have maintained position in this slab (Toxics Link 2015: 15).

Toxics Link (2016) conducted a survey on 'awareness about e-waste rules' in 2015, covering 2,030 respondents from five cities of India – Delhi, Mumbai, Chennai, Kolkata, and Bengaluru. 50% of people interviewed are acquainted with the term e-waste; the lowest among Kolkata, Delhi and Chennai cities, and highest in Mumbai city. After almost five years of the *Rules, 2011*, 66% respondents had no knowledge on the rules; among the aware respondents (34% of total), 12% had heard about the rules but did not know the details. In response to, 'who is responsible for management of e-waste/toxic waste', most respondents gave multiple answers making more than one to all the stakeholders (government, producer, consumer) responsible – most Kolkata respondents claimed the government to be the exclusive responsible entity.

Regarding toxicity of e-waste, Mumbai respondents know the least (almost 90% are unaware), and all respondents of Chennai are aware. Sources of information included newspapers (34%), media (22%), internet (16%), friends (14%), product manuals (11%), and other (2%). More than half of the respondents (51%) hand over their toxic e-waste to *kabaadiwalas*, which most likely end up reaching to the informal sector with crude methods of recycling, 36% discarded to second hand market or exchanged them for new equipment, 16% gave away to their friends, relatives or maids, 0.7% people handed them to the licensed recycler. 61% EEE users do not know about hazardous nature of e-waste; Kolkata reported the least awareness while 50% of Bengaluru respondents reported awareness. About 30% of the total respondents know that e-waste could have adverse impact on health and environment.

Four states, namely Kerala, Odisha, Tamil Nadu, and Telangana, have taken initiatives for implementation of EPR under the *Rules, 2016*. The analysis of performance of EPR under the *Rules, 2016*, and role of the regulatory body is described in detail in Chapter 5.

Notes

1 'Liability' refers to the responsibility for proven environmental damages caused by the product in question. The extent of the liability is determined by legislation and may embrace different parts of the life cycle of the product, including usage and final disposal.
2 'Economic responsibility' means that the producer will cover all or part of the expenses, for example, for the collection, recycling or final disposal of the products he is manufacturing. These expenses could be paid for directly by the producer or by a special fee.
3 'Physical responsibility' is used to characterise the systems where the manufacturer is involved in the physical management of the products and/or their effects.
4 'Informative responsibility' signifies several different possibilities to extend responsibility for the products by requiring the producers to supply information on the environmental properties of the products they are manufacturing.
5 consumers are given a refund when returning the products to the dealer or treatment facilities after their use. In many developing countries, informal sector operates and therefore this scheme has little relevance.
6 It is a tax paid in advance by manufacturers to cover the cost of collection or recycling of a product or sometimes paid by consumers as a separate tax, reflecting in the bill against the product purchased.
7 This goal talks about establishing effective collection of end-of-life products from consumers, promote environmentally sound treatment and efficient recycling, use of secondary raw materials and the production of sustainable goods, and reduce the amount of waste for final disposal.
8 This goal leads to make products easier to dismantle, reuse, and recycle. Thus, the total environmental impact of a product decreases and waste prevention is stimulated, and the financial burden for waste management is transferred from the public sector to the manufacturers.
9 The environmental costs, at least, include costs for pollution prevention and the collection, recycling and treatment of waste. These environmental costs should be incorporated into the price of products. As a consequence, the consumer, and not the taxpayer, bears all costs related to the waste he has produced, which is more socially fair.
10 Nine countries follow this model: Belgium, Czech Republic, Ireland, Italy, France, Netherlands, Norway, Portugal, Spain.
11 Three countries follow this model: Austria, Germany, Sweden.
12 Eight countries follow this model: France, Spain, Belgium, Netherlands, Italy, Czech Republic, Slovenia.
13 Six countries follow this model: Romania, Bulgaria, Slovakia, Malta, Latvia, Lithuania.
14 Austria, Belgium, France, Spain, Germany, Ireland, Cyprus, Luxembourg, Portugal, Sweden, Greece, Latvia, Malta, Lithuania, Czech Republic, Slovak Republic, Italy,

Slovenia, Estonia, Romania, Bulgaria, Turkey, Norway, Finland, Serbia, Israel, Netherlands, Poland, Macedonia and Bosnia.
15 For further details, refer Sander 2007: XVIII–XX.
16 This is used in Indian context. Paper trading refers to 'instead of procuring e-waste, fake invoices and paper trails are procured to show e-waste movement and recycling' (Singhal 2019: 153).
17 For more information on PROs in India, see Singhal (2019).
18 In 2014, criteria were: sufficiency of information on Website (maximum of 15 points), ease of accessibility to information (maximum of 10 points), take-back system (maximum of 30 points), number of collection points (maximum of 20 points), information with Customer Care or the helpline provided (maximum of 10 points). In 2015, the criteria were refined and elaborated, such as, Sufficiency of information on Website (A maximum of 10 points), Ease of accessibility to information (A maximum of 10 points), Information provided in the booklet (A maximum of 20 points), Take-back system (A maximum of 15 points), Products RoHS Compliant (A maximum of 15 points), Collection centres in all states/UTs (A maximum of 20 points), Authorization from CPCB or SPCBs (A maximum of 5 points), Submitted Annual returns under E-waste Rules, 2011 for the year 2014–2015 (A maximum of 5 points), Number of collection Points (A maximum of 15 points), Awareness campaigns conducted (A maximum of 15 points), Amount of space allocated for e-waste recycling in Product Advertisements (A maximum of 15 points), Any other initiative taken (A maximum of 10 points), Information with Customer Care or the helpline provided (A maximum of 10 points), Take back centre operational (A maximum of 20 points), and Tied up with an authorised recycler for environmentally sound recycling and disposal of e-waste collected through Take back programme (A maximum of 15 points).
19 In 2014, the company achieving points between 75 and 85 are 'good performance'; with points between 50 and 74 are 'fair performance'; with points between 25 and 49 are 'not so good performance'; and points between 0 and 24 are 'bad performance'. In 2015, the company achieving points between 150 and 200 are 'good performance'; with points between 100 and 149 are 'fair performance'; with points between 50 and 99 are 'not so good performance'; and points between 0 and 49 are 'bad performance'.

3
TOXICITY AND IMPACTS ON ENVIRONMENT AND HUMAN HEALTH

> *The composition of WEEE/E-waste is very diverse and differs in products across different categories. It contains more than 1,000 different substances, which fall under "hazardous" and "non-hazardous" categories. Broadly, it consists of ferrous and non-ferrous metals, plastics, glass, wood and plywood, printed circuit boards, concrete and ceramics, rubber and other items.*
>
> United Nations Environment Programme (2007: 12)

Toxicity, recycling, and regulations

In this chapter, toxicity of e-product and e-waste due use of hazardous and non-hazardous substances, chemicals, and persistent organic pollutants (POPs) is at the centre. The toxicity is a manifestation of a substance/toxin on a living organism, a tissue, or a cell; it is observed in form of cancer, malfunctioning of nervous systems, reproduction processes, respiratory systems, etc. on the human body. Recycling is at the focal point that links environment, and health concerns. 'A conundrum is created as to whether e-waste recycling is an "economic boom or an environmental doom"' (Oteng-Ababio 2012: 153). From a legal standpoint, toxicity is well-defined, but legal enforcement depends on a range of issues, such as, design of e-product makes it easy to dissemble and less hazardous; productivity, cost, availability recycling technology; resource efficiency; and final disposal that ensures least leaching to soil and water to prevent health hazards.

Almost every smart device and e-product includes printed circuit boards (PCB), which contribute to almost 30% of total e-waste. PCBs are made of mainly three elements: metals, non-metal (ceramics and fibre glasses), and organic substances (resins) (Figure 3.1).

Much e-waste is considered hazardous waste from a toxicological standpoint (Puckett et al. 2002: 29), which deliberates on toxins/pollutants. E-waste is not

DOI: 10.4324/9780429285424-3

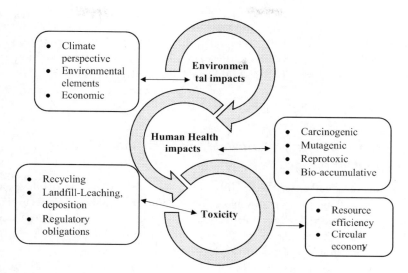

FIGURE 3.1 Toxicity, environmental, and health impacts

biodegradable and gets accumulated in the environment: in the soil, air, water, and in living things. The pollutants of e-waste have adverse impacts on health, especially through water sources and the food supply chain of livestock, fish, and crops.

> The e-waste that is end-treated in a landfill leads to leaching of toxic metals and chemicals into the soil…low temperature burning causes the emission of dioxins from PVC components. Also waste material is just dumped into nature, and in water bodies.
>
> (Baldé et al. 2015: 35)

The end-of-life of EEE including open and manual dismantling, shredding, burning, leaching and uncontrolled dumping directly harm the exposed workers, and reach environment through contaminating soil, ground water, surface water, and polluting air. The e-waste that is end-treated in an incinerator leads to emissions of GHG and mercury (ibid.).

A vast literature exists on toxicity of e-waste, covering use of different methods to document toxins generated or released during recycling processes. There are three main groups of substances that may be released during recycling and material recovery, and which are of environment concern: (i) original constituents of equipment, such as lead and mercury; (ii) substances that may be added during some recovery processes, such as cyanide; and (iii) substances that may be formed by recycling processes, such as dioxins (Lundgren 2012: 18). Dioxins[1] can be released when PVC parts are incinerated at a low temperature. Similarly, massive literature exists on toxicity of e-waste, covering use of different methods to test leaching effects of metals since late 1990s, for example, Milli Q (MQ) water, Synthetic Precipitation

Leaching Procedures (SPLP, a mild leaching agent with no buffering), Toxicity Characterisation Leaching Procedure (TCLP),[2] and Waste Extraction Test (WET) (Yadav et al. 2014). Of them, most articles are laboratory-based tests and findings of a specific e-product; very few field studies are found. A vast literature exists on toxicity of a specific e-product, such as cell phones (feature and smart phones), PCBs (used in every e-product), computers, and so on.

Significance of recycling technique and technology in e-waste management

Recycling occupies critical space in the discourse of e-waste management, and is considered to be the best possible solution. With proper recycling, recoverable resources are collected, which further save other resources, such as, energy, water, and other material footprints; also boost economy. Consequently, the reduction in landfill may result into reduction in toxic effects on environment, and human health. Landfilling has been the least favourable waste management option, mainly because proper treatment to e-waste reduces release of toxins; lesser the toxicity, lesser the adverse impacts on environment, and human health.

Recycling, if done in an environmentally sound manner, needs considerably less energy than mining ores in nature; prevents secondary and tertiary emissions; creates economically and environmentally sustainable businesses (optimise ecoefficiency); and considers the social implications and the local context of operations (e.g. employment opportunities, available skills, and education etc.) (UNEP 2009: 16).

I: Environmental concerns

The report of UNEP (2010) titled, *Assessing the environmental impacts of consumption and production: Priority products and materials* has focused on 'how different economic activities currently influence the use of natural resources and the generation of pollution,' and looked at the economy via three perspectives – production, consumption, and resources – in conjunction with environmental concerns, such as, climate change, water use, toxic emissions, use of fossils for heating, the production and use of electrical appliances is of comparable importance, causing the depletion of fossil energy resources, climate change, and a wide range of emissions-related impacts (UNEP 2010: 2). 97% of all life cycle waste is generated during the production of input materials (Miliute-Plepiene and Youhanan 2019: 16) (Figure 3.2).

While elaborating impacts on environment and human health, describes toxicity from two important frameworks: first, life cycle thinking,[3] or 'life cycle impact assessment' (LCIA);[4] and second, regulatory provisions imposed/evolved through legislations at international and national level. For example, the *Basel Convention* to regulate transboundary movements of e-waste; and the *RoHS Directive* applicable to EU countries, which restricts the use of lead, cadmium, mercury, hexavalent chromium, PBB and PBDEs) in new electronic devices; and a regulatory method

Toxicity, environment, human health 71

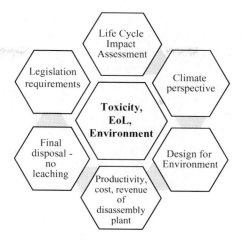

FIGURE 3.2 Toxicity, EoL solution, and environmental concerns

of 'total threshold limit concentrations,' which refers to use of hazardous elements and its threshold specified under the regulatory framework of every country. The existing literature also describes toxicity by linking it to recycling by the informal sector to large extent across several countries with rudimentary methods; and 'design for environment' of every e-product. It is argued that if the design of every e-product is simplified and different materials are assembled in a manner which makes disassembly/dismantling of e-waste smoother, toxicity question could be dealt effectively. The experiences of Guiyu of China, and Ghana in Africa represent challenges of unregulated transboundary movements, and functioning of the informal sector leading to damage of environment and human health to a level of crisis.

The life cycle thinking identifies environmental impacts from the climate perspective (resource use, global warming potential, change in the ozone layer, energy consumption, water use, carbon foot prints, etc.); economic (recoverable and reusable materials – metals, plastic, etc.); and EoL solution/treatment to e-waste, i.e. its recycling, final disposal and impact on environmental elements (impacts on air, soil, and water – acidification, eutrophication and pollution); and impact on human health, such as carcinogens, mutagenic, reprotoxic, and bio-accumulative. Manufacturing of e-products have direct effect on climate change; every product has a carbon footprint and is contributing to human-made global warming.

Production process, treatment to e-waste, and its impact on environment

Typical environmental concerns are resource use, global warming potential, energy consumption, water use, carbon footprints, potentials for damaging ozone layer (GHG emissions), deteriorating soil and water quality, etc. Global warming could be calculated for the life cycle stages of a product or service based on CO_2 equivalent (or carbon equivalent) emission; ecological footprints, etc. The ecological footprint can also be expressed in units like water intensity, total material requirement, and total amount of waste. Different environmental impacts are induced from the generation of air emissions, effluents, and waste (Table 3.1).

Every e-product has the highest footprint in the group in terms of waste. For instance, the life cycle of one smartphone is associated with the production of 86 kg of waste (Miliute-Plepiene and Youhanan 2019: 16). The digitalisation across the world has added more than 1.5 billion mobile phone units in 2017 accounting for 225,000 tons of material usage during manufacturing (considering an average weight of 150 g/unit) (statista.com) (Table 3.2).

TABLE 3.1 Emissions from primary production of metals used in a personal computer

Metal	Emissions of CO_2 from primary mining per tonne of metal (in tonnes)	Amount of metal in one PC (in kg)	Emissions of CO_2 from primary mined metals in one PC (in tonnes)
Steel	2.04	6.193	0.01263372
Aluminium	10.02	0.549	0.00550098
Lead	3.2	0.00658	0.000021056
Nickel	19.53	0.0127	0.000248031
Copper	3.4	0.413	0.0014042
Gold	16,991	0.00026	0.00441766
Silver	144	0.0017	0.0002448
Palladium	9,380	0.00012	0.0011256
Total	**26,553**	**7.17**	**0.0256**

Source: YES Bank and TERI-BCSD (2014: 9).

TABLE 3.2 Comparison of use of energy and water consumption in production of metals from e-waste and ores

	Energy use (MJ per kg of metal extracted)		Water use (Em3 per tonne of metal extracted)	
Metal	E-waste	Ores	E-waste	Ores
Magnesium	10	165–230	2	2–15
Cobalt	20–140	140–2,100	30–100	40–2000
PGM	1,400–3,400	18,860–254,860	3,000–6,000	100,000–1,200,000
Rare Earths	1,000–5,000	5,500–7,200	250–1,250	1,275–1,800

Source: EU (2018: 11).

Mapping of environmental impacts of a cell phone

The average energy consumption for material extraction is 23 MJ (megajoules) for one mobile phone; 120 MJ energy is consumed during manufacturing of components – ICs (integrated circuit), capacitors, and resistors; total energy consumption for assembly of a phone is 2 MJ; and 30 MJ is assumed as energy consumption for packaging and transportation (Yu et al. 2010: 4137). Mobile phones contain various valuable metals (copper, gold, and silver) along with some toxic or hazardous metals (Pb, Cd, Hg, As, Ni, and Cr).

Approximately half of the elements of the periodic table go into the production of a mobile phone including neodymium, terbium, and dysprosium (UNEMG 2017: 140).

According to Dave Holwell, an economic geologist at the University of Leicester, a tonne of old phones (weighed without their batteries) yields about 300 g of gold. There is about 1 g of gold in 35–40 mobile phones (Magazine Monitor).

Responsibly recycling one million cell phones can recover 20,000 lbs (approx. 9,072 kg) of copper, 550 lbs (250 kg) of Silver, 50 lbs (22.6 kg) of gold, and 20 lbs (9 kg) of palladium (www.ban.org).

In 2009, for 2.7 billion mobiles in use, they accounted for about 125 million tonnes CO2e, which is just over 0.25% of global emissions (Berners-Lee 2010). 'An Apple iPhone emits 70 kg of carbon particles and 81% of the carbon particles are emitted during its manufacturing' (www.attero.in).

Extraction and production of raw materials generate 80% of total greenhouse gas (GHG) emissions, compared to 14% from mobile phone use, and just 1% from EoL treatment (quoted in ILO 2019b: 6) (Figure 3.3).

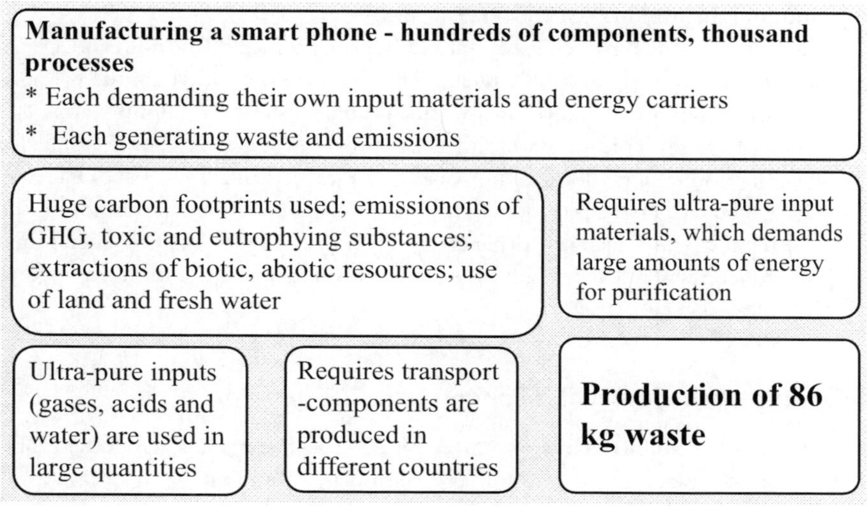

Manufacturing a smart phone - hundreds of components, thousand processes
* Each demanding their own input materials and energy carriers
* Each generating waste and emissions

Huge carbon footprints used; emissiononos of GHG, toxic and eutrophying substances; extractions of biotic, abiotic resources; use of land and fresh water

Requires ultra-pure input materials, which demands large amounts of energy for purification

Ultra-pure inputs (gases, acids and water) are used in large quantities

Requires transport -components are produced in different countries

Production of 86 kg waste

FIGURE 3.3 Environmental mapping of a smart phone manufacturing
Source: Adapted from Hertwich et al. (2010: 37)

Mapping of environmental impacts of a computer

'Manufacturing a tonne of laptops and potentially 10 tonnes of CO_2 are emitted' (PACE and WEF 2019: 13). Manufacture of one computer and monitor takes 530 lbs (240 kg) of fossil fuel, 48 lbs (21.8 kg) of chemicals, and 1.5 tons of water (www.attero.in). For a laptop computer, 'about 1,200 kg of waste is produced over its life cycle' (Miliute-Plepiene and Youhanan 2019: 16). 'Recycling one million laptops saves the energy equivalent to the electricity used by 3,657 homes in a year.' (www.attero.in)

The annual life cycle burden of a computer is 5,600 MJ (megajoules), however, only 34% of life cycle energy consumption occurs in the use phase. The rest of the energy is needed for the mining, manufacturing, packaging, and transportation processes that are required in making a computer. An average computer is made up of over 30 different minerals (silica, iron, aluminium, copper, lead, zinc, nickel, tin, selenium, manganese, arsenic, and cadmium) which are non-renewable resources; they are mined and extracted from the earth. 500 million PCs comprise about 2,872,000 tonne of plastics, 718,000 tonne of lead, 1,363 tonne of cadmium, and 287 tonne of mercury (Puckett et al. 2002: 437). Manufacturing of one desktop computer takes 245 kg of fossil fuels, 22 kg of chemicals, and 1,500 litres of water (Kuehr et al. 2003). Reduction of waste is achieved through reuse and recycling. From a climate perspective, GHG emissions are avoided with proper waste treatment and disposal. An estimate says reuse and recycling of 40 personal computers may lead to avoidance of CO_2 emissions from 2.1 barrels of oil consumed (Agarwal and Mullick 2014: 8).

Amount of fossil fuels used to produce a computer are equivalent to approximately nine times the computer's weight. Approximately half of the elements of the periodic table go into the production of a mobile phone including neodymium, terbium, and dysprosium. (UNEMG 2017: 140).

The environmental impact/footprint of the primary metals (precious and special metals) production is significant, which are mined from ores in which the precious and special metal concentration is low. In mining, wastewater, sulphur dioxide is created, and energy consumption and CO_2 emissions are large. For example, to produce one tonne of gold, palladium, or platinum, CO_2 emissions of about 10,000 tons are generated. The annual demand for gold in EEE is some 300 tonnes [in the year 2007] at average primary generation of almost 17,000 tons CO_2 per tonne of gold mined, which leads to gold induced emissions of 5.1 million tons in total' (UNEP 2009: 10).[5]

Mapping of environmental impacts of a CRT monitor

There were 83.3 million CRT monitors by 2002 in the market across the globe; they begin to replace by LCD (liquid crystal display) monitors.

There are 14 processes involved in producing, using, and disposing of a CRT. The major components of the complete CRT monitor are the tube, plastic casing, and associated PWB assemblies. The glass components contain approximately

70% lead oxide. The total number of inventory items for the CRT profile was 770; of them, almost 274 chemicals were classified as potentially toxic. Overall, 18,000 MJ of energy was reported per CRT monitor produced within the manufacturing stage; roughly 87% of this can be attributed to the glass manufacturing energy alone.

During production, carbon monoxide released from the production of LPG was the top contributor at 22%, followed by nitrogen oxides (9%) from electricity generation in the use stage, and by arsenic (9%) in the production of lead that is eventually used in the CRT glass, and phosphorus (6%) and fluorides (4%) (Socolof et al. 2005).

'The average 14-inch monitor uses a tube that contains an estimated 2.5–4 kg of lead. One CRT television or computer monitor can contain 4–8 pounds (1.8–3.6) of lead' (www.ban.org).

Linkages between resource recovery and improvement in environment

For special and precious metals, the environmental footprint of recycling is much smaller than for primary production; for example, aluminium recycling uses only 1/20 of the energy required for primary production. The environmental impacts per kilogram for the production of precious metals (silver, gold, platinum, and palladium) is higher than for base metals (iron, copper, aluminium, lead, and nickel); yet recovery of both types of metals may yield a commercial profit, which may generate a new scope of work for the new generation. An example of PCBs is presented here – as a resource and as a hazardous object.

Among environmental concerns, saving CO_2 emission is one of the major considerations. Therefore, harvesting the resources from used e-products substantially less carbon-dioxide emissions than mining in the earth's crust is preferred as part of e-waste management. According to WorldLoop,

> every tonne of e-waste collected and recycled; 1.44 tons of CO_2 emissions are avoided…with the 954 tons of e-waste collected and recycled by WorldLoop's projects, 1,374 tons of CO_2 emissions[6] have been avoided (That's 734,759 m^3 of CO_2, which is slightly bigger than the Statue of Liberty).
>
> (www.worldloop.org)

The other dimension of environment is to look at e-waste as a resource versus a hazardous object. The following Box 3.1 presents an example of a PCB.

E-waste recycling chain

E-waste recycling chain comprises of four main steps: (i) collection; (ii) pre-processing (sorting – classification, separation[7]/manual dismantling or disassembly,[8] de-pollution); (iii) end-processing that includes physical and chemical processing; and (iv) refining process. Every single step in the recycling chain is closely interlinked in both an upstream and downstream direction (Table 3.3).[9]

BOX 3.1: PCBS AS A RESOURCE AND AS A HAZARDOUS OBJECT

As a resource – recovery from PCBs	As a hazardous object – impact on health
The substances present in large quantities in e-waste are PCBs, Poly Vinyl Chloride (PVC), fibreglass, epoxy resins, lead, tin, copper, silicon, Beryllium, carbon, Iron and Aluminium (Darshan and Vidhya Lakshmi 2016: 1). Copper (4,500,000 t/year globally), tin (90,000 t/year globally), Antimony (65,000 t/year globally), cobalt (11,000 t/year globally), silver (6,000 t/year globally), lead, nickel, etc. (Toxics Link 2019b: 5). The intrinsic material value of global e-waste was estimated to be 48 billion euro in 2014. The material value is dominated by gold, copper and plastics contents (Baldé et al. 2015: 9).	Plastics in a PCB contain organobromine compounds, denominated Brominated Flame Retardants (BFRs) such as the brominated bisphenols – TBBPA or PBDEs, which are endocrine disruptors, interfere with hormones involved in growth and sexual development, effects on immune system, highly toxic to the foetus; produce hormonal changes; and are carcinogenic. The chlorinated compounds, such as, the polychlorinated biphenyl, and the polychlorinated dioxins are present in flame retardant substances, which are bioaccumulable and highly toxic. The halogenated compound is PVC, such as those based on organotin (organic compounds of carbon and tin), lead, and cadmium. Flexible PVC includes phthalate esters, which change sex hormone levels, alter development of genitals.

TABLE 3.3 Three tier treatment processes for recycling e-waste

Tier/level	Process
First	⇨ Decontamination – Removal of all liquids and gases (if required; e.g. CRT) ⇨ Dismantling – manual/mechanised breaking ⇨ Segregation
Second	⇨ Hammering ⇨ Shredding ⇨ Special treatment processes – electromagnetic separation, eddy current separation, density separation using water
Third	**Recycling processes** ⇨ Chemical – refinery/metal smelter (plastic/metal) ⇨ Mechanical – shredding, breaking (plastic/glass) ⇨ Thermal – power generator/cement kiln (plastic) **Recovery processes** ⇨ Reverberatory furnace, blast furnace, electrolytic (lead, Cu) ⇨ Leaching, smelting, electrolytic (precious metals)

Source: Wath et al. (2011: 257) – revised by the author.

The first stage of recycling is collection from consumers once the EEE have reached their EoL. This phase is crucial, as this ensures that the collected e-waste is not mixed with others; and less dependent on technical solution, and highly influenced by socio-economic factors, such as level of awareness and disposal by the users, awareness and integrity of vendors who provide least cannibalised e-waste, and so on.

During second stage, de-pollution process includes one or several shredding processes aimed at reducing the size of devices and elimination of potentially hazardous components. Once reduced in size, the shredded components in e-waste undergo mechanical sorting, where different sorting technologies are applied. Miliute-Plepiene and Youhanan (2019: 29) has provided details about what is achieved at the end of this stage, and what happened to the residues, as follow:

> Regardless of the approach and the chosen technology, in the pre-processing stage four groups of materials are extracted: (i) hazardous materials (e.g. batteries), (ii) valuable components, which could be reused/resold on the market after dismantling, (iii) valuable recyclable materials (copper, aluminium, plastics) that will be sold for further material recovery, and (iv) residues – non-hazardous materials (ceramics, some plastics etc.), that are not suitable for recycling. This fraction is likely to be disposed of in landfills or incinerated.

During the third stage – physical recycling, usually – size reduction takes place through disassembling, dismantling, chopping, shredding, crushing etc. Also, physical separation of ferrous and non-ferrous parts takes place vis-à-vis magnetic parts, current connecting parts, electro-static, etc. For chemical recycling, different methods are employed, such as, magnetic method for recovering ferrous fractions (iron, nickel, and cobalt), gasification, melting process (pyro-metallurgy[10]), hydrometallurgy,[11] and bio-metallurgy.[12]

During refining processes, plastics, fuels, oil-based resins, metals, glass, methanol, filler materials, and phenolic composites are separated. Non-recyclable materials usually end up in waste incinerators or landfills. For metal recovery,[13] physical recycling is practiced across the world (Debnath et al. 2018). The metal recovery involves various thermal and chemical treatments depending on their merits and demerits. Thermal treatment avoids the liquid effluent disposal problems associated with wet chemical extraction methods. Thermal incineration combined with pyro-metallurgical treatments is applied in commercial use for metal recovery from PCBs (Chatterjee and Kumar 2009: 899).

Mainly three kinds of substances are released during recycling: (i) the substances used in manufacturing of electrical and electronic equipment; (ii) those substance are used in recycling process (auxiliary substances); and (iii) by-products, which are formed during the transformation of primary constituents. The by-products are: fly ashes, fine particles, fumes, waste water, etc; of them, fly ashes, fine particles, and fumes are transported to other places via air while waste water becomes leachate/effluent and contaminate surface and the sediments contaminate ground waste (Awasthi et al. 2016: 260).

Recycling and risks

If not properly managed, hazardous substances may pose significant human health and environmental risks. Toxic substances can be found within the following types of emissions or outputs: (i) leachates from dumping activities; (ii) particulate matter (coarse and fine particles) from dismantling activities; (iii) fly and bottom ashes from burning activities; (iv) fumes from mercury amalgamate "cooking," de-soldering and other burning activities; (v) wastewater from dismantling and shredding facilities; and (vi) effluents from cyanide leaching and other leaching activities. Among them, most researchers have expressed concern about manual disassembly, and acid-leaching operations[14] for value of valuable components from wires and cables, CRTs, and PCB.

A particular hazard associated with the disassembly stage is the possibility of accidental release and spillage of hazardous substances upon breakage of the shell, such as mercury, which is found within light sources as well as switches. The primary hazards of mechanical treatment methods are associated with the size reduction and separation steps, which can generate dusts from plastics, metals, ceramics, and silica. Open-air storage raises concerns regarding the possibility of lead and other substances leaching out into the environment. In addition, with lack of access to running water, toxins are transmitted orally via people's hands when eating (quoted in Lundgren 2012: 18–20).

Toxics Link (2014a, 17) report has mentioned potential hazards of e-waste recycling by informal sector in India. While breaking and removal of copper yoke CRTs, lead, barium, and other heavy metals leach into groundwater. During PCB disordering and removing computer chips, air emission of these substances remains in air for long time; and while processing dismantled PCBs, that is, open-air burning to remove the metals, tin and lead contaminate immediate environment including surface and ground waters, and brominated dioxins, beryllium, cadmium, and mercury emissions take place. For treating chips and other gold plated components, chemical stripping method (using nitric and hydrochloric acid), along river banks Hydrocarbons, heavy metals, brominated substances, etc. are discharged directly into river or left on the banks, which acidifies the river destroying fish and flora.

II: Human health concerns

E-waste, toxicity, and its impact on human health

> 76% of workers in informal recycling operations in India suffer from respiratory ailments like asthma, bronchitis, choking, coughing, irritation, breathing difficulties and tremors among others…this is primarily due to primitive and polluting methods of processing e-waste, lack of safety measures, awareness, and negligence.
>
> (www.attero.in)

Complex processes are employed for recycling of e-waste in India, such as, manual disassembly, heating PCBs to recover solder and chips, acid extraction of metals from complex mixtures, melting and extruding plastics, and burning plastics to isolate metals. Mixtures of concentrated nitric acid and hydrochloric acids are used for the extraction of gold and copper respectively. Various volatile compounds of nitrogen and chlorine are known to be emitted during such processes. The heating of PCB for de-soldering and removal of chips exposes workers to fumes of metals, particularly those in solder (often lead and tin), and other hazardous substances that can be potentially released. Such practices often exacerbate pollution by creating hazardous chemicals and additional pollution (Toxics Link 2019b).

Three most prevalent and hazardous technologies for treating e-waste adversely impact environment and human health.

Incineration

Incineration is a process of destroying waste through burning. The gases released during the burning and the residue ash are often toxic, especially when incineration, or co-incineration of e-waste with neither prior treatment nor sophisticated flue gas purification. Studies of municipal solid waste incineration plants have shown that copper, which is present in PCBs and cables, acts as a catalyst for dioxin formation when flame retardants are incinerated. These BFRs when exposed to low temperature (600–800°C) can generate extremely toxic PBDDs and Polybrominated Furans. PVC is also found in e-waste in significant amounts, which is highly corrosive when burnt and also induces the formation of dioxins; its incineration also leads to the loss of valuable elements that can be recovered if sorted and processed separately (Toxics Link 2014a: 18).

Open-air burning

Open burning is used mostly for waste disposal, at relatively low temperature; this is far more polluting than controlled incineration process. Inhalation of open fire emissions can trigger asthma attacks, respiratory infections, and cause other problems such as, chest pain, coughing, wheezing, and eye irritation. Chronic exposure to open fire emissions may lead to diseases such as emphysema (lung condition that causes shortness of breath) and cancer. Open-air burning of PVC releases hydrogen chloride, which on inhalation mixes with water in the lungs to form hydrochloric acid, which may lead to corrosion of the lung tissues, and other respiratory complications. Often open fires burn with a lack of oxygen, forming carbon monoxide, which poisons the blood when inhaled. The residual ash becomes airborne, and is dangerous if inhaled (ibid.: 19).

Landfilling

This is one of the most widely used methods of waste disposal; it is well known that all landfills leak. The leachate (cadmium, lead, and mercury) often contain heavy metals and other toxic substances that contaminate groundwater resources.

Even state-of-the-art landfills, which are sealed to prevent toxins from entering the ground, are not completely tight in the long-term.

There are three major concerns regarding landfills and its impact on environment are – its leach, vaporization effects, and its proneness to uncontrollable open fires and release of toxic fumes. Older landfill sites and uncontrolled dumps pose a much greater danger of releasing hazardous emissions. From the PCBs and CRT monitors, lead is found to leach from their glasses. The land filled BFR plastics or plastics containing Cadmium, both PBDE and Cadmium may leach into soil and groundwater. The land filled condensers emit hazardous polychlorinated biphenyls. Besides leaching, vaporization is also a concern in landfills – volatile compounds (mercury or di-methylene mercury) are released through vaporisation (ibid.: 19).

Historical mapping of toxicity, environment, and human health

Despite some of the more stringent regulations apply, as much as 75% of generated e-waste is unaccounted for. There is evidence that e-waste is transported internationally from many countries to destinations where informal recycling and disposal take place, often in small workshops with little or no regulation (Brigden et al. 2005: 18); impacts have already been reported in many countries, particularly in China and India in Asia, in some African countries, including Ghana. A study by Greenpeace in 2008 found severe chemical contamination in ash contaminated soil samples from open burning sites at both Agbogbloshie and Korforidua, and in sediment from a shallow lagoon at the Agbogbloshie site. Most samples contained numerous toxic and persistent organic chemical pollutants, high levels of many toxic metals, due to treatment of e-waste in these areas. The nature and extent of chemical contamination found at these sites in Ghana were similar to those previously reported for e-waste open burning sites in China, India and Russia (ibid.). As such this study did not attempt to quantify damage caused to the environment or human health, but its results do indicate that the exposure of workers and bystanders to hazardous chemicals may be substantial.

During 1990s and early 2000s, several studies[15] have established increased exposure to toxic chemicals associated with e-waste recycling, for both workers and local residents, including for chlorinated dioxins and furans (PCDD/Fs), certain PBDEs, and the toxic metal lead. For example, in China, children have been found to have significantly higher levels of the toxic metal lead in their blood compared to children in a neighbouring area and recycling workers may commonly carry significantly higher concentrations of certain PBDEs in their blood compared to the general population; higher tissue levels of chlorinated dioxins and furans; workers involved in high temperature processes, such as at lead smelters, can be significantly exposed to lead fumes, and workers using lead based solders may also be exposed to lead-bearing dusts and fumes; where soils and dusts are contaminated with lead, children can be particularly exposed through hand-to-mouth transfer (quoted in Brigden et al. 2005: 9,18). Workers in electronics recycling facilities in Europe have

BOX 3.2: MAPPING HEALTH HAZARDS OF CELL PHONES

Mapping health hazards of a cell phones

The common brands referred are – Apple, Blackberry, Samsung, Sony Ericsson; types referred are – cell phones, iPhone, and smartphones.

The battery, circuit board, and display screen are key components of a mobile phone. The materials and weight (in per cent) (approx.) are: steel (5%), copper (13%), aluminium (one per cent), plastics (57%), glass fibre (2%), and others (22%). It contains hazardous materials, such as beryllium (Be), BFRs, cadmium (Cd), chlorine (Cl), lead (Pb), lithium (Li), and mercury (Hg). Of them, beryllium can cause pneumonia, lung damage, increased cancer risk, and DNA damage while the cadmium can cause psychological disorder, cancer, and can damage liver and kidney, and sperm damage leading to birth defects and headaches. Mercury can damage the brain and DNA, disrupt nervous system, sperm damage, birth defects, skin rashes and headaches (GIZ and MESTI 2019: 43).

been found to have higher blood levels of PBDEs than other workers, probably as a result of inhalation of contaminated dust (Sjodin et al. 2001; Sjodin et al. 2003) (Box 3.2).

Broadly, the exposure to toxic chemicals is through inhalation, dust ingestion, dermal exposure, and oral intake. Inhalation and dust ingestion impose a range of potential occupational hazards including silicosis, toxic exposure to dioxins, mercury and other metals and carcinogens through inhalation of fumes while processing e-waste or from local drinking water and food sources contaminated by e-waste processing by-products. Electrical shocks are another occupational hazard (Lepawsky and McNabb 2010: 181). The natural presence of these metals in a given place is generally very low. However, their amount found in the soil of any hazardous landfill as a result of human activity can be very high. For example, Chromium does not remain in the atmosphere but get deposited in soil and water. Drains from industries that manufacture or handle products containing zinc, lead, or other metals can discharge particles of these elements into water streams. Certain environmental conditions and soil characteristics facilitate their filtration into groundwater; thus, these elements can become part of the food chain. For example, Cadmium adheres strongly to organic matter and can be incorporated by plants, thus entering the food chain. The polychlorinated biphenyls, BFRs, PVC, or CFCs are known as persistent organic pollutants. They are characterised by their being persistent, highly toxic, bioaccumulable, and transported over long distances. Chlorine chemistry produces more than 11,000 organochlorine compounds, most of them are harmful to people, animals and the environment in general (Pont et al. 2019: 7–8).

Table 3.4 summarises with four columns: (i) type of elements[16] – halogenated compounds, heavy and other metals, and others; (ii) occurrence in EEE; (iii) how

TABLE 3.4 Pollutants and their occurrence in WEEE, and impact on human health

Element	Occurrence in EEE	Human intake	Toxicity and impact on human health
1. Halogenated compounds Chlorofluorocarbons (CFCs) – known for causing degradation in ozone layer	As solvent and refrigerants. In air-conditioner.	Through environment – air, soil, water. Through inhalation.	Exposure to stronger ultraviolet rays can cause skin cancer, cataracts, and weak immune system. Direct exposure to some types of CFCs can cause loss of consciousness, shortness of breath, and irregular heartbeat; can also cause confusion, dizziness, cough, sore throat, shortness of breath, and redness and eye pain. Direct contact with the skin with some types of CFCs can cause burns from cold or dry skin.
Polybrominated diphenyl ethers (PBDE)	For casing	Environmentally persistent chemicals, some of which are highly bio-accumulative, through ingestion and inhalation.	Suspected endocrine disruptors, demonstrating an ability to interfere with hormones involved in growth and sexual development, effects on immune system are also reported.
Polychlorinated biphenyls[a]	Found in older e-products. Transformers, capacitors, softening agents for paint, glue, plastic	Widely spread through the environment – air, water, soil. Ingestion and inhalation.	In these compounds, the degree of toxicity increases as the chlorine content increases. The common symptoms of chronic intoxication are: nausea, vomit, weight loss, oedema, and lower abdominal pain.
PVC (forms organ chlorinated substances when it is burned, emitting dioxins that end up in the environment)	Massive use – in most e-product	Through environment; ingestion and inhalation.	Can cause many types of cancer and birth defects.
Triphenyl phosphate	Casings of computer monitors		A strong inhibitor of a key enzyme system in human blood. Known to cause contact dermatitis in some individuals, a possible endocrine disruptor.

Toxicity, environment, human health **83**

2. Heavy and other metals			
Aluminium (Al), atomic number 13			Affects brain and kidneys.
Antimony (Sb)	Variety of industrial use – as flame retardant, similar to arsenic	Through nose – dust and fumes	Severe skin problems, stomach related problems. Antimony trioxide is classified as carcinogenic for human.
Arsenic (As)	Semiconductors, solid lasers, diodes, microwaves, LEDs (Light Emitting Diodes), solar cells	Pulmonary	Poisoning causes symptoms kidney and liver damage, vascular disorder, loss of blood pressure, metallic taste in the mouth. Other effects include numbness of limbs, muscle cramps, and in extreme cases, death. Over longer period this could be carcinogenic – skin, bladder, lung cancer.
Barium (Ba) atomic number 56	Electron tubes, filler for plastic and rubber, lubricant additives, CRT.	In form of dust and through water pipes – ingestion and inhalation.	These compounds are poisonous and cause swelling in brain, muscle weakness, difficulty in breathing, increased blood pressure, arrhythmia, stomach pain, and damage to heart, liver, and spleen.
Beryllium (Be) atomic number 4	A good conductor of electricity, heat, and is non-magnetic – in computers	Inhalation of dust, fumes, or mist	Is the most toxic metal known; classified as a carcinogenic for humans. The most commonly known effect is called berylliosis, a dangerous and persistent disease of the lungs that can even damage other organs, including the heart. Can also causes allergic reactions in people who are hypersensitive to chemicals. People poisoned by this may feel weakness and fatigue.
BFR – proofing agent (include PBBs, PBDEs, TBBPA)	Casing, circuit boards (plastic) –		Highly toxic to the foetus, produce hormonal changes, and are carcinogenic

(*Continued*)

84 Toxicity, environment, human health

TABLE 3.4 (Continued)

Element	Occurrence in EEE	Human intake	Toxicity and impact on human health
Cadmium (Cd), atomic number 48	A plastic stabiliser. Batteries, pigments, solder, alloys Ni-Cd Cd plating to prevent corrosion and chip resistance on circuit boards; in infrared detectors, semiconductors, fluorescent screens in CRT and solar cells.	Orally in form of dust and vapour – contaminated fumes, via food chain (low concentrations found in vegetables, cereals, and tubers rich in starch).	This is classified as carcinogen for humans. Fumes and compounds are chronically toxic – accumulated in liver and kidneys and create poisoning. Cadmium oxide and Cadmium sulphate are carcinogenic, damaging DNA. May have irreversible effect on cardiovascular system, bones, and testicular function.
Chlorine (Cl), atomic number 37	PVC, flame retardants, insulating materials		
Chromium (Cr), atomic number 24 / Hexavalent Chromium	Dyes / pigments, switches, solar	Orally via food chain, drinking Cr-laden water, pulmonary intake via the skin (allergic reactions)	Cr oxide and alkali metal chromates are toxic to human organism and have caustic effect on the skin and respiratory tract. Get accumulated in spleen, bone marrow, liver, kidney, lungs, womb and testes, and damage them. May damage DNA.
Cobalt (Co), atomic number 60	Insulators		
Copper (Cu), atomic number 29	Conducted in cables, copper ribbons, coils, circuitry pigments		Copper dust create symptoms – allergies, liver damage, breathing trouble; zinc deficiency; on skin leads to eczema.

Toxicity, environment, human health **85**

Lead (Pb), atomic number 82	Lead rechargeable batteries, solar, transistors, lithium batteries, PVC (polyvinyl chloride) stabilisers, lasers, glass components of CRTs and LCD/LEDs, thermoelectric elements, soldering agent.	Build-up in body through repeat exposure. Deposited in teeth and bones, get accumulated over time.	Cause damage of kidneys, liver, and nervous system; central and peripheral nervous system; affects brain development and intelligence in children. May influence progression of Alzheimer disease. Can also cause anaemia, hypertension, renal dysfunction, immunotoxicity, and reproductive toxicity.
Lithium (Li), atomic number 3	Mobile telephones (Li-ion batteries), photographic equipment, video equipment (batteries)	Touch – while removing, affected if leakage in the batteries	Due to Lithium poisoning neurological disorders are reported, which can be accompanied by cardiac and gastrointestinal alterations. Severe cases can present fatal cardiovascular complications.
Mercury (Hg), atomic number 80	Components in copper machines and steam irons; batteries in clocks and pocket calculators, relays, and switches, LCD backlights, thermostats, censors	Oral and pulmonary intake, through skin by resorption, food chain particularly via fish	Impact depends on its form – elementary, inorganic or organic). Advanced toxicity can lead to loss of teeth, kidney failure, severe neurotrauma, affects lungs, even death. The inhalation of mercury vapour can be harmful to the nervous and immune systems, the digestive system, and the lungs and kidneys. After inhalation or ingestion of different mercury compounds or after skin exposure to them, neurological, and behavioural disorders can be observed, with symptoms such as tremors, insomnia, memory loss, neuronuscular effects, headache, or cognitive and motor dysfunctions.

(*Continued*)

TABLE 3.4 (Continued)

Element	Occurrence in EEE	Human intake	Toxicity and impact on human health
Nickel (Ni), atomic number 28	Alloys, batteries, relays, semiconductors, pigments	Exposure through skin, ingestion, and inhalation	Most common adverse effect is an allergic reaction. People poisoned can develop problems like asthma and chronic bronchitis; nose, larynx, lung and prostate (in men) cancer; lung embolism; respiratory failure; birth defects and, heart diseases.
Silver (Ag), atomic number 47	Capacitors, switches (contacts), batteries, resistors	Not documented	Not documented
Tin (Sn), atomic number 50	Soft solder, fusible alloys, flame-proofing agent, plastic stabilizers		
Zinc (Zn), atomic number 30	Steel, brass, alloys, disposable and rechargeable batteries, luminous substances	Inhalation	Zinc is an essential nutrient for the human body related to the growth and proper functioning of the immune system. Ingestion and inhalation of excessive doses of zinc can cause, among others, diarrhoea, cramps, sickness, vomit, loss of appetite, depressed immune system function, altered formation of red blood cells, and reduced levels of HDL cholesterol.
3. Others Acid			Sulphuric and hydrochloric acids are used to separate metals from circuit boards. Fumes contain chlorine and sulphur dioxide, which cause respiratory problems. They are corrosive to the eye and skin.

Asbestos – it covers all naturally occurring fibrous materials consisting of silicon dioxide, calcium, iron, magnesium or aluminium oxide, and magnesium silicate	Irons, boilers, toasters (heat insulation)	These fibres can reach lungs leading to lung cancer.
Dioxins and furans from waste incineration		Can cause variations in serum lipid levels, enzymic dysfunction, and gastrointestinal alterations; reduction in testosterone.
Liquid crystals	Displays	
Nonylphenol (NP)	A chemical widely known as a breakdown product of nonylphenol ethoxylate (NPE) detergents	Food / human diet, placenta, breast milk
	Build up through the food chain	Capable of causing damage to DNA and even sperm function.

Source: Janz and Bilitewski (2008: 93), Maharashtra Pollution Control Board (2007: 4–7); 'IT's underbelly', *Down to Earth*, vol. 19, no. 1, May 16–31, 2010; and Toxics Link (2014: 47–49), GIZ and MESTI (2019: 26–27) and Pont et al. (2019: 6–8).

[a] The materials used in PVC are classified as hazardous substances according to the Agency for Toxic Substances and Disease Registry (ATSDR), a federal public health agency of the USA Department of Health and Human Services.

contamination takes place – which process and through which part of human body; and (iv) details about toxicity and its impact on human health. Thus, every element is linked with its occurrence in EEE, how that element is entering human body, and its impact human health (Table 3.4).

Informal recycling operations, toxicity, and health hazards in India

In India, informal sector treating e-waste is one of the focal points of the debate on resource recovery, adverse impact on environment as well as human health. Two major arguments are: because of rudimentary recycling methods are employed by the informal sector players health hazards are rampant; resource recovery is much lesser than the scientific methods, advanced technology and infrastructure for recycling e-waste; and higher proportion of waste directly going to landfill, contaminating soil and water with high level of heavy metals. In order to measure contamination, trace elements method is used wherein soil, air dust, and human hair are collected from e-waste recycling sites (a recycling facility and backyard recycling units), and concentration of various elements (including metals) are traced/measured (Ha et al. 2009).

The collection, storage, and transportation of e-waste are though need safety features in order to avoid environment and health hazards, but these are not much discussed in the existing literature vis-à-vis recycling methods and resource recovery. In the existing literature, dismantling and segregation of different parts – electronics, glass, plastics, and others – are considered to be relatively safer processes.

UNEP (2009, 57) report has argued regarding informal pre-processing technologies, accepting that deep-level manual dismantling is preferred by most of the informal recyclers, because this is beneficial to separate the whole equipment into purer fractions. This approach is rather preferable in developing countries due to the reason that the labour cost is comparatively low and the work force abundant. Systematic deep-level dismantling serves as a good preparation for the refinery, reuse, and material recycling in the next phase. The report has recognised that all other informal activities bear great adverse environmental and social impacts and often are also less attractive from an economical point of view than innovative technologies as identified by the UNEP. Based on informal practices, the report has further made four groups to show informal sector is decreasing / increasing. Among the country specific barriers, UNEP (2009, 65) had further mentioned, there is little change observed on most of them – legal, technology and skills, and business and financing; for example, no definition of roles and responsibilities of stakeholders, no proper solution for hazardous fractions contained in e-waste, difficulties to access the materials and direct competition with the informal sector, no secure financing of non-profitable recycling operations, and so on.

In the existing literature, impact on environment and human health mentioned as process (release of toxins), end result (type of toxins) or in generalised manner;

either of them is rarely quantified through macro studies / statistics. E-waste and toxicity in India were reported as early as in 2002.

> The E-waste recycling and disposal operations found in China, India, and Pakistan are extremely polluting and likely to be very damaging to human health. Examples include open burning of plastic waste, exposure to toxic solders, river dumping of acids, and widespread general dumping.
>
> (Puckett et al. 2002: 4)

BAN/Puckett (2005) repeated similar concerns in the following study conducted in 2005, saying,

> the situation becomes worrying in situations where studies in China and India have shown that unregulated disposal of such wastes can contaminate soil, groundwater, and air, as well as affect all those involve in their processing, as well as the nearby communities.

Release of toxins is reported by the Greenpeace report (2005: 5) as, 'street dust samples from the recovery units in Delhi detected alarmingly high concentrations of lead, cadmium, mercury, tin, organochlorines, Chlorinated Benzenes, PBDEs, and Polychlorinated Namphalenes (PCNs) and Polychlorinated biphenyls.' The PBDE and Polychlorinated biphenyls are known BFRs; they are much higher in concentration at the estates where e-waste is treated, compared to the ones from the residential or other commercial areas where significantly less concentrations of metal residues were detected (Toxics Link 2019b: 8).

Another study, measuring trace elements, conducted in Bangalore and Chennai in December 2006, collecting samples of air, soil, and hair of male workers engaged in recycling process, from storage areas outside the main building of an e-waste recycling facility and backyard recycling sites in the slum areas. The study revealed that though informal e-waste recycling technology extracts valuable metals rapidly, the recovery is inefficient and incomplete. Generally, manganese (Mn) and copper were high in all the soils. High level of bismuth (Bi), copper (Cu), indium (In), lead (Pb), stannum (Sn), stibium (Sb), and zinc (Zn) were found in all the soil samples of recycling sites. Silver, Cadmium, and mercury (Hg) concentrations were higher in soils; presence of mercury in recycling sites indicate that the crude extraction methods of gold using mercury are contributing to the higher mercury contamination in the soils of the slum areas. Higher concentration in air of chromium, manganese, carbon monoxide, copper, indium, stannum, stiumb, thallium (Tl), lead, and bismuth from recycling sites compared to city area. Generally, zinc concentration in human hair was the highest, followed by copper, lead, and manganese. On the other hand, hair thallium level was quite low. Other pollutants were getting discharged into the local environment, causing soil, air, water, and plant pollution because of high penetration rate (Ha et al. 2009: 12–14).

90 Toxicity, environment, human health

Two recent field base investigation reports (CSE 2015; Toxics Link 2019b) have found direct linkages between toxicity, health hazards, and rudimentary methods used for e-waste recycling. The informal sector recyclers process e-waste to recover metals, including copper, aluminium, gold, and silver. As a result of informal e-waste recycling in Moradabad, State of Uttar Pradesh, soil in the area has been contaminated with zinc and copper by up to 5–15 times more than the prescribed safety limits. Even the water from the nearby Ram Ganga River was found contaminated with Chromium and Cadmium by up to 1.3–2 times higher than normal limits along with traces of cancer causing elements like mercury and arsenic (CSE 2015; www.attero.in).

The *Guidelines for environmentally sound management of e-waste* published by the MoEF and CPCB (2008: 64–70, 74–79) provides details on thresholds of total 20 pollutants (e.g. beryllium, cadmium, chromium, lead and their chemical combinations created during the treatment to e-waste) and risk of every substance/pollutant as per the Indian regulation, in comparison with European standards of the then. These guidelines have been in use after the *Rules, 2011* and *Rules, 2016* are enacted. However, Singhal (2019b: 22) observed that 'the categorization of products and components in Schedule 1 of the E-waste Rules [2016] are currently not based on the toxicity potential.' (emphasis added). He further adds, 'even though servers, routers and switches have similar toxicity potential, only servers are included in the targets for collection…Include all WEEE in categories of e-waste and bring in toxicity-based criteria for identification of product categories to be covered' (ibid.).

Notes

1. For example, copper is a catalyst for dioxin formation and copper electrical wiring is coated with chlorine-containing polyvinyl chloride (PVC) plastic which also contributes to the formation of dioxins.
2. TCLP is considered to be important toxicity indicator; it is designed to determine the mobility of chemical substances in liquid, solid, and multiphase wastes, is widely used in research to test potential hazard levels (Chen et al. 2018: 2). The regulatory level for lead in the U.S. is a TCLP of 5.0 mg/L. TCLP levels for monitors due to lead concentrations in the glass test out to be on average about 18.5 mg/L for lead (quoted in Puckett et al. 2002: 29).
3. The life cycle thinking is from materials extraction to waste treatment, usually called "from cradle to the grave".
4. Usually, in LCIA, USEtox model is used to determine the trends of potential impacts on human health (cancer and non-cancer disease) and ecological toxicity (Singh et al. 2019: 2).
5. Refer UNEP (2009: 10) for more details on emission of CO_2 for demand for EEE and primary production of metals – copper, cobalt, tin, indium, silver, palladium, platinum and ruthenium.
6. The CO_2 emission could be broken down as follow: 1,030 tons of CO_2 avoided because no virgin materials had to be produced; 331 tons of CO_2 avoided because of local recycling activities; 13 tons of CO_2 avoided because of energy recovery of non-recyclables;

The total CO_2 emissions avoided amount to 4.5 times the emissions produced taking into account collection, pre-treatment and transporting of e-waste following the Bo2W model (http://worldloop.org/e-waste/bo2w-impact-on-co2-emissions/) accessed on 1 July 2020.
7 Collected e-waste from diversified sources is segregated in various categories such as components, modules, metals, glass and plastics depending on the saleability for highest economic returns.
8 The disassembly methods are of two types, non–destructive and destructive. Non–destructive recovers the certain disassembled parts for reuse while the destructive disassembly separates each material type for recycling processes. For more details refer Chatterjee and Kumar 2009.
9 For further details, refer UNEP (2009); Miliute-Plepiene and Youhanan (2019).
10 Pyro-metallurgical method is employed when the metals are present in a complex matrix with other non-metals and ceramics etc., in order to recover metals. Smelting, refining, incineration, combustion are the common processes in this route; typically smelting is followed by electro-chemical refining (Debnath et al. 2018: 4). For more details, refer Shamsuddin (1986).
11 Hydro-metallurgical methods used for metal extraction from primary ores. Leaching (cyanide leaching, thiourea leaching, thiosulfate leaching) is carried out by means of acid, alkali or other solvents to leach out metals in form of soluble salts. Impurities are removed with the gangue materials and the isolation of metals from the solution is achieved by processes such as adsorption, solvent extraction etc. Final forms of metals are achieved through electro-refining or chemical reduction processes. Copper and other precious metals such as gold, silver, etc. can be recovered. Usually, nitric acid; sulphuric acid and muriatic acid based solutions are used for primary leaching for recovering precious metals (quoted in Debnath et al. 2018: 4–5). For more details, refer (Darnall et al., 1986; Kuyucak and Volesky 1988; Niu and Volesky 1999).
12 Bio-metallurgical processes can be classified into two types: (i) Biosorption; and (ii) Bioleaching. Biosorption means adsorption of metals by means of adsorbents prepared from waste biomass or abundant biomass. Metal recovery from E-waste by biosorption has been achieved by using algae, fungi, bacteria, hen eggshell membrane, ovalbumin, alfalfa, etc. For bioleaching mainly three groups of bacteria associated – autotrophic bacteria, heterotrophic bacteria, and heterotrophic fungi. Typically bioleaching occurs in four steps – Acidolysis, Complexolysis, Redoxolysis, and Bio-accumulation (quoted in Debnath et al. 2018: 5). For more details, refer Schinner and Burgstaller (1989), Brandl et al. (2001).
13 For more details, refer Hanapi, B.M., Tang, B.S. 2006. 'Selective Liquid-liquid extraction of precious metals from semiconductor wastes', *Department of Chemical Engineering Faculty of Chemical and Natural Resources Engineering University Teknologi, Malaysia.* For more details on different types of processes, refer the following articles: Hyunmyung, Y., Yong-Chul, J. 2006. 'The practice and challenges of electronic waste recycling in Korea with emphasis on extended producer responsibility (EPR)', *IEEE International Symposium on Electronics and the Environment,* 8–11 May, pp. 326–330; and Xuefeng, W., Yuemin, Z., Chenlong, D., Xiaohua, Z., Hongguang, J., Shulei, S. 2005. 'Study on metals recovery from discarded printed circuit boards by physical methods', *Electronics and the Environment,* Proceedings of IEEE International Symposium, May, pp. 121–128.
14 In these processes, levels of metals, including dissolved arsenic, chromium, lithium, molybdenum, antimony, selenium, silver, beryllium, cadmium, cobalt, copper, nickel, lead and zinc to be treated properly.

15 For details, see ATSDR. 1999. 'Toxicological Profile for cadmium,' *United States Public Health Service, Agency for Toxic Substances and Disease Registry* (July); Chan, J.K.Y., Xing, G.H., Xu,Y., Liang,Y., Chen, L.X.,Wu, S.C.,Wong, C.K.C., Leung, C.K.M.,Wong, M.H. 2007. 'Body loadings and health risk assessment of polychlorinated dibenzo-p-dioxins and dibenzofurans at an intensive electronic waste recycling site in China,' *Environmental Science and Technology*, 41: 7668–7674; Malcoe, L.H., Lynch, R.A., Kegler, M.C., Skaggs, V.J. 2002. 'Lead sources, behaviors, and socioeconomic factors in relation to blood lead of native American and white children: A community-based assessment of a former mining area,' *Environmental Health Perspectives* 110 (Supplement 2): 221–231; Qu, W., Bi, X., Sheng, G., Lu, S., Fu, J.,Yuan, J., Li, L. 2007. 'Exposure to polybrominated diphenyl ethers among workers at an electronic waste dismantling region in Guangdong, China', *Environment International*, 33(8): 1021–1028; Schutz, A., Olsson, M., Jensen, A., Gerhardsson, L., Borjesson, J., Mattsson, S., Skerfving, S. 2005.'Lead in finger bone, whole blood, plasma and urine in lead-smelter workers: extended exposure range,' *International Archives of Occupational and Environmental Health*, 78(1): 35–43.
16 For permissible limit of each element, refer MoEF and CPCB (2008: 79–83).

4
TREATING E-WASTE, RESOURCE EFFICIENCY, AND CIRCULAR ECONOMY

> *In the face of sharp volatility increases across the global economy and proliferating signs of resource depletion, the call for a new economic model is getting louder. In the quest for a substantial improvement in resource performance across the economy, businesses have started to explore ways to reuse products or their components and restore more of their precious material, energy and labour inputs. The time is right, many argue, to take this concept of a 'circular economy' one step further, to analyse its promise for businesses and economies, and to prepare the ground for its adoption.*
>
> Ellen Macarthur Foundation (2013: 6)

This chapter focuses on recycling-resource efficiency-circular economy themes in the context of resource use and sustainable development. These themes are linked based on the idea that if e-products are designed to last longer, and if more e-waste is recovered, reused, and recycled throughout the life cycle, there will be a reduced demand for virgin materials and less waste will be generated from the extraction of raw materials, packaging and transport (ILO 2019b). The circular economy (CE) approach brings in shift 'from a problem to a resource' and promotes e-waste as a resource; the environment approach stresses on increasing recycling, and consequently resource efficiency (RE) from e-waste so that its final disposal would increasingly be environmentally sound manner. In this gamut of themes, proper recycling techniques and technology, recycling infrastructure are desired, proper disposal of residues avoiding leaching and contamination of soil and water, and proper working conditions for the workers to prevent health hazards (Figure 4.1).

The chapter begins by linking treating e-waste, resource with safe environment, and CE as desired outcomes, followed by explaining the difference between linear and circular economy. Recycling, REs, and resource use are briefly talked about in order to enhance the CE. Towards end, urban economy, informal sector dealing with e-waste, resource recovery, and possibility of CE in India are discussed in detail.

DOI: 10.4324/9780429285424-4

94 Resource use, efficiency, circular economy

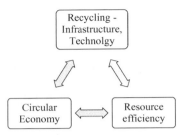

FIGURE 4.1 Recycling, resource efficiency, and circular economy

Safe environment, resource use, and circular economy

The parlance of e-waste-based economy incorporate three stages of e-products – production, consumption, and disposal; also includes demand and supply of e-products, economic growth, critical resources used, and value of material recovery. The parlance of e-waste linked with environment has expressed concerned about pollutants/toxins and pollution/contamination; release of toxins/toxicity due to process failures – worker's protection and human health; fossil use; energy efficiency/use; footprints of land, water, and raw materials based on their use; and final fate of by-products (UNEP 2009). When electricity dominates the life cycle energy of a product, global warming impacts often mirror energy use impacts because electricity generation emits large amounts of carbon dioxide (CO_2), a global warming gas (Socolof 2005: 1,289). When e-waste is seen as a resource that is properly managed, it can support livelihoods, generate employment, provide access to technology and/or enable technological upgrading, skills and knowledge transfer, and provide capital to produce second-hand commodities/materials and to recover materials (Lepawsky 2015).

Availability of critical resources, their use and reuse

Many critical materials are used in the manufacturing processes of EEE, as such in a very small quantities; each material is important with its properties. Scarcity of virgin materials, especially rare earth metals, and need for reducing mining and extraction of virgin materials has contributed to this shift – focus on CE as desired outcome. The EU has listed 27 critical raw materials'[1] (CRM) in 2017, which are 'for society and welfare' – rare earth elements[2] (light rare earth elements, heavy rare earth elements, and platinum group metals.[3] The criticality of these materials is defined by two main criteria: importance to the economy and high supply risks (Miliute-Plepiene and Youhanan 2019: 8). This list is prepared based on historical data rather than a forecast. 'Recovering resources from e-waste and maintaining a closed-loop of resources also minimise the stress on the virgin resource supply chain. As industries encounter scarcity of resources and higher production costs, closed-loop production becomes increasingly important' (Patil and Ramakrishna 2020: 2).

The economic viability is comprised of

> process costs; impact on process costs (and yields) of preceding and subsequent steps in the recycling chain; quality and market value of output streams; process stability/vulnerability to changes in feed composition; labour cost; availability of skilled/trained labour, capital access; investment security; intellectual property security; critical size/economies of scale; available markets for output fractions; availability and sources of feed material; infrastructure in place; etc.
>
> (Patil and Ramakrishna 2020)

Increased scale of EEE production has led to increased scale and intensity of resource use leading to manifold increase in demand for natural resources, especially materials to find a balance between developmental needs and minimising the negative impacts associated with resource use. Concerns over resource depletion and constraints manifesting in resource supply constraints, price shocks, and rapid degradation of natural resource base have become more pronounced. Therefore, judicious use of resources through a combination of conservation and efficiency measures for economic, social, and environmental sustainability is suggested, and now have become part of CE. The International Resource Panel (IRP) established by UNEP in 2007 provides 'independent scientific assessments on sustainable use of natural resources and their environmental impacts and policy approaches to promote decoupling economic growth from environmental degradation' (NITI Aayog and EU 2017: 4–8).

Under the EPR, environment protection and sustainable development have been introduced as critical components as well as the expected outcome. Therefore, in the discourse of e-waste management, judicious resource use, resource recovery, and REs have been brought in along with the CE as a value addition as well as the most desirable outcome since almost a decade. More specifically, this shift in perspective regarding e-waste management has taken place after the EU Commission adopted a CE package consisting of a communication and an action plan and proposals for revised legislation on waste on 2 December 2015 (EU 2018: 8). Thus, there is a shift in e-waste management; i.e. 'from a problem to a resource'.

The *Recycling – from e-waste to resources*, by UNEP in 2009 is one of the first reports that has discussed resource recovery, e-waste recycling technologies, and market potential. The resource recovery includes:

> variety of substances that are recovered; recovery and yield for individual materials; rating of recovered materials with respect to economic and environmental value; technology used; interfaces to other steps in the chain; requirements of the next processing step and also requirements to preceding step; etc.
>
> (UNEP 2009: 17)

Recovery of resources

The recovery of metals is considered as a profitable business across the globe in present time, which results in local, trans-boundary, and global trade. The UNEP report (2007) presented data on resource recovery. Details of different constituents of five e-products (cellular phone, computer, television set, refrigerator and freezer, and washing machine)[4] are presented in the following table. The table presents weights of different e-products and recoverable materials provide a glimpse of possibility of recovery (Table 4.1).

After a decade, the PACE and WEF (2019) report reiterated aforementioned UNEP's articulation; linking e-waste, environment sustainability, health of humankind, and need to re-evaluate and reconsider e-waste for the benefit of industry by creation of new jobs, consumer, and workers, in order to grab an opportunity to shaping a future that works for all in the CE and development of the nation. 'Working electronic goods and components are worth more than the materials they contain. Therefore, extending the life of products and re-using components brings an even larger economic benefit' (PACE and WEF 2019: 5). The report shared an estimate,

> e-waste represents a huge opportunity. The material value alone is worth $62.5 billion (EUR 55 billion), three times more than the annual output of the world's silver mines and more than the GDP of most countries. There is 100 times more gold in a ton of mobile phones than in a ton of gold ore.
>
> (ibid.)

TABLE 4.1 Constituents of e-waste

Appliance	Average weight (in kg)	Iron (Fe) weight (%)	Non-Ferrous weight (%)	Glass weight (%)	Plastic waste (%)	Weight of electronic components (%)	Weight of other component (rubber, wood, ceramic, etc.) (%)
Cellular phone	0.08–0.1	8	20	10.6	59.6	–	1.8
Computer	29.6	53.3	8.4	15	23.3	17.3	0.7
Television set	36.2	5.3	5.4	62	22.9	0.9	3.5
Refrigerators and freezer[a]	48	64.4	6	1.4	13	–	15.1
Washing machine	40–47	59.8	4.6	2.6	1.5	–	31.5

Source: UNEP (2007: 32), and MoEF and CPCB (2008: 71–74) compiled by the author.
[a]For details on material recovered, see Wath et al. 2011: 256. 39 elements are recovered, including rare earth.

Circular economy: recycling, resource recovery, and resource efficiency

The concept of CE is increasingly occupying centre-stage in the political, economic, and policy discourse as a strategy to improve REs and reduce the environmental footprints of consumptions, especially the virgin material. 'The 'resource efficiency' is the ratio between given benefit or result and the natural resource required for it' (quoted in NITI Aayog and EU 2017: 7); this definition is adopted from German Federal Environment Agency (2012).

The idea of the CE traces its origins to the 1960s and in particular Kenneth Boulding's essay, titled *The Economics of the Coming Spaceship Earth* in 1966. The concept focused on nature's cycles of nutrients where different species co-exist in symbiotic relationships with each other; CE is inspired by the ideas found in industrial ecology, focusing on understanding and rationalising the interaction between the biosphere and anthroposphere (Miliute-Plepiene and Youhanan 2019: 24; Ellen MacArthur Foundation website[5]). One of the inherent limitations of this conception of CE is that human elements and costs are not recognised.

In the waste management context,

> the circular economy implies reusing waste back into the production cycle to produce new products and uses instead of wasting such materials with embedded resources. Therefore, steps to achieve a circular economy are an important part of resource efficiency; however, resource efficiency encompasses a wider range of strategies through the entire life cycle of products: Mining/Extraction →Design →Manufacturing/Production →Use/Consumption →Disposal/Recovery.
>
> (NITI Aayog and EU 2017: 7)

Resource efficiency is:

> a strategy to achieve the maximum possible benefit with least possible resource input. Fostering resource efficiency aims at governing and intensifying resource utilization in a purposeful and effective way. Such judicious resource use brings about multiple benefits along the three dimensions of sustainable development – economic, social and environmental.
>
> (ibid.: 15)

Resource efficiency concern is discussed in the context of:

> extraction of both biomass and fossil fuels has doubled, while extraction of metal ores has tripled and the extraction of non-metal minerals has nearly quadrupled during the period... in Asia, where the extraction of primary materials more than five times in just 40 years, particularly after 1990.
>
> (ibid.: 8)

Linear economy model versus circular economy

'There is also growing recognition that the prevailing linear model of "take, make, use and dispose" generates waste that could — and should — be reduced throughout the life cycle of electronic and electrical products' (ILO 2019a: 2), as this model has consequences for society, a negative impact on health and contributes to climate change (PACE and WEF 2019).

The CE in the context of waste management is simply conceived with the following components and their linkages: raw materials; design; production/remanufacturing; distribution; consumption/use, reuse, repair; collection; recycling – residual waste in between the collection and recycling (EU 2018: 9).

Historically, the CE model was developed on the use of biodegradable materials in the manufacture of consumer goods, which can be returned to nature without causing any environmental damage. This principle is not applicable to e-waste as such, because of no biodegradable materials are used. But this is certainly applicable in the context of the product design, product materials, manufacture of environmentally friendly products (eco-design), the selective disposal of waste for its subsequent recycling or enrichment to put them back into the production chain. Thus, in economic and industrial system, reusability of products and raw materials, and the restorative capacity of natural resources occupy centre-stage. It also attempts to minimize value destruction in the overall system, and to maximise value creation in each link in the system (Bastein et al. 2013: ix) (Figure 4.2).

The recycling 'technique' and 'technology' are often used synonymously, which needs to be distinguished in the context of e-waste.

> The term 'technique' refers to methods of creating new tools, establishing products of tools and the capacity for constructing such artefacts; the definition of 'technology'[6] implies the know-how required to develop and apply techniques and technical procedures. Thus, it exists embodied in machinery and equipment and unembodied in blueprints, technical instructions, manuals etc.
>
> (UNEP 2009: 2)

Technology is skills, processes, and combination of techniques; therefore, systematic dismantling of an electronic device is considered as part of recycling chain of e-waste.

When the concept of CE applies to both, biological, and technological cycles of e-waste, it distinguishes between technical and biological cycle. For the technical cycle, it focuses on to recover and restore products, components, and materials through technical processes like reuse, repair, remanufacturing and (in the last resort) recycling (Miliute-Plepiene and Youhanan 2019: 25). Thus, CE is considered to be a well thought out, rational waste management strategy along with smart production system. This system promotes maintenance and repair work, intensive reuse, and increased recycling.

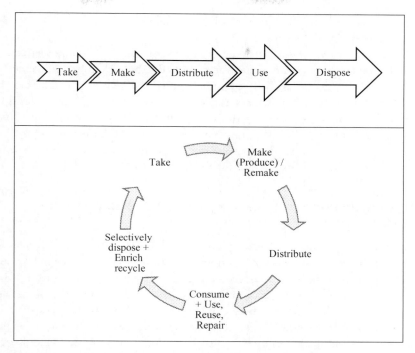

FIGURE 4.2 Linear economy model versus circular economy model
Source: Adapted from Miliute-Plepiene and Youhanan 2019: 24

Potentials of urban mining in circular economy

Urban mining is increasingly recognised as an important component of resource strategies of public authorities, not only because it contributes to environmental protection, but also because it is a source of valuable recyclable materials. In the last 40 years, demand for metals has increased by 87%. In this context, organised urban mining is seen as a potentially benefitting process for the CE, especially versus virgin mining, that is, extraction of metals from their natural setting in ores. As virgin extraction is difficult to be continued on sustainable manner, circulation of materials extracted from recycled products is preferred and promoted as part of the CE. According to some studies, urban mining of rare metals can recycle, globally, less than 1% of their embedded content; and depends on the type of devices and the potential value of the embedded raw materials.

Zeng et al. (2018: C) have tried to calibrate costs of urban mining for e-waste based on difficulty of recycling or recyclability. According to them, it encompasses fees paid for collection, labour, energy, material, transportation, residue disposal, and capital costs of equipment and buildings. Recyclers can generate revenues from three sources: from selling recovered materials; from selling recovered components, and from the government subsidy or funds. Previous studies indicate that resources in e-waste significantly differ in recyclability, therefore, costs of urban mining vary for different resources in e-waste.

Urban mining claims to contribute to environmental conditioning (detoxification of hazardous materials, conservation of natural resources) and (gainful employment). However, two major challenges are identified: unless in-depth understanding and data of material and substances available, effective recovery of resources from anthropogenic stock and transition to a CE is a challenge; and more complex compositions of e-waste stream. The development of urban mines requires innovative technologies as well as good urban mining governance that ensure a sustainable supply of secondary raw materials through recycling (Arora et al. 2017).

Recycling and resource efficiency related challenges to the circular economy

Recycling and RE are critical components of CE. A few external barriers are identified as challenges to the CE – from collection to recycling techniques and technology. For example, unintended consequences of existing regulations (e.g. definitions of waste that hinder trade and transport of products for remanufacturing), and sometimes policymakers to detect and capture CE opportunities; lack of experience among companies; and unaccounted externalities, such as, carbon emissions). Sometimes, economic feasibility of material recycling from e-waste, especially rare metals, is in question; mainly on the count of the process is complicated, the costs of waste collection, logistics, and the level of technology involved, and small quantities of precious metals collected as against the costs (Miliute-Plepiene and Youhanan 2019) (Figure 4.3).

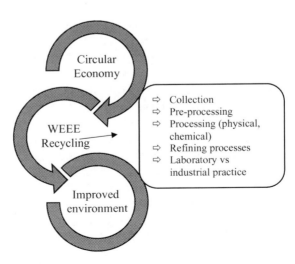

FIGURE 4.3 Recycling, circular economy, and improvement in environment

The process of recycling is closely linked to e-waste collection, as how much resources would be recovered is determined by the collection. The total recycling efficiency depends on the recovery rate. The amount of availability of metallic and non-metallic components decides the type of recycling. Also, there exists a distinct difference between laboratory practices and industrial practices. Environmentally sound recycling of e-waste requires infrastructure (sophisticated technology and processes, appropriate air pollution control devices for the fugitive and point source emissions), which is infrastructure very expensive, and requires specific skills, and training for its operation. Such costs need to be factored into as part of the CE.

The efficiency of the entire recycling chain depends on the efficiency of each step and on how well the interfaces between these interdependent steps are managed. For example, for a certain device/metal the efficiency of collection is 50%, the combined dismantling pre-processing efficiency is 70% and the materials recovery efficiency 95% (which all are rather optimistic assumptions), the resulting net metal yield along the chain would be only 33% (UNEP 2009: 12).

Recycling of critical metals is not easy. Precious metals in PCBs are generally recovered due to their high economic value and positive relationship to recovery costs. Recycling of gallium, germanium, indium, and rare earth metals is challenging as they are dispersed in products and require high volumes of waste in one place to make recycling more economically efficient. Moreover, recovery and purification of specific metals from very low quantities in e-waste (Miliute-Plepiene and Youhanan 2019).

Proper recycling of complex materials requires the expertise to recognise or determine the presence of hazardous or potentially hazardous constituents as well as desirable constituents or those with materials having recoverable market value. For example, 'some precious metals (platinum, palladium, gold, silver) and cobalt is significantly better with rates above 50%. While such as tantalum, indium, gallium, lithium and lanthanides, present poor recycling rates, lower than one percent' (Buchert et al. 2012: 2).

Significance of recycling technique and technology in e-waste management

Recycling occupies critical space in the discourse of e-waste management, and is considered to be the best possible solution. With proper recycling, recoverable resources are collected, which further save other resources, such as, energy, water, and other material footprints; also boost economy. Consequently, the reduction in landfill may result into reduction in toxic effects on environment, and human health. Landfilling has been the least favourable waste management option, mainly because proper treatment to e-waste reduces release of toxins; the lesser the toxicity, the lesser the adverse impacts on environment, and human health.

Recycling, if done in an environmentally sound manner, needs much less energy compared to mining ores in nature; prevents secondary and tertiary emissions; creates economically and environmentally sustainable businesses (optimise ecoefficiency);

and considers the social implications and the local context of operations (e.g. employment opportunities, available skills, and education) (UNEP 2009: 16).

Urban mining, recycling, resource use, resource efficiency, and circular economy in India

Urban mining and e-waste

Urban areas are considered as the main source of wastes; e-waste is mainly generated in urban settings.[7] It is estimated that such WEEE constitutes 8% of the total municipal solid waste generated in urban areas of India. Urban mining in the context of e-waste management refers to collection and recycling of raw material from used products, buildings, and waste in general; with regard to e-waste, it refers to reclaiming raw materials/recovery of critical metals from e-waste (including post-consumer electronic products), metals embedded in buildings (e.g. cables) and deposits after waste treatment (e.g. landfills, also called 'landfill mining'). 'Landfill mining' refers to extracting valuable materials from concentrated e-waste fractions in landfills.

> E-waste disposal mixed with solid municipal waste is posing a greater threat for environmental degradation…E-waste contains valuable materials including metal, plastics and glass, which are of the 95% of the total e-waste by weight. The populated PCBs/ connectors are of 3–5% of the total e-waste.
> (Chatterjee and Kumar 2009: 894)

One of the firsts estimates was provided by Chatterjee and Kumar (2009) a decade ago; i.e., details of recovered material from recycled PCs;[8] from assorted e-waste (containing PC, TV, Mobile Phone etc.);[9] and value of metals recovered from PCBs (Chatterjee and Kumar (2009: 896). The following table present details of metals recovered from 1,000 kg of PCBs, and their perception value of metals based on prevalent rate in 2009, and perception value of metals based on prevalent rate in 2020. Table 4.2 provides the details.

TABLE 4.2 Metal recovered from 1,000 kg of PCBs and perception value based on prevalent market rate (2009)

No.	Recovered metal	Weight (in g and kg)	Approx. cost (USD) in year 2009
1.	Gold (Au)	279.93 g	6,115 (@685.00 per 31 g)
2.	Precious metals (Pt, Pd, In)	93.31 g	3,852 (@ 1,284.00 per 31 g)
3.	Copper (Cu)	190.512 kg	1,470 (@ 3.50 per 453.59 g)
4.	Aluminium (Al)	145.152 kg	448.00 (@ 1.28 per 453.59 g)
5.	Lead and Tin (Pb, Sn)	30.844 kg	144.16 (@2.12 per 453.59 g)
6.	Silver (Ag)	450 g	213.15 (@ 14.70 per 31 g)

Source: Chatterjee and Kumar (2009: 896).

In Indian context, the government is talking of the situation in terms of the waste continuum and not in terms of the resource continuum. The governance processes between international institutions, governments, private sector, and civil society are still in the early stages of development.

> Even after the recommendations of the TSR Subramanyam Committee (High Level Committee) report,[10] we are talking in terms of wealth from waste. The government may intend to talk about urban mining from a resource perspective but when it comes to the policy, or the supporting instruments that have to be in place, the policies are weak.
>
> (Arora et al. 2017: 220)

A Parliamentary Standing Committee rejected the High Level Committee's report, and recommended appointment of a new committee. Thus, there is continuity of waste continuum regime, wherein creating wealth from waste, and consequently, process of recycling occupies centre-stage in India.

Resource use in India

In India,

> extraction of primary raw materials increased by around 420% between 1970 and 2010, which is lower than the Asian average but higher than the world average. While extraction of biotic materials only increased by a factor of 2.4, extraction of abiotic materials, particularly of non-metallic minerals, show remarkable augmentation.
>
> (NITI Aayog and EU 2017: 10)

Thus, India has experienced a remarkable growth of GDP (Gross Domestic Product), resource consumption and resource productivity but lagged behind on resource productivity increase compared to other countries (ibid.).

Recycling facility and resource efficiency related

The report *A strategy on resource efficiency* was jointly prepared by EU and NITI Aayog (2017), which links RE as a key element to sustainable development and the goals – 2, 6, 7, 8, 9, 11, 14, and 15. It further says the extraction and consumption of natural resources is not only an ecological challenge but also an economic and social issue.

> The Indian Resource Panel (InRP), through an overarching framework on resource efficiency, strives to decouple economic growth as far as possible from resource use, reduce burden on the environment and strengthen the sustainability and competitiveness of the Indian economy. **The focus of the outputs from the InRP is on abiotic resources** that are not used for

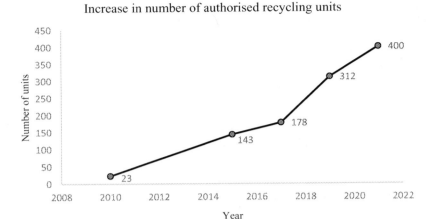

FIGURE 4.4 Number of recycling units in India (2010–2021)

energy production (ores, industrial minerals, construction minerals) to be supplemented by the material use of biotic resources in future.

(NITI Aayog and EU 2017: 5)

As mentioned in *GEM 2020*, 17.4% of e-waste is recycled annually worldwide; in India it is 1%. As the demand for materials is growing, recycling and urban mining are gradually becoming matters of interest, as sources for providing required materials.

After introduction of the draft e-waste rues in 2010, number of formal recycling units has been continuously increasing, as shown in the Figure 4.4.

Recent thinking on recycling and resource recovery, as described in the MeitY and NITI Aayog report (2019: 31),

> India can adopt measures for secondary raw materials management to foster security of resources...India needs to invest in processes and technology which can recover resources from the waste that is generated in the consumption process so that they can be channelized back into the production process. This will reduce the dependence on imports, enhance resource security for production, lead to development of skilled jobs and a better work force, higher GDP and an economy which will be resilient to external economic and trade shocks.

The Strategy paper on resource efficiency, GoI (2019)

Soon after amending the *Rules, 2016* in *2018*, the GoI prepared four strategy papers, one of them is specifically on EEE sector. The *Strategy on resource efficiency in electrical and electronic equipment sector* was prepared by MeitY and NITI Aayog (2019), which compares different aspects of e-waste as well as the methods/technology employed different stakeholders – by indigenous technologies developed by MeitY, and informal sector in India[11] versus formal processes of recycling / through recycling infrastructure (Umicore, Belgium). The following table presents the details (Table 4.3):

The REs strategy for EEE sector with a focus on utilisation of secondary materials recovered from end-of-life EEE also finds congruence with three ongoing missions and programmes of the GoI: Make in India, Digital India, Skill India and Swachh Bharat (Clean India).

Among various impacts including economic benefits, safe e-waste disposal in an environmentally friendly manner is anticipated, which expected to provide a fillip to the Swachh Bharat Mission (MeitY and NITI Aayog 2019: 42). Focus on cleanliness is represented as lesser degree of pollution and contamination in the environment.

Centre for Materials for Electronics Technology (C-MET), MeitY, and Central Institute of Plastics Engineering and Technology (CIPET), Ministry of Chemicals and Fertilisers have developed indigenous technology for the recovery of precious metals and plastics from e-waste respectively. After laboratory scale experiments, these technologies are yet to be upscaled to industry level use. Provision of technology to informal actors who are willing to formalise will allow benefits in the form

TABLE 4.3 Comparative of recycling processes, recovery, and cost calculations

Parameters	Indigenous technologies developed by MeitY	Informal sector – India	Umicore, Belgium
Materials recovered from	Gold, Silver, Platinum, and Palladium, Plastics of different varieties	Gold, Silver, Platinum, Palladium, and Lead	17 metals including Gold, Silver, Platinum, and Palladium
Efficiency of recovery of materials	Between 80–97%	20–30%	Above 95%
Input costs involved	INR 25,000 per 100 kg	INR 7,000 for a 100 kg batch	Includes Ore which increase input costs, as higher amount of energy is required
Capital costs involved	INR 25 crores to start the recycling process	In-house facility	More than Euro 200,000,000 already invested
Operational costs	INR 700,000–1000,000 per month	INR 15,000–25,000 per month	Not Available
Profit margins	Approx. 50–80%	Approx. 15–25%	Not Available

Source: MeitY and NITI Aayog 2019: 41–42, compiled by the author.

of enhanced resource recovery and incomes, safe and non-hazardous workplace, and mitigation of environmental pollution in the vicinity (Arora et al. 2019a: 72).

Recently, in the EU-India summit held in July 2020, a joint declaration to scale-up EU-India cooperation in the areas of REs and CE is adopted. 'The declaration establishes an India-EU Resource Efficiency and Circular Economy Partnership bringing together representatives of relevant stakeholders from both sides, including governments, businesses (including start-ups), academia and research institutes' (European Commission News, 15 July 2020).

Two issues need further deliberations, discussions, and due initiatives in the context of RE and CE in India: first, RE primarily focus on material recovery, especially the metals; no attention is paid to recovery of toxic elements and their final disposal. In this way, environment aspects, especially environment protection, are undermined. Second, material recovery through appropriate technology is conceived, which is minus human labour. This contrasts the classical understanding of economy, wherein labour and employment are absent.

Notes

1 Antimony, baryte, beryllium, bismuth, borate, cobalt, coking coal, fluorspar, gallium, germanium, hafnium, helium, light rare metals, heavy rare metals, indium, magnesium, natural graphite, natural rubber, niobium, platinum group metals, phosphate rock, phosphorus, scandium, silicon metal, tantalum, tungsten, vanadium.
2 The light rare earth materials consist of eight elements: Lanthanum (La), Cerium (Ce), Praseodymium (Pr), Neodymium (Nd), Promethium (Pm), Samarium (Sm), Europium (Eu), Gadolinium (Gd). The heavy rare earth materials consist of nine elements: Dysprosium (Dy), ytterbium (Yb), yttrium (Y), Erbium (Er), Gadolinium (Gd), Holmium (Ho), Lutetium (Lu), Scandium (Sc), Terbium (Tb), Thulium (Tm) (Buchert et al. 2012: 1). There is a minor change in the list prepared by EU, which is as follow: heavy rare earth elements: dysprosium, erbium, europium, gadolinium, holmium, lutetium, terbium, thulium, ytterbium, yttrium; light rare earth elements: cerium, lanthanum, neodymium, praseodymium, samarium; and platinum group metals: iridium, platinum, palladium, rhodium, ruthenium (EU 2018: 5).
3 Platinum group of elements (also called as platinoids, platinides, platidises, platinum group, platinum metals and platinum family elements) are six noble, precious metallic elements clustered together in the periodic table: Ruthenium (RU), Rhodium (Rh), Palladium (Pd), Osmium (Os), Iridium (Ir), and Platinum (Pt).
4 For more details, refer MoEF and CPCB (2008: 71–74).
5 https://www.ellenmacarthurfoundation.org/circular-economy/concept/building-blocks accessed on 8 March 2020.
6 The term 'technology' reflects four different dimensions: (i) the specific configuration of techniques and thus machinery and equipment designed to production process or for the provision of services, which can be summarized under the term "technical hardware"; (ii) the scientific and technical knowledge, formal qualifications and experienced-based knowledge (also called 'know-how'); (iii) the management methods used to link technical hardware and know-how, known under organization; and (iv) the physical good or service emerging from the production process and thus entitled 'product' (quoted in UNEP 2009: 2).

7 The ASSOCHAM-NEC (2018a) report mentioned 70% of e-waste was generated in ten states, notably those with the largest urban centres.
8 In formal recycling, 99% materials were recovered, 1% was sent for secured landfill. Recovered material from 1,000 kg PCs were as follow: 23% plastics (230 kg); 5% metals from cables (50 kg); 29% non-ferrous metals (290 kg); 20% ferrous metals (200 kg); and 4% (40 kg) metals from PCBs.
9 Saleable materials recovered from 1,000 kg assorted E-waste (containing PC, TV, Mobile Phone etc.) include 23% mild steel, 8% stainless steel, 27% glass, 27% plastics, 3% Copper, 3% Aluminium, 8% other materials, and 1% hazardous materials. These details do not include precious metals related details.
10 The High Level Committee under chairmanship of Mr. TSR Subramanian was appointed to review various acts Administered by the MoEFCC has submitted its report on 18 November 2014. The *Environment (Protection) Act, 1986* has also been reviewed. This committee proposed changes in legal and policy framework, amendments in specific environment laws.
11 Recycling units in India are mainly engaged the extraction of copper and its compounds. Extraction processes involve alkali and acid treatment. The metal sludge formed is allowed to settle at the bottom of the drum used and after separation of the precipitated metal the acid solution is discarded. The sludge is then sun dried, powdered and sold for production of metal sheets and further uses. Apart from copper and aluminium compounds certain precious metals like gold and silver are also extracted in the process. Additionally, plastic casings made of PVC or ABS [Acrylonitrile butadiene styrene] are sold to plastics recycling units located in industrial areas of Delhi for the manufacture of granules and toys (Dimitrakakis et al. 2006: 7).

5
E-WASTE MANAGEMENT THROUGH LEGISLATIONS IN INDIA

> *Legislation on e-waste should encourage a better product design at the production stage. This is the key to facilitate recycling and to produce products that are easier to repair or more durable. In addition, policies should point towards both a more efficient use of resources to improve production processes and to the recovery of valuable materials incorporated in EEE.*
>
> Baldé et al. 2017: 49

The trend of dealing with e-waste related problems with overarching legislation/regulatory framework is increasing and expanding across the globe. Current e-waste legislation in different countries mostly include restrictions on e-waste import/export, e-waste disposal in environmentally sound manner, recycling specific categories of e-waste, and Extended Producer Responsibility (EPR); India is no exception. The existing regulations aim at safe environment and protection of human health; recently, recycling and resource efficiency, as part of enhancing the circular economy are added thrust.

The discourse on e-waste management incorporates many other aspects, such as, green technology for e-products, DfE, resource recovery, and need for economically feasible technology, circular economy focusing on resource efficiency and management of secondary material, efficiency of informal sector, and aspiration to move towards formal economy. This chapter examines how, to what extent, these different aspects of the discourse on e-waste management have been incorporated in the existing regulatory framework of India.

The chapter is presented in four sections. The first section presents historical process – Indian government's considerations and actions for dealing with e-waste, that is, from 1989 onwards, linking with international conventions and agreements, and adopting regulatory framework in the present time. This section briefly overviews the *Rules, 2011*. The second section provides overview of and *Rules, 2016* and *Amendment Rules 2018*, and documents implementation related experiences. The third section analyses EPR as a statutory and enforcement strategy for effective of e-waste management in India, and flags the issues regarding fulfilment of the aspiration to move towards circular economy in the country. As part of this section, role and performance of the regulatory bodies in enforcement, monitoring, and evaluation of the Rules are examined. The regulatory bodies include the CPCB (Central Pollution Control Board), SPCBs (State Pollution Control Boards)/ PCCs (Pollution Control committee), and MoEFCC[1] (Ministry of Environment, Forests, and Climate Change) as a nodal Ministry for the Rules. The fourth section is on evolving jurisprudence on e-waste management, which is in very nascent state. An overview on the litigation at the National Green Tribunal (NGT) and State High Courts, proceedings, and judgements is presented, and cases are analysed to articulate the jurisprudence.

I: Historical backdrop of regulatory regime for e-waste in India

The historical backdrop of regulatory regime for e-waste needs to be understood with its criss-cross of the legislative and the executive as well as hazardous waste and municipal waste.

Environmental law and regulations: executive and legislative criss-cross

The management of e-waste was under the purview of the Division of Hazardous Waste Management, CPCB[2] after the enactment of the *Environment Protection Act, 1986*, ('EPA, 1986' henceforth). The *EPA, 1986* confers the power to enact regulations concerning environmental issues on the executive. Since then, the 'precautionary principle' and the 'polluter pays principle' have both become part of Indian environmental policy (Skinner et al. 2010: 18).

In furtherance to the implementation of the objectives of the *EPA, 1986*, the *Hazardous Waste (Management and Handling) Rules* ('HWM Rules' henceforth) were enacted in 1989. As per the *HWM Rules, 2008* 'hazardous waste' is defined as,

> any waste which by reason of any of its physical, chemical, reactive, toxic, flammable, explosive or corrosive characteristics causes danger or is likely to cause danger to health or environment, whether alone or when in contact with other wastes or substances.

These *Rules* were amended in the year 2000 primarily to bring them in line with the *Basel Convention*; were further amended in 2002, and were notified on 20 May 2003 as *The Hazardous Wastes (Management and Handling) Rules, 2003*. The amendment made in the *HWM Rules* in 2003 streamlined the list of processes and waste streams, based on their characteristics – dividing different processes and waste streams into three schedules.[3]

The Indian Constitution assigns solid waste management (SWM) as a primary responsibility to the Municipalities under the Twelfth Schedule (LARRDIS 2011:

54). Article 243W empowers the State Legislatures to frame legislations in respect of waste management. The *Municipal Solid Wastes (Management & Handling) Rules, 2000* ('MSW Rules' henceforth) were enacted by the Central Government which came into force from 25 September 2000. The report prepared by Research Unit of the Rajya Sabha (LARRDIS 2011: 56) mentioned,

> While the Municipal Solid Waste (Management and Handling) Rules regulate the disposal of municipal solid wastes in an environmentally acceptable manner and the Hazardous Waste (Management, Handling & Transboundary) Rules define and regulate all aspects of the hazardous waste, there are no specific environmental laws for the management and disposal of e-waste. None of the existing environmental laws has any direct reference to the electronic waste or its handling as hazardous in nature. However, there are several provisions in these laws which have been applied to various aspects of the electronic waste.

Until 2008, Indian government did not come up with any specific regulatory framework for e-waste. The beginning was – 192nd Report on the 'Functioning of the Central Pollution Control Board' by the Department-related Parliamentary Standing Committee[4] on Science and Technology, Environment and Forests (henceforth 'the Standing Committee') in 2008. This report mentioned in its para 12.2 that

> e-waste is going to be a big problem in the future as the modern lifestyle seeps and the living standards increase with economic growth. The Committee feels that CPCB should conduct studies to make future projections and devise steps to check the menace.

The Central Government drafted the *Hazardous Material (Management, Handling and Transboundary Movement) Rules, 2007*, which were notified on 24 September 2008 as the *Hazardous Wastes (Management, Handling and Transboundary Movement) Rules, 2008* (henceforth 'Rules, 2008') by the MoEF of Environment and Forests in supersession of the *HWM Rules, 2003* except in respect of things done or omitted to be done before such supersession. The MoEF was appointed as the nodal Ministry to deal with the transboundary movement of the hazardous wastes and to grant permission for transit of the hazardous wastes through any part of India under the *Rules, 2008*.[5] The *HWM Rules, 2008* 'contained additional provisions on e-waste handling within India as per the *Basel Convention*. These provisions require every person planning to recycle or reprocess e-waste to obtain prior authorization from the relevant SPCB' (Skinner et al. 2010: 18).

No exclusive e-waste regulation until 2011

The e-waste problems were once discussed in the Rajya Sabha on 23 December 2005, when Shri Vijay J. Darda, Honourable Member from Maharashtra, presented Private Member's Bill[6] on 'The Electronic Waste (Handling and Disposal) Bill, 2005'

(LARRDIS 2011: 53). However, the Bill was lapsed in July 2010 with the expiry of the tenure of the honourable member in the Rajya Sabha. Since then, questions have been raised in Lok Sabha and Rajya Sabha regarding e-waste management. During Lok Sabha in 2010,[7] the CPCB shared information regarding hazardous waste in India, 'there are 36,165 industries in the country generating about 6.2 million MT hazardous waste every year, of which landfillable waste is 2.7 million MT, incinerable waste 0.41 million MT and recyclable hazardous waste 3.08 million MT' and beside this, over 10,000 items, including hazardous items, are imported to India; these items are classified under various heads (quoted in LARRDIS 2011: 55).

Prior to the Rules, 2008, the 'Guidelines for Environmentally Sound Management of E-Waste' (henceforth 'the Guidelines, 2008') were published by the MoEF in May 2008. The *Guidelines, 2008* provided very detailed guidance on different aspects of e-waste in seven chapters and 11 annexures, as follow: identification of various sources of e-waste and classification and composition of e-waste; provided an overview of regulatory regime for e-waste at national and international levels; approach and methodology for handling and disposal of e-waste in an environmentally sound manner, such as, e-waste composition and recycle potential of items of economic value; identification of possible hazardous contents in e-waste; the recycle, reuse and recovery options; treatment and disposal options; the environmentally sound e-waste treatment technologies; and for establishment of integrated e-waste recycling and treatment facility. Along with these, the Guidelines emphasised the concept of EPR. Different annexures have covered details about e-waste – definitions under different regulations; hazardous substances in e-waste; recoverable quantities in different EEE, such as CRT, TV, refrigerator; trade value chain; and process flow of an integrated facility. These guidelines were not enforced until 2010.

If e-waste management is considered to be important in the context of environment; the 'environment' being a concurrent subject,[8] the Central Government has competence to legislate on e-waste. When the 186th Report of Standing Committee on Subordinate Legislation[9] (2015–2016) scrutinised the effectiveness of the *MSW Rules* in 2009, and expressed concern on the inadequate and ineffective the State laws, acknowledged the financial and technological constraints faced by Municipalities in the implementation of the Rules (LARRDIS 2011). With increasing urbanisation, increasing landfills, and concern for public health, it was stressed upon to enact a law. This situation again revealed that,

> while the MSW Rules regulate the disposal of municipal solid wastes in an environmentally acceptable manner and the *Hazardous Waste (Management, Handling & Transboundary) Rules* define and regulate all aspects of the hazardous waste, there are no specific environmental laws for the management and disposal of e-waste. None of the existing environmental laws has any direct reference to the electronic waste or its handling as hazardous in nature. However, there are several provisions in these laws which have been applied to various aspects of the electronic waste.
>
> (Quoted in LARRDIS 2011: 56)

The Mayapuri Radiological incident, also known as Cobalt-60 tragedy in Delhi in 2010 highlighted again a necessity for e-waste management under a regulation. This incident also highlighted direct contravention with the Export-Import Policy. For instance, implicit ban on the import of hazardous waste under the *HWM Rules*, e-waste was continued to be imported. The licenses for such import were provided for by Directorate General of Foreign Trade, as e-waste was categorised in the Schedule 2, and List A of Schedule 3. This incidence also became a reason for e-waste regulation.

However, until mid-2012, there was no dedicated regulation in force for e-waste management. Table 5.1 provides and overview of regulations under which e-waste management was covered until 2011.

The *E-waste (Management and Handling) Rules, 2011* came in force from 1 May 2012. Several efforts for policy dialogues and advocacy by civil society actors/agencies are described in detail for enactment of regulation on e-waste.

Brief introduction of *E-waste (Management & Handling) Rules, 2011*

Increasing quantum of domestic e-waste with rapid urbanisation, use of hazardous substances and toxic pollutant, contamination of soil and water due to leaching of pollutants, etc. together finally became instrumental in enacting this regulation. Minimal information is provided here, as these Rules are now repealed after *E-waste Management Rules, 2016* are enacted.

The *E-waste (Management and Handling) Rules, 2011* were notified in May 2011 and became effective from 1 May 2012.[10] These rules shall apply to every producer, individual or bulk consumer involved in the manufacture, sale, purchase and processing of EEE or components specified in Schedule-I,[11] collection centre, dismantler and recycler of e-waste (The Gazette of India 2010). The Batteries (as governed by *Batteries (Management and Handling) Rules, 2001*) Micro and Small Enterprises (as governed by *Micro, Small and Medium Enterprises Development Act, 2006*), and Radioactive Wastes (as governed by *Atomic Energy Act, 1962*) were kept out of purview of these Rules.

The *Rules, 2011* had six chapters, three schedules, and six forms – to be filled by different stakeholders. The salient features of the Rules, 2011 include (i) responsibilities of producers, collection centres, consumer of bulk consumer, dismantler, recycler; (ii) procedure for seeking authorisation and registration for handling e-waste; (iii) procedure for storage of e-waste; (iv) reduction in the use of hazardous substances in manufacturing of EEE; (v) duties of authorities; and (vi) annual report filing were mentioned.

The Rules have duly addressed the aspects of definition of e-waste, mechanism for collection, and end-of-life solution or recycling of e-waste, etc. which are important components of e-waste management. There are three highlights of these Rules focusing on ESM of e-waste: introduction of EPR; list of EEE items to be considered as e-waste; RoHS specifications;[12] and obligations of the concerned stakeholders, such as authorisation, maintenance of records, and filing annual returns.

E-waste management 113

TABLE 5.1 Overview of Indian regulations under which e-waste was managed

Year of notification	Title of the rule	How was e-waste managed
1986	Environment Protection Act (*Waste Rules* under Sections 6, 8, and 25 of *EPA*, 1986)	No specific definition of e-waste, as this Act is an umbrella act that covers hazardous wastes and provides broad guidelines to address it control of generation, collection, treatment, transport, import, storage, and disposal of wastes listed in the schedule annexed to these rules
	Section 2(e)	As hazardous – containing hazardous substance
1989	The Hazardous Wastes (*Management and Handling Rules*)	Categories of waste under three schedules – e-waste with specified hazardous substances
1992	Policy statement issued by the Government of India	Abatement of pollution – waste minimisation and control of hazardous wastes – e-waste with specified hazardous substances
2001	Batteries (*Management and Handling*) Rules	Exclusively cover lead acid batteries – thinly linked with e-waste
2000	Municipal Solid Wastes (*Management and Handling*) Rules, 2000	Earlier e-waste was part of MSW
2003	The Hazardous Wastes (*Management and Handling*) Amendment Rules, 2003 (Basel Convention and its Application to E-waste (Annex-VII)	Rules 3: WEEE including all components, subassemblies and their fractions[a] except batteries falling under these rules (listed in Part A, list A and B of the Schedule 3) – e-waste with specified hazardous substances; its movement and disposal to be controlled, recovery or reclamation and recycling operation to be looked into, need for environmentally sound technologies for its recycling
2006	National Environment Policy	As part of soil pollution action plan, it mentioned, 'Develop and enforce regulations and guidelines for management of e-waste, as part of the hazardous waste regime' – not specific action plan was mentioned
2008	Guidelines for Environmentally Sound Management of E-Waste	As a prelude to the *Rules, 2011* e-waste was classified according to its various components and compositions; mainly emphasised on the management and treatment practices of e-waste. The guideline incorporated concepts such as EPR
2008	Hazardous Wastes (*Management, Handling and Transboundary Movement*) Rules, 2008	Prior to the introduction of the 2011 Rules, e-waste was included in Schedule IV of the *HWM Rules, 2008*, making it registration mandatory for recyclers handling e-waste with the CPCB

(*Continued*)

TABLE 5.1 (Continued)

Year of notification	Title of the rule	How was e-waste managed
2011	The e-waste (Management and Handling) Rules, 2011	The EEE defined – equipment which is dependent on electric currents or electro-magnetic fields to be fully-functional, and 'e-waste' means WEEE, whole or in part or rejects from their manufacturing and repair process, which are intended to be discarded. EPR applied to EEE producer, collection centre, consumer, or bulk consumer, dismantler, recycler

Source: Bhaskar and Turaga (2017: 4), Maharashtra Pollution Control Board (2007: 13–16), LARRDIS (2011: 53–66), MeitY & NITI Aayog (2019: 27); Singh and Thomas (2016: 30). Compiled by the author.
ªMetal wastes and waste consisting of alloys; Waste having as constituents or contaminants, excluding metal waste in massive form; Waste lead acid batteries, whole or crushed; Unsorted waste batteries excluding mixtures of only list B batteries; and Glass waste from CRTs and other activated glass destined for direct reuse and not for recycling or final disposal. Electrical and electronic assemblies (including printed circuit board, electronic components and wires) destined for direct reuse and not for recycling or final disposal (quoted in Maharashtra Pollution Control Board 2007: 13–16).

The responsibilities for producers were defined in line with the principle of EPR, that is collection of e-waste generated during manufacturing of EEE and channelisation to the registered dismantler or recyclers; setting up collection centres or take-back system either individually or collectively; financing and organising a system to meet the cost involved in ESM of e-waste generated from the EoL. The collection centres have to obtain authorisation from the respective SPCB or from CPCB in case of Union Territory. These Rules are aiming at mitigating some of the risks associated with the informal sector operations and ensure that the waste flows in the clean channel.

Limitations of *E-waste (Management & Handling) Rules, 2011*: in conception and execution

There is a focus on recycling; thus, the other critical aspects of EPR were overlooked, such as, e-product design, increasing life of e-product through repair and refurbish. Recyclers are mandated for recovery of materials, but quality control aspect of the recovered materials and its selling were completely overlooked. Due to such limitations, quality recycling was not ensured; in absence of resource efficiency, the concept of CE remains half-heartedly addressed.

Specifications for collection centres were mentioned but *Rules, 2011* were silent on the problems related regular flow of e-waste, logistics, and its costs, etc. This may result into ineffective functioning of collection centres and negligible quantum of collection of e-waste. Most consumers or bulk consumers get monetary value in exchange of the discarded e-gadgets at the doorstep; such arrangement dissuade them to go to the collection centre for the due disposal of e-waste. Awareness raising may or may not lead to such behavioural change of consumers or bulk consumers. Moreover, status quo in such situation may lead to strengthening of collection of e-waste by the existing channel set by the informal sector.

No target, neither collection nor the recycling amount of e-waste (in weight, item-wise) was specified under the EPR. There was no provision for punishment/penalty charges in case of non-compliance of these Rules. The operations by informal sector – from collection to recycling, and selling secondary materials – were not addressed at all. This implied that in absence of scientific/environmentally sound manner, threat to environment and health hazards, and restricting business opportunities in e-waste sector would remain a challenge. Also, there was no mention about the monitoring by the CPCB and SPCBs of producers' performance under the EPR. The studies by Toxics Link examining effectiveness of EPR under the *Rules, 2011* is covered in the Chapter 2.

II: *E-waste (management) Rules, 2016* and *E-waste (management) Amendment Rules, 2018*

Prior to the *E-Waste (Management) Rules, 2016* (henceforth 'Rules, 2016'), a committee on subordinate legislation was appointed. The Committee presented its report in August 2016, which recommended 'a separate legislation on e-waste instead of handling it under the Environment Protection Act' (2016: 52). Despite the recommendation of the Committee for separate legislation, the MoEFCC continued with e-waste management with the Rules.

The *Rules, 2016* were notified on 10 June 2015 and became effective from 1 October, 2016.[13] The *Rules, 2016* were in exercise of the powers conferred by sections 6, 8 and 25 of the *Environment (Protection) Act, 1986* (29 of 1986), and in supersession of the *E-waste (Management and Handling) Rules, 2011*.

The *E-waste (Management) Amendment Rules, 2018*, were published on 30 October 2017 and became effective from 22 March 2018[14] (henceforth 'Amendment Rules, 2018'). The *Amendment Rules, 2018* have specified procedure for authorisation by the producer, PRO, recycling unit, revised forms (I and III) and EPR targets. Along with this, Schedule III is substituted (in Rule 5 and 13 of the *Rules*, 2016) with collection targets (in weight) for producers and increase in targets every year.

The specific objectives of *Rules, 2016* as follow: (i) to implement EPR; (ii) to promote and encourage establishment of an efficient e-waste collection mechanism; (iii) to promote environmentally safe and sound recycling by channelising e-waste to authorised dismantlers and recyclers of e-waste; (iv) to minimise illegal recycling / recovery operations; and (v) to reduce hazardous substances in EEE (Anand Kumar 2019: 4).

Brief introduction to the *Rules, 2016* and *Amendments Rules, 2018*

The *Rules, 2016* has seven chapters, four schedules, and seven forms – to be filled by different stakeholders. The salient features are: (i) responsibilities of manufacturer, producer, collection centre, dealer, refurbisher, consumer of bulk consumer, dismantler, recycler, and the State Government; (ii) procedure for seeking authorisation and registration for handling e-waste; (iii) procedure for storage of e-waste; (iv) reduction in the use of hazardous substances in manufacturing of EEE; (v) duties of authorities; and (vi) annual report filing were mentioned.

The *Amendment Rules, 2018* have amended Rule 5 (targets related), 13 (grant and renewal of authorisation), 16 (verification of compliance for RoHS), 21 (violation of provision), 22 (aggrieved persons and appeal), 23 (collection, storage, transportation, segregation, refurbishment, dismantling, recycling and disposal of e-waste shall be in accordance with the guidelines published by the CPCB), and Schedule III (revision in e-waste collection targets and others).

Highlights of *Rules, 2016* and *Amendment Rules, 2018*

The *Rules 2016* are the revised version of the *Rules, 2011*, with new additions and some changes are made in the old provisions while the *Amendment Rules, 2018* have specified more details on points of authorisation, collection targets, etc.

Continued provisions of the *Rules, 2011* are as follow: responsibilities of stakeholders, RoHS compliance, maintaining records by the stakeholders, annual return to be filed by the stakeholders, specifications for storage and transportation of e-waste, reporting of any environment damage, accidents, etc. to the specified authorities, etc.

New additions in the *Rule, 2016* are observed on the following points: first, the list of stakeholders have added manufacturer, dealer, refurbisher, and State Governments for ESM of e-waste. The definition of 'bulk consumer'[15] is expanded, by bringing all state and central government agencies, educational, and financial institutions, companies registered under the *Factories Act 1948*, and *Companies Act, 2013*. Second, list of items of EEE in the Schedule-I is expanded, adding more e-products as e-waste, especially fluorescent and other mercury containing lamps, and a few more item of IT products. Urban local bodies to ensure e-waste pertaining to orphan products is collected and channelised to authorised dismantler or recycler. Four new stakeholders – manufacturers, dealers, refurbishers, and PRO have been added. The following Table 5.2 provides an overview of the provisions under the *Rules, 2016*.

Salient changes in *Rules, 2016* and *Amendment Rules, 2018* compared to *Rules, 2011*

1. The scope of EPR is expanded and spelt out; this point is dealt in the following section. Under EPR, PRO registration and authorisation, the producer linked channels, and scope for collection and recycling of e-waste are expanded with additional options like DRS, e-waste exchange, targets for collection, etc. for fulfilling responsibilities of producers. These additions are considered to be 'ease of implementation' by many actors working for e-waste management. Every producer is mandated to prepare EPR Plan for implementation including meeting collection targets, estimating the quantity of e-waste generated

TABLE 5.2 An overview of *E-waste (Management) Rules, 2016* and *Amendment Rules, 2018*

Stakeholder, Rule	Responsibilities assigned under the Rules
Manufacturer, Rule 4	Collection and channelisation of e-waste; seeking authorisation form SPCB; maintaining records of the e-waste generated, handled and disposed; and filing annual returns to the concerned SPCB before 30 June in the financial year
Producer, Rule 5	Authorisation for EPR; implementing EPR by allocating finance and setting up collection and channelisation of e-waste and end-of-life solution; mechanism used for channelisation of e-waste; for disposal in Treatment, Storage and Disposal Facility, a pre-treatment is necessary to immobilise the mercury and reduce the volume of waste to be disposed of; providing contact details for EPR related activities, and for import of EEE; creating awareness; providing information on the implementation of DRS[a] to ensure collection of EoL; provide necessary details to consumers; periodically update information and maintain records; and filing annual returns
Amendment Rules, 2018, Rule 5, 13, Schedule III	Targets to be specified; EPR targets will be applicable as per Schedule III; transfer or sale of assets by the producers the liability under EPR shall be transferred to the buyer; and a PRO to obtain registration and authorisation
Collection centre, Rule 6	collection of e-waste; ensuring that the facilities are in accordance with the standards or guidelines issued by the CPCB for storage, and transportation; maintaining records; and filing annual return
Dealer, Rule 7	Collect e-waste on behalf of the producer; refund the amount as per take-back system or DRS (Deposit Refund Scheme); ensure safe transportation to authorised dismantler or recycler without any damage to environment during storage and transportation
Refurbisher, Rule 8	Collect e-waste generated during the process of refurbishing and channelise the waste to authorised dismantler or recycler through its collection centre and provide information; obtain authorisation from the concerned SPCB; ensure safe storage and transportation to authorised dismantler or recycler; and file returns before 30 June in the financial year; and maintain records of the e-waste handled
Consumer or Bulk consumer, Rule 9	Ensure channelisation of e-waste through prescribed channel; bulk consumers maintaining records; and filing annual return
Dismantler, Rule 10	Ensure prescribed standards for dismantling facility; obtain authorisation from the concerned SPCB; no damage is caused to the environment during storage and transportation of e-waste, and during dismantling processes; maintaining record of e-waste collected, dismantled, and sent to authorised recycler; filing annual returns; and not processing any e-waste for recovery or refining of materials, unless authorised

(*Continued*)

118 E-waste management

TABLE 5.2 (Continued)

Stakeholder, Rule	Responsibilities assigned under the Rules
Recycler, Rule 11	Ensure prescribed standards for recycling facility and processes; obtain authorisation from the concerned SPCB; ensure no damage is caused to the environment during storage and transportation of e-waste, and during the recycling processes; residue generated during recycling process is disposed of in an authorised treatment storage disposal facility; maintaining record of e-waste collected, dismantled and recycled; and filing annual returns
State governments, Rule 12	Made responsible for ESM through authorised agency (Department of Industry, Department of Labour or any other); ensure that earmarking or allocation of industrial space or shed for e-waste dismantling and recycling units; recognition and registration of workers involved in dismantling and recycling; facilitate workers for setting up dismantling facilities; undertaking industrial skill development activities for the workers; annual monitoring and to ensure safety and health of workers involved in dismantling and recycling; prepare integrated plan for effective implementation of these provisions, and to submit annual report to the MoEFCC

[a]Deposit Refund Scheme – an additional fee to be paid during the purchase of the e-product, which is compensated (with interest), when they return their obsolete electronics.

from their EoL products, outlining a scheme for collection and channelisation of their EoL products or products with same EEE code to authorised dismantlers/recyclers; estimated budget for implementing EPR; outline the scheme of creating awareness; and declaration on RoHS compliance. For implementation, every producer will provide every e-product with a unique serial number or individual identification code and take responsibility for all previously generated waste labelled with their name. 'Setting up targets will aid the evaluation of the performance of firms and the ministry.' (Agarwal 2016)

2. Pan India EPR Authorisation for all producers of EEE (including importers, e-retailers/on-line sellers/eBay etc.) from CPCB is mandatory. Without authorisation, selling, or placing of EEE in the market by any producer penal provisions. Authorisation of recyclers are also mandatory; however, they do not have to produce data on quantum of e-waste recycled. This will replace state-wise EPR authorisation; 'provide single window clearance making the process of getting approval for e-waste management strategy easier and quicker' (*op. cit.*).

3. Expansion of definition of 'bulk consumers' has become inclusive; and filing annual return by them also is looked upon as this would help in creating database and bring in transparency. The 'bulk consumers' are believed to be the largest quantity e-waste generators; they can ensure that e-waste generated by them is handed over to the authorised PRO, producer take-back system or to the authorised dismantler/recycler who is a part of producer's take-back channel/channelisation system.

4. Maintenance of records (Form-2 based) and filing annual return (Form-3 based), which could be made available for scrutiny by the SPCB would be useful in two ways – creating database, and a tool for monitoring.
5. Provision as 'liability of manufacturer, producer, importer, transporter, refurbisher, dismantler, and recycler for paying financial penalties for any violation' (Section 21) is introduced.; however, details about exact nature of violation, and extent of penalties for violation, non-compliance, etc. are not clearly mentioned in the guidelines for these Rules. It is believed that the penalty applicable under the *EPA, 1986* would be applicable in case of violation.
6. Maintaining records by all key players, and filing annual returns by producers may help in building reliable data related to e-waste disposal ensuring EoL as well as accountability, for monitoring on compliance, bringing transparency in the system.
7. CFL and other mercury containing lamps have been added in the list of e-waste items.
8. Collection mechanism-based approach has been adopted, in which collection centres, collection points, take-back system, etc. would contribute to enhancement of collection. Additional channels like PRO, DRS have been brought in for channelisation of e-waste. A PRO can be third-party professional e-waste management entity that can set up entire mechanism – from collection to recycling, would create competitive interest in the sector. Collectives of producers/PROs may manage collection centres on collective basis, thereby reducing costs, and enhancing collection. The applicability of DRS seems challenging in the competitive electronic sector in terms of price / cost making, marketability, etc.; user's behaviour – reselling the product, give away, etc. before its EoL; vis-à-vis a thinking of refunding to the consumer on returning the product, and thus incentivising channelling back of the end-of-life products.
9. States governments are bound to undertake skill development activities for the workers, their involvement in e-waste management process. Linking e-waste management with other government schemes like Skill India may open up new avenues/business opportunities.

III: Analysing performance of EPR and CPCB as regulatory mechanisms

Table 5.3 presents an overview on EPR as regulatory, enforcement, and awareness creation strategy under the *Rules, 2016* and *Amendment Rules, 2018*.

Anand Kumar (2019), Additional Director, CPCB has portrayed EPR as a mix of three types of strategies – legal/regulatory, management, and enforcement strategy by the CPCB for e-waste management in India, as part of his presentation while discussing with ITU. As part of legal/regulatory strategy, three components are important: (i) pan Indian EPR authorisation for all producers of EEE; (ii) ensuring that producers prepare EPR plan and achieve targets for e-waste collection, and enhance recycling; and (iii) ensuring RoHS compliance.

TABLE 5.3 EPR as regulatory, enforcement, and awareness creation strategy under the *Rules, 2016*

EPR components	Stakeholders			
	Producer	Retailer (also as producer)	Consumer	Government
Regulatory	Obtain registration and authorisation Set target for collection and inform the regulatory body Report back to the regulatory body (maintain record keeping, fling return, violation)	Create 'Take-back' and collect e-waste / product created	Receive communication for awareness Receive facilitation for disposal of e-waste	Provide guidelines for effective implementation of the *Rules* Prepare integrated plan for implementation – labour issues, infrastructure building, facilitation to industry, etc. Issue certification and authorisation – producer, PRO, recycler after due diligence Ensure (inspect, monitor, evaluate) that producer meet the targets, and comply Act upon accident reported
Enforcement	Budget allocation Set up operational mechanism directly/through PRO Coordinate with various stakeholders	Collect e-waste as part of producer	—	Create mechanism to inspect, monitor, evaluate compliance by the stakeholders Create enabling environment for legal compliance by the stakeholders
Awareness creation	Educate consumers on RoHS, disposal, impacts, facilitation provided, etc.	Provide necessary information to consumers	May use information to act upon/e-waste disposal	Facilitate, monitor, evaluate EPR obligations of producers Undertake awareness programmes

Source: GIZ (2019: 30). Modified by the author.

As part of management strategy, one of the most important aspects of EPR is the collection and channelisation of e-waste, and necessary records are maintained, such as, amount of e-waste collected, channelised, and recycled, reporting of activities that damages environment, and annual returns filed by producers. Producers are required to create collection and recycling mechanism directly or through a PRO. As per EPR authorisation, product code-wise annual collection targets[16] of e-waste have been assigned to producers. Producers, authorised dismantlers/recyclers, PRO, etc. are key players for this management strategy.

As part of enforcement strategy, role of CPCB, SPCBs, and PCCs as regulatory agencies is critical. The CPCB and SPCBs need to check whether producers' action plan with specific activities along with parameters and methodology is in place; whether every key player is implementing clearly defined responsibility; and whether RoHS report compliance, maintaining records by producers and key players, and annual returns are filed by producers. To check enforcement, the CPCB needs to launch and use Progress Review Portal (comprehensive software based) for reviewing progress/status of implementation.

Implementation of EPR

The assessment of implementation of these Rules could be carried out on the following three strategic points (regulatory, enforcement, and awareness); recycling related issues including infrastructure, resource recovery reports, etc.; monitoring mechanism and its activation by the CPCB, its impact / consequence, etc.; and how state governments and SPCBs have progressed.

As policy instrument

Arora et al. (2019a: 69) opined that EPR as a policy statement

> is a short-sighted administrative planning tool of 5, 10 and 15-year plans. It fails to address the need for undertaking innovation by the industry towards system design thinking for integrated assessment of long-term supply and ensuring adequacy of metallic resources through collection and recycling of e-waste.

Awareness related

Effectiveness of EPR under the *Rules, 2016* has been carried out through a study by Toxics Link in 2019. Total 54 Brands were evaluated on the basis of the decided criteria[17] (action taken by producers towards fulfilling their responsibility under the Rules) and given score,[18] following the research of 2014 and 2015 (Toxics Link 2014b, Toxics Link 2015). The study was conducted of 50 producers based on secondary data, that is, producer website, helplines numbers provided on the producer's websites, and information provided by SPCBs in public realm. Major findings of these reports are briefly shared here: five brands belonged to 'poor category'; 29 companies belonged to 'below average rating'; 13 companies belonged to 'average rating' and seven companies featured in 'good rating'. Among them, large number of cell phone companies scored 'below average rating' (Toxics Link 2019a). This report indicates that 'there is a need to strengthen the regulatory bodies and improve enforcement. Producers may be submitting plans on paper, but are they being translated on ground? – this certainly needs to be checked and verified' (ibid.: 23).

Among the key recommendations, Toxics Link (2019a) stresses upon a need for the enforcement against free riders, to ensure fairness to the producers that carry out their EPR responsibility, and the good performers could be incentivised; building up national registry and/or third-party audits could be considered for identifying free riders; the government need to create EPR fund, at the time of getting an authorisation – as an insurance in case the producer wishes to exit the market and in such case, the orphan products[19] are taken care of; and small or medium scale producers who are still not aware of their responsibilities of EPR could be reached out to and to be motivated for performing their responsibilities.

State's initiatives

Not many states have drafted a separate state level policy for e-waste. has studied this issue in detail. The following Table 5.4 provides and overview of state's initiatives for e-waste management, implementing EPR.

Recycling related issues

Different aspects of recycling of e-waste include ability to recover/optimising recovery; recycling capacity and infrastructure; sustainability of recycling including quality, quantum, and selling of recovered/secondary material. Among these, information from the existing literature is available on recycling capacity versus quantum of e-waste generated; and recycling infrastructure required.

Overall implementation scenario of *Rules, 2011* and *Rules, 2016* in the year 2017–2018 and 2018–2018 is presented in the following Table 5.5. The number of authorised producers and collection centre under *Rules, 2011*, they are mentioned

TABLE 5.4 State's initiatives for implementation of EPR for e-waste management

State	Initiative for EPR implementation for e-waste management
Kerala	Clean Kerala Company, Government of Kerala – a recycling enterprise is set up; a few more places have been identified to set up collection centres
Odisha	The state government has directed concerned producers to collect/take-back the discarded products whilst implementing the DRS
Tamil Nadu	Waste segregation is emphasised; focus on e-waste
Telangana	Launched a comprehensive set of policies in consultation with the Telangana State Pollution Control Board in 2017, especially on creating awareness and nurturing a culture of reusing and recycling. Inventory of e-waste was prepared in 2016

Source: Malhotra (2020: 22–27). Compiled and revised by the author.

TABLE 5.5 Recycling facility in India as on 24 March 2021

No.	Name of state	No. of authorised dismantler/recycler	Total recycling capacity (MTA)
1.	Andhra Pradesh	03	6,600
2.	Assam	01	120
3.	Chandigarh	02	6,600
4.	Gujarat	19	50,507.02
5.	Goa	01	103
6.	Haryana	39	133,532.1
7.	Himachal Pradesh	02	1,500
8.	Jammu & Kashmir	03	705
9.	Jharkhand	02	660
10.	Karnataka	71	53,722
11.	Maharashtra	99	94,750.5
12.	Madhya Pradesh	02	9,600
13.	Odisha	05	5,690
14.	Punjab	04	7,250
15.	Rajasthan	26	90,769
16.	Tamil Nadu	32	132,049
17.	Telangana	12	70,892
18.	Uttar Pradesh	68	382,570.2
19.	Uttarakhand	05	19,971
20.	West Bengal	04	1950
	Total	**400**	**1,068,542.72**

separate as 153 and 159 respectively. Eventually, the number of authorised producers has increased in 2018–2019 almost 10 times compared to *Rules, 2011*. Similarly, number of registered dismantler/recycler (capacity in tonnes) has gradually increased to 400 units with capacity of 1,068,542.72 MT (metric tonne)[20] as on 24 March 2021, reported by the CPCB on its website. This capacity is almost 30% of the total e-waste generated every year in India, which shows that there are formal recycling facilities located in 20 of the 29 Indian states (CPCB 2021).

Given recycling capacity of 782,080.62 MT through authorised units in 2019–2020, Gaikwad (2019: 4) posed a question regarding economic benefits that India would achieve,

> the critical issue is to find ways of linking market information for e-waste with appropriate financial incentives for consumers, and upskilling informal sector players in handling and processing methods that are linked to readily available and mature e-waste recycling technologies.

Performance of regulatory bodies – CPCB, SPCBs, and MoEFCC

It is believed that EPR's effective performance require close monitoring and evaluation to complete the loop of e-waste management in environmentally sound manner. In this context, the regulatory bodies occupy critical importance. One of the apparent features of the regulatory body is that most of the functions are centralised.

The CAG (Comptroller and Auditor General) of 2015[21] has provided details regarding its performance based on duties of CPCB[22] mentioned in the *Rules, 2011* and the Schedule III, which are presented in the following (Table 5.6).

The regulatory body, its institutional mechanism, capacity, and effectiveness, are dealt in detail Chapter 7.

IV: Legal cases and judicial directives

This section presents legal cases where the *Rules, 2011*[23] and *Rules, 2016* are invoked by December 2019. Of total five cases, three are fought at the NGT for protection of environment, one at the High Court of Tamil Nadu for proper treatment of e-waste, separate from the MSW, and one at the High Court of Kerala against Cochin Port for taking necessary permissions from Marine Pollution Control Office, CISF and Customs under the MARPOL.[24] The first two cases were examined as violations of the *Hazardous and Other Waste (Management and Transboundary Movement) Rules, 2016* while the third was considered under the *Rules, 2016* by the NGT. The fourth case *Madurai Farooq Ahmed vs. The Tamil Nadu Pollution Control Board* was fought at the Tamil Nadu High Court in 2019 invoking the *Rules, 2016*, ordering that e-waste should be treated separately from the MSW. The fifth case *K.N. Unnikrishnan vs. Cochin Port Trust & Ors.* is regarding marine pollution but the judgement has separately mentioned about the proper disposal of e-waste in the sea or on the seacoast, preventing marine pollution; as e-waste is not linked MARPOL convention.

The first case *M.C. Mehta Vs. Union of India & Ors*[25] is keeping the environment at centre, concerned primarily with the quality of life and assigning power to the SPCB and the State Government for imposing penalty for polluting Ramganga river. The principal bench of the NGT, its Order on 3 May 2017, noted that

> huge quantity of hazardous waste generated from the e-waste processing, which is in powder form is being dumped indiscriminately on the bank of river Ram Ganga at Muradabad [Moradabad]...this hazardous waste is highly polluting and would introduce heavy metals into the river which will be injurious to human health and environment.
>
> (pp. 1–2)

And mentioned that all the local authorities responsible including UPPCB (Uttar Pradesh Pollution Control Board), Uttar Pradesh Jal Nigam, Government of Uttar Pradesh Irrigation Department in particular, and local police. Therefore, all these institutions should collectively operate to ensure protection of environment and public health. The Tribunal Ordered 'to constitute a Committee[26] which will ensure removal of such hazardous waste from the bank of river Ramganga within

TABLE 5.6 CAG reporting performance of CPCB for e-waste management (2015)

Duty of CPCB	Performance, follow up action taken
Co-ordination with SPCBs/PCCs	Even after getting reports in disparate manner by 18 bodies, CPCB did not pursue with them regularly for furnishing necessary information
Preparation of Guidelines for ESM of e-waste	CPCB brought out (June 2012) *Guidelines on implementation of E-waste (Management and Handling) Rules, 2011,* in which regulatory and safety requirements for collection centre, dismantling and recycling facilities were described
Conduct assessment of e-waste generation and processing	CPCB did not conduct any independent assessment of e-waste generation and processing in India after 2005. Thus, CPCB was unaware of the quantity of e-waste generated and collected in the country and consequently did not assess the scope and magnitude of e-waste management activities to be covered under the Rules. CPCB had scarce information on the quantity of e-waste being generated and processed in the country
Recommend standards and specifications for processing and recycling e-waste	–
Documentation, compilation of data on e-waste and uploading on websites of CPCB	CPCB could only upload the list of recyclers and dismantlers as received from SPCBs / PCCs. Only category wise details of e-waste collected; product-wise quantity of e-waste collected was not furnished by Andhra Pradesh (2012–2013), Assam, Bihar, Himachal Pradesh, Tamil Nadu, Uttar Pradesh, Punjab, Chandigarh and Delhi
Conducting training and awareness programmes	No training/awareness programmes were conducted by CPCB regarding implementation of the Rules. The Punjab Pollution Control Board had admitted that there was lack of awareness/co-ordination among various stakeholders regarding treatment of e-waste
Submit Annual Report to the Ministry	Only 15 SPCBs and three PCCs submitted annual reports for the year 2012–2013 and 2013–2014 in a combined way. Based on these reports, the CPCB submitted the annual report to the Ministry/MoEFCC in 2015. No further action was initiated based on the data submitted in the annual reports either by CPCB or MoEF. Mechanism of collection of data relating to e-waste through Annual Reports by SPCBs / PCCs as well as by CPCB was ineffective
Any other function delegated by the Ministry under these rules	–

(Continued)

TABLE 5.6 (Continued)

Duty of CPCB	Performance, follow up action taken
Enforcement of provisions regarding reduction in use of hazardous substances in manufacture of EEE	CPCB initiated (March 2014) an implementation framework on RoHS enforcement based on self-regulation[a] model. As verification of compliance to RoHS required separate infrastructure for testing of hazardous substances and laboratory infrastructure available at CPCB was not sufficient for testing of EEE samples under RoHS compliance, CPCB proposed to enter into an MoU with Centre for Materials for Electronics Technology, Hyderabad (C-MET)[b] for a period of three years. The framework including MoU with C-MET was approved by MoEF in November 2014
Set targets for compliance to the reduction in use of hazardous substance in manufacture of EEE	As of May 2015, CPCB had not entered into MoU with C-MET and was still in the process of developing infrastructure for testing of EEE to enforce RoHS regulation. Consequently, no random verification of hazardous substances could be done by CPCB. The proposed self-regulation model was also yet to be enforced
Incentives and certification for green design/products	CPCB was required to develop incentives and certification for green design/products. However, as of May 2015, no action was taken in this regard
In case of non-implementation of EPR	CPCB was required to set up a committee to examine the issue of fixing targets for the purpose of monitoring of EPR compliance based on the life and type of the product, usage and consumption patterns and other relevant factors and also taking into consideration the level of compliance achieved during the first two years… committee was not constituted as of May 2015
	MoEF replied (July 2015) that due to poor compliance by producers, it was decided to amend the Rules, due to which committee was not constituted

Source: CAG report (2015: 105–115). Compiled by the author.

[a] Self-regulation model had put primary responsibility of reduction of hazardous substances on producers and included provisions such as development of a Central Registry of Producers, mechanism for self-declaration by producers on RoHS compliance, data base on various EEEs being placed in the market by producers; only random verification on RoHS was to be done by CPCB.

[b] C-MET is an autonomous society under the Department of Electronics and Information Technology

one week from today.' The Order further mentioned that 'all the industries concerned…shall be informed that any person throwing such a waste…shall be liable to pay environmental compensation of Rs. 50,000 to Rs. 1 lakh [100,000 INR] depending on the quantum of the waste being thrown' (p. 5).

The second case *Mahendra Pandey Vs. Union of India &Ors*[27] is about disposal of e-waste and the black powder generated in the process, as informed by the CPCB's inspection in September, 2015. This activity was seen as a violation of the NGT's order in the case of *M.C. Mehta Vs. Union of India & Ors.* in 2017. On 26 June 2018, during an inspection by the CPCB and UPPCB, the level of mercury and heavy metals was found higher in water samples than permissible limits. This was seen as a serious failure of the District Administration; the Chie Secretary of Uttar Pradesh was called upon in the next hearing of the Tribunal on 10 September 2018. In the next hearing, the Chief Secretary submitted an action plan. The progress was again reviewed on 9 October 2018. In the Order of 16 October 2018, it is mentioned that the work of removal of the hazardous waste from the bank of River Ramganga has commenced from 8 October 2018 and was to be completed in 105 days, with completion of environment impact assessment by 31 December 2018. The NGT directed the CPCB 'to prepare a Standard Operating Procedure (SOP) under Rule 10 of the Hazardous Waste Management Rules, 2016 to deal with such issues which can apply pan India' (p. 3).

The third case *Shailesh Singh Vs. State of U.P. & Ors*[28] is regarding the grievance against unauthorised recycling collection/dismantling units, burning, selling of E-waste and other solid waste on the roadside/bank of rivers in violation of the *E-Waste (Management) Rules, 2016* and *Environment (Protection) Act, 1986*. The NGT directed the MoEFCC, UPPCB, and CPCB to prepare an action plan for enforcement of the Rules and taking appropriate action against those violations. A compliance report dated 14 December 2018 was filed before this Tribunal which was considered on 12.02.2019; the report consisted of the challenges in performing different tasks and responsibilities. Further, the report mentioned that the e-waste inventory would be prepared by December 2019. The matter is pending.

The fourth case (writ petition) *Madurai Farooq Ahmed vs. The Tamil Nadu Pollution Control Board*[29] was regarding contamination of water at the Shakirabad area of Tamil Nadu in 2019. The petitioner submitted that the Vaniyambadi Municipality is erecting a Solid Waste Dumping and Micro Composting Process unit, at Shakirabad, Vellore is being set up without proper clearance from the Pollution Control Board.

> The local body shall ensure that the e-waste, bio-medical waste and industrial hazardous wastes shall not be brought to this Municipal waste processing facility and shall be disposed in accordance with the e-waste Management Rules, 2016, Bio-Medical Waste Management Rules, 2016 and Hazardous and other Wastes (Management and Transboundary Movement) Rules, 2016 respectively.

The fifth case *K.N. Unnikrishnan vs. Cochin Port Trust & Ors*[30] is about marine pollution. Though e-waste is not linked to MARPOL, the judgement has specially mentioned disposal of e-waste in order to prevent marine pollution; saying that

> Cochin Port Trust has enlisted the Collection of garbage from ships to private garbage collectors who are granted yearly license to collect both dry and wet wastes. E-wastes and battery wastes and items not specified in MARPOL Annex V are not collected (enclosed Annexures I to V).

(p. 5)

Evolving jurisprudence of e-waste management

The jurisprudence of e-waste management is as such in its nascent stage; nonetheless, these cases have reflected judicial awareness and proactive directives for disposal and treatment of e-waste in the broader context of a safe environment. The NGT orders established supreme importance of healthy and wholesome environment and making district administration, local authorities, and regulatory bodies (CPCB, SPCBs, and MoEFCC) for the *Rules, 2016* responsible for the spread of pollution; directing these authorities to work in co-ordination by forming a committee and preparing a report based on field visits and inspection; asked for compliance reports; and followed up for e-waste inventory and its digital platform as a monitoring tool.

'Actually, electronic waste is a threat to deplorable quality of the environment because of its disposal is very hazardous process' (Singh and Thomas 2016: 4). The orders/judgements of the State High Courts reflect that until the *Rules, 2016*, e-waste was considered under *HWM Rules* or *SWM Rules*, not explicitly mentioned as a harmful waste with hazardous substances, and so on. The NGT orders indicate that e-waste issues are examined from the perspective of 'pollution', and thus penalty, action plan for Clean Ramganga, etc. are directed. Thus, a scope of linking e-waste with international conventions like MARPOL on marine pollution is also opened up. The Constitution of India guarantees the right to lead healthy life as a fundamental right under the Article 21; e-waste has been addressed through the *EPA, 1986* under the Article, yet to be dealt exclusively.

Jurisprudence of e-waste when looked from an angle of actionable points, that is, the executive executing the actionable points, and complying with the judicial orders / verdicts, the scenario leaves us in doldrums. Formation of committee for inspection of polluting site; giving time to prepare action plan; allowing leeway for execution of tasks, which were pending for more than four years (for example, preparing SOP, inventory, environment impact assessment report, etc.); etc. are usual way of dealing with the existing problems by the judiciary. In the case of *M.C. Mehta Vs. Union of India & Ors. (2014)*, the tribunal has mentioned about penalty. 'So far there is no data on the convictions under EPA [*Environment Protection Act, 1986*] related to electronic waste… Judiciary has not dealt with the punitive issues related to electronic waste which results in a legal vacuum' (Chaudhary 2018: 5). In the case of *Mahendra Pandey Vs. Union of India &Ors. (2017)*, the pending tasks of preparing SOP, preparing inventory, etc. were to be completed by December 2019. However, no updates are available on these tasks are available. This scenario leaves us in doldrums.

Comparison: Indian legislation with international legislature

The existing e-waste legislation in different countries mostly include restrictions on e-waste import/export following the *Basel Convention*, regulations for recycling specific categories of e-waste following the classification by the UNU for harmonising statistics, and the EPR (discussed in detail in Chapter 2). As such, there is no uniformity in e-waste legislation across all the countries; each country's e-waste legislation is drafted to address her (the country) specific problems, the legislation is mostly not holistic, leading to different management issues, for example, monitoring e-waste recycling.[31] Broadly, most countries face problems of lack of adequate public awareness, the dominance of the recycling sector by an uncontrolled, ill-equipped informal sector that pollutes the environment, lack of adequate recycling facilities, and poor financing of hazardous waste management activities (Forti et al. 2020: 71), which cannot be always managed by a single piece of legislation. However, most aspects of e-waste management are legislation driven in India; this argument is dealt in detail in the following chapter.

Bernd Kopacek (2019: 74–76) has identified similarities and differences regarding e-waste in India and Europe. Driving regulation, that is, EPR is the same for both. However, the mindset of the Indian citizen is completely different from Europe; using e-products for longer time (sometime through repairs) in India is common, and attach a value to the waste while Europeans have adopted the concept of a "throw away" and submit waste at the collection centre free of charge. In India most recycling takes place in informal way and lack state-of-art processing while in Europe, at 65% recovery is assured, along with compliance of the *WEEE Directive* – recycling and recovery targets. The difference in the *WEEE Directive* and *Rules, 2016* are highlighted in terms of *modus operandi* for collection target based on life span of an e-product in Europe and India respectively. He has foreseen two major challenges for treating e-waste – first, rapid technological advances (including 3D printing) make it necessary to keep up with the fast progress and develop constantly new recycling processes. Second, more and more chemical processes may take over because the e-products become a more and more complex mix of materials. For India, repair sector and collection services are the best practices; and India can start with smaller scale mobile treatment technologies and then step by step upgradation of their capacity.

Notes

1 Renamed MoEFCC from Ministry of Environment and Forests (MoEF) in 2014.
2 Section 3 of the *Environment (Protection) Act*, 1986, gives all-encompassing powers of setting standards, laying down procedures and supervision on the Central Government. CPCB is an autonomous body under MoEF.
3 The *Schedule 1*, with 36 industrial processes generating hazardous waste, and 123 waste streams. The *Schedule 2* with 79 types of waste substances, with concentration limit is to be used for classification/characterization of waste stream as hazardous/non-hazardous in case of dispute. Lists the concentration limits of constituents in the wastes. This E-waste or its fractions come broadly under this Schedule. *Schedule* 3 provides a separate list of hazardous wastes to be applicable only for imports and exports; it is divided hazardous waste into two parts, A and B (similar to the Basel Convention Annexes VIII and IX). Part A of the Schedule deals with two lists of waste to be applicable only for imports and exports purpose. Export and import of items listed in List A and B of Part A are permitted only as raw materials for recycling or reuse. Electrical and electronic scraps as a hazardous

waste are covered under serial number A1180 in List A, which is hazardous under the rules; and serial number B1110 in List B, which is not hazardous and is meant for direct reuse and not for recycling or final disposal.

4 A standing committee is constituted as and when required in pursuance of the provisions of an Act of Parliament or Rules of Procedure and Conduct of Business in Lok Sabha. Every Committee undertake detailed scrutiny of a Bill being piloted, allows views of the concerned stakeholders, and thus increases expertise on the topic under scrutiny for the Parliament.

5 For more details, refer LARRDIS (2011: 61–65).

6 The Bill criticised the improper way of disposal as the electronic products contain many components which are hazardous to health and environment, and therefore a regulation of electronic waste disposal is necessary. The Bill also stressed upon need for prescribing norms and fixing responsibilities and duties on manufacturers, recyclers and consumers with regard to the disposal of electronic waste and for all matters connected to it, for proper handling and disposal of millions of tonnes of electronic waste in India (LARRDIS 2011).

7 'E-waste', Lok Sabha Unstarred Question No. 5449, dated 28 April, 2010

8 'Environment' is not included in any of the list (List I, II or III) in distribution of legislative power by the Constitution of India. Any matter not included in the list shall be subject matter of Central government.

9 Subordinate legislation is the legislation made by an authority subordinate to the legislature. Such legislation is to be made within the framework of the powers so delegated by the legislature. The Supreme Court of India has specified need and importance of subordinate legislation:

> most of the modern socio-economic legislations passed by the legislature lay down the guiding principles and the legislative policy. The legislatures because of limitation imposed upon by the time factor hardly go into matters of detail. Provision is, therefore, made for delegated legislation to obtain flexibility, elasticity, expedition and opportunity for experimentation. The practice of empowering the executive to make subordinate legislation within a prescribed sphere has evolved out of practical necessity and pragmatic needs of a modern welfare State.

Available at: https://rajyasabha.nic.in/rsnew/practice_procedure/book13.asp (accessed on 3 July 2020).

10 The draft rules – 'E-waste (Management and Handling) Rules, 2011' were published in the Gazette of India, Part II, Section 3, Sub-section 3(ii), vide number S.O.1035(E) dated the 12 May 2011 inviting objections and suggestions from all persons likely to be affected thereby, before the expiry of the period of sixty days from the date on which the copies of the Gazette containing the said notification were made available to the public.

11 IT equipment (19 items) and consumer electrical and electronics equipment (5 items, excluding centralised air-conditioning plants) including their components and consumables put on the market in India.

12 RoHS to ensure that the products do not contain Lead, Mercury, Cadmium, Hexavalent chromium, Poly Brominated Biphenyls or PBDE above a specified threshold. The reductions have to be achieved by 1 May 2014, two years from the dates when the rules become effective. Certain applications and components of EEE manufactured or placed in the market six years before the date of commencement of these rules, listed in Schedule 2 (Annexure-II) are exempted from the above requirements (CPCB 2011).

13 The draft rules – 'E-waste (Management) Rules, 2015' were published by the Government of India in the Ministry of Environment, Forest and Climate Change *vide* number G.S.R. 472(E), dated the 10th June, 2015 in the Gazette of India, Extraordinary Part II, section 3, sub-section (ii) inviting objections and suggestions from all persons likely to be affected thereby, before the expiry of the period of sixty days from the date on which the copies of the Gazette containing the said notification were made available to the public.

14 The Amendment rules – 'E-waste (Management) Amendment Rules, 2017' were published by the Government of India in the Ministry of Environment, Forest and Climate Change *vide* number G.S.R. 1349(E), dated 30 October, 2017 in the Gazette of India, Extraordinary Part II, section 3, sub-section (ii) inviting objections and suggestions from all persons likely to be affected thereby, before the expiry of the period of sixty days from the date on which the copies of the Gazette containing the said notification were made available to the public.

15 A bulk consumer includes central government or state government institutions, financial institutions (Banks), educational institutions (schools, colleges, universities, etc.), hospitals and other health care facilities (having turnover of more than one crore or have more than 20 employees), multinational organisations, international agencies, hotels, partnership and public or private companies registered under the Factories Act 1948, and companies Act 2013.

16 The quantum of targets is specified as per schedule III and schedule III A of *Amendment Rules, 2018*.

17 Criteria for evaluating implementation of EPR are: authorisation for CPCB (maximum of 5 points), Take-back policy (maximum of 20 points), RoHS compliance of the product (maximum of 20 points), submitted annual returns under E-waste Rules, 2016 & amendment Rules, 2018 for the year 2017–2018 (maximum of 5 points), e-waste collection target achieved as per Rules, 2016 (maximum of 20 points), information with Customer Care or the helpline provided (A maximum of 10 points), take-back centre operational (A maximum of 20 points), tied up with an authorised recycler for environmentally sound recycling and disposal of e-waste collected through take-back programme (maximum of 15 points), sufficient information on the brand's website (maximum of 10 points), information provided in the booklet (maximum of 15 points), Collection centres/ pick up in all states/UTs (maximum of 15 points), ease of accessibility to information on public domain (maximum of 10 points), awareness campaign conducted (maximum of 15 points), any other initiative taken (maximum of 10 points).

18 The company achieving points between 150 and 200 are 'good rating;' with points between 100 and 149 are 'average rating;' with points between 50 and 99 are 'average rating;' and points between 0 and 49 are 'poor rating.'

19 The companies which are closed down but their e-products are in the market and/or likely to existing as e-waste.

20 The number of e-waste recyclers have increased substantially from 23 registered recycling facilities in 2010, to 143 dismantlers/recyclers in 12 States in 2015, 178 units and capacity of 438,086 tonnes in 2017, and 275 dismantlers/recyclers in 16 states/ union territories in 2018 with a total recycling capacity of about 0.5 million ton per annum. There were 312 authorised recycling units with capacity of 782,080.62 MT (metric tonne) as on 27 June 2019.

21 Based on information received from SPCBs/PCCs in February 2013/July 2014/March 2015

22 As per Rule 15 (1) of the *Rules, 2011*, SPCBs/PCCs were required to prepare an annual report in the format prescribed under Form 5 of the Rules, and submit the same to

CPCB by 30th September every year. As per Rule 15 (2), CPCB was to prepare the consolidated annual report on Management of e-waste and forward it to MoEF along with its recommendations before 30th December of every year.

23 The *Toxics Link vs. UoI & ors.* (case no. 183/2014) was disposed of on the ground that MoEFCC have placed *E-waste Management Rules, 2016* in the public domain on 16 March 2016, repealing the Rules, 2011. The Tribunal did not see any purpose in prosecuting the present application in light of the newly introduced *Rules, 2016*. For more information, visit https://www.casemine.com/judgement/in/5b17d55b4a93267801004e7f (accessed on 4 August 2020).

24 International Convention for the Prevention of Pollution from Ships is the main international convention covering prevention of pollution of the marine environment by ships from operational or accidental causes.

25 This case is *M.C. Mehta Vs. Union of India & Ors. And Anil Kumar Singhal Vs. Union of India & Ors. And Society for Protection of Environment & Biodiversity & Anr. Vs. Union of India & Ors. And Confederation of Delhi Industries & CETP Societies (An Organisation of CETP Societies) Vs. D.P.C.C. & Ors. And J.K. Srivastava* Vs. Central Pollution Control Board & Ors. And Swami Gyan Swarop Sanand Vs. Ministry of Home Affairs & Ors. Original Application No. 200/2014.
(M.A. No. 486 of 2017, M.A. No. 488 of 2017, M.A. No. 502 of 2017 & M.A. No. 503 of 2017) (C.W.P. No. 3727/1985) And Original Application No. 501 of 2014 (M.A. No. 404 of 2015) And Original Application No. 146 of 2015 And Appeal No. 63 of 2015 And Original Application No. 127 of 2017 And Original Application No. 133/2017 (W.P. (C) No. 200/2013).

26 This Committee to be headed by the District Magistrate, Muradabad, and a senior nominee of the Member Secretary of UPPCB, Irrigation Department, Uttar Pradesh Jal Nigam, Muradabad Municipal Corporation and Muradabad Nagar Nigam and DSP of the concerned area as members of the Committee.

27 Original Application No. 621/2018 (Earlier O.A. No. 58/2017)

28 Original Application No. 512/2018

29 Writ Petition No.21344 of 2019, dated 21/8/2019 in the High Court of judicature at Madras. Retrieved from http://www.judis.nic.in W.P.No.21344 of 2019 (accessed on 23 June 2020).

30 Writ petition WP(C).No.32389 OF 2011(S), on FRIDAY, THE 31ST DAY OF JANUARY 2020 / 11TH MAGHA, 1941. Retrieved from https://indiankanoon.org/doc/22472661/ (accessed on 23 June 2020).

31 See Patil and Ramakrishna (2020) for further details; they have listed and categorised different countries e-waste policy/legislation and their objectives. Also see Forti et al. 2020 for legislation related details organised region-wise in the *GEM 2020*.

6
STRATEGIES AND INITIATIVES FOR DEALING WITH E-WASTE IN INDIA

> The growing production of waste electric and electronic equipment (WEEE) justifies the increasing attention of both institutional and industrial organizations. The fast adoption of legislations, rules, and practices leads to a great dis-homogeneity in the technical, organizational and cost models adopted world-wide.
>
> Elia and Grazia Gnoni (2015: 271)

This chapter encompasses pan-Indian initiatives for dealing with e-waste management, ranging from building knowledge base through research and social action by different stakeholders to technological and legal advancements and industrial initiatives. All these initiatives are organised on time scale, in a manner, to capture every initiative in its context with its evolutionary journey. The chapter is divided into two sections: the first section covers the period of 2001–2012, until the *Rules, 2011* were enforced in May 2012; and the second section elaborates on law driven implementation, post-2012. The first section covers milestones and activities, such as, getting to know ground reality and creation of information and knowledge base; initiatives to reach out to masses through media reports and to the stakeholders/sector players; and dialogues and advocacy with different government agencies for separate legislation on e-waste. Thematically, information is provided on e-waste generation[1] (computers, and mobile phones) and its quantum; e-waste flow (domestic and imported[2]); trade chain and informal sector; recycling scenario (Toxics Link 2003, 2004a, 2004b; Mehra 2004); role of awareness in e-waste management; and role of CSOs and newspapers in identification of policy/legal points by non-government actors; EPR and take-back campaign; and fostering formal-informal sector partnership. The second section elaborates on law driven implementation, which includes initiatives by the GoI (awareness campaigns; strategy papers on resource efficiency, linking e-waste management with three missions – Digital India, Clean India, and made in India, etc.); expansion of discourse on e-waste management

DOI: 10.4324/9780429285424-6

through economic aspects of EPR (tax structure, business opportunities created, producers' budget allocation for PROs' functioning, financing for e-waste management, etc.); industry development through start-ups (PROs, recycling units); and starting of academic courses on e-waste management.

An attempt is made to link global and local – how and what/which global thinking and doing have reached India and which Indian actors have acted upon, including the government. The discussions and discourse on regulatory framework for e-waste management in the Chapter 5 are the contexts for this chapter. While narrating initiatives or actions, names of the specific actors (research organisations, bi-lateral agencies, industrial actors, stakeholders under the *Rules, 2016*, etc.) are consciously not spelt out because of two reasons. The first reason is to avoid cherry picking (naming a few may become a promotion of the named ones, and implied neglecting the others) in the given competitive scenario in the industry/e-waste sector; and the second is to document pan-Indian initiatives comprehensively – making thoughts, perceptions, discussions and debates, transitions/shifts, etc. more important as an academic objectivity and pursuits. Thus, the chapter leaves an open space and yet recognises those actors and initiatives that are not named or covered may have taken place in India.

I: Overview of pan-India initiatives for dealing with e-waste during 2000 and 2012

The years 2000 and 2012 are believed to be founding years for building up the discourse and actions for e-waste management in India; a game changer in the larger context of growth of electronics industry as one of the promising engines for economic development in India. These years were beginning of enforcement of two international regulations – the *Basel Convention* across the world, and the *WEEE Directive* in EU countries; regulating transboundary movements of e-waste, and specific guideline for e-waste management and introduction of EPR respectively. India had amended *Hazardous Waste Management Rules* in 2003 in light of the *Basel Convention*, and later in 2008; and introduced *E-waste Management and Handling Rules, 2011* towards end of 2010.

The global thinking on e-waste management had begun in late 1990s on the following issues: growing quantity of e-waste; landfills as well as leaching of toxins to soil and water, and its hazardous impact on environment and human health; safe disposal/treatment of e-waste as a necessity because of its toxic composition; developed countries shipping e-waste to developing countries, sale of 'grey goods'; and EPR and waste management.

India is an example of economic growth and environmental protection indicators are at odds with one another. Indian electronic industry, especially IT industry witnessed huge growth, that is, from 1998 to 2002, there was a 53.1% increase in the sales of domestic household appliances, both large and small; and the growth in PC ownership per capita in India between 1993 and 2000 was 604% compared to a world average of 181%. As a result, the total PC base during this period has grown from an estimated 450,000 PCs–4,200,000 PCs. On the other hand, India ranks an abysmal 101st on the 2005 Environmental Sustainability Index, and for Environmental Governance gets only the 66th rank, with a score of −0.10 (the highest being Iceland with 1.65, and the lowest Iraq with −1.52) (quoted in Sinha-Ketriwal et al. 2005: 498). 'MAIT (2007) provided figures, total PC sales, between October and December 2006 were 1.39 million units, registering a growth of 28% over the same period a year before.' (Quoted in Arora et al. 2019b: 69–70.)

As part of domestic e-waste, large quantity of e-waste is generated by consumers and manufacturers. The e-waste from manufacturers is generated in the form of defective printed wiring boards, IC chips, and other components, which are discarded in the production process. All types of e-waste are being recycled in the country. The unorganised recycling units as part have been developed organically as a natural branching of the established scrap industry, which has been market-driven and driven by economic necessity associated with poverty. For these units, main incentive is financial profit, not environmental or social awareness (Sinha-Ketriwal et al. 2005). Materials recovery interest small scale recyclers, and entire communities, including children, earn their livelihoods by foraging metals, glass, and plastics from the e-waste.

Getting to know ground reality, knowledge base created

The first report on e-waste scenario in Asia (including India) was published by the BAN and SVTC (Silicon Valley Toxics Coalition) in 2002 with the contributions of three country representatives[3] (Puckett et al. 2002). This report revealed how the USA and other rich economies that use most of the world's e-products, generate most of the e-waste, and exporting the e-waste crisis to the developing countries of Asia. It stressed on unjust, inappropriate export of pollution to a particular region (China, India, and Pakistan) simply because it is poorer. After showing e-waste impacts – environmental[4] and occupational, and legal implications of e-waste export, it drew attention to – how from a legal standpoint, the issue has become murky and is dependent on how seriously a government intends to deal with the hazards (ibid.: 27). As part of recommendations, this report stressed upon making implementation of the *Basel Convention*; making producer responsible; activating product take-back system; encouraging design for longevity, upgradability, repair and reuse, and for recycling. Thus, most actors of e-waste sector were made aware of Indian ground reality in the global scenario – e-waste export by rich countries, its hazardous impacts, limitations of Indian laws to deal with e-waste dumping vis-à-vis the *Basel Convention* as well as the *WEEE Directive* in European countries and its implementation.

The 'Indo-German-Swiss E-waste Initiative'[5] was started in 2003–2004 for knowledge partnership through an understanding between MoEF and EMPA,[6] working on a mandate for SECO (Swiss State Secretariat for Economic Affairs) and GTZ,[7] Germany (renamed as GIZ in 2011). This was commissioned under BMZ and ASEM (Advisory Services in Environmental Management) Programme. This programme was instrumental in supporting the WEEE strategy group, which was establishing national WEEE baselines, and assisting in implementing WEEE pilot projects. A national workshop on 'Electronic Waste Management' was organised jointly by CPCB, MoEF,[8] EMPA, Switzerland, and GTZ in New Delhi during March, 2004. This workshop emphasised urgency of inventorisation and micro-level intervention to tackle the potential problem of e-waste in India. Two-pronged strategy was adopted: first, at the macro level, national level desk study was proposed; second, a national level working group was formed (Arora et al. 2019b). The working group included multiple stakeholders, such as regulatory authorities,[9] industry associations,[10] NGOs,[11] recyclers (formal and informal), research institutions, and experts in the field like EU and UNEP. This consortium was to take initiatives to improve recycling practices, providing fiscal incentives, and evolving standards for recycling, formulating legislative tools, providing cleaner production options to manufacturers using fewer toxic components, and take steps to check illegal imports of e-waste in the country. The CPCB commissioned by the proposed desk study to IRGSSA,[12] its report was published in 2005.[13]

The multiple stakeholder group undertook various initiatives, such as, awareness raising among consumers, corporate houses, government agencies, manufacturers, and informal recyclers; capacity-building of government agencies, producers of EEE, formal and informal recyclers; occupational health safety measures for informal recyclers; improving recycling recoveries; and policy advice. Training was carried out by GTZ based on a tool – PREMA (Profitable Environment Management) for informal recyclers of Delhi and Bangalore cities. One of the lessons learned by this training was that 'not much can be achieved by aiming to improve the methods of metal extraction, as the processes cannot be improved unless they are carried out in an environmentally safe, risk-free, and economically efficient manner.' (Arora et al. 2019b: 77.)

IRGSSA was to carry out a study covering the following: rapid assessment for quantification, characterisation, future projections for e-waste, documenting e-waste management in different cities, and plans for new management systems. This report estimated e-waste generation (computers) based on 'the average penetration levels of PC in a population of 1,000…According to this estimation, total e-waste generated in India was 146,180 tonnes' (quoted in Sinha 2019a: 28–29). Maharashtra was at the top among 35 State and Union Territories with 20,270.6 tonnes followed by Tamil Nadu with 13,486.2 tonnes, and Andhra Pradesh with 12,780.3 tonnes. Among them,

> some of the important sectors like railways, defence, and health generate very large volumes of e-waste…individual households are perhaps the lowest contributors to e-waste for PCs…[but] large-scale generation from consumer durables, such as TVs, refrigerators, air conditioners, and washing machines.
>
> (ibid.: 31)

This shows that the e-waste generation was linked to production and consumption pattern; production was linked to lifespan of an e-product and introduction of newer technology in short span of time.

Domestic generation of e-waste

Most of the studies on estimation of e-waste are based on the market supply method, while some studies use end-of-life models (Subramanian 2014: 27). A few reports on inventory of e-waste are based on models of obsolescence and not based on actual physical inventories; this trend was observed until 2008. The statistics of production, exports, and sales of each product and their average life have been considered in these studies. For example, average life of a PC was assumed to be 5 and 7 years and of a television (TV) to be 15 and 17 years. It was also assumed that 100% of electronic units sold in one particular year would become obsolete at the end of the average life. These perceptions of life of e-waste were based on urban conditions; the conditions are far from it considering the rural scenario (Chatterjee and Kumar 2009: 895).

A report was jointly prepared by GTZ and BIRD in 2007, which is one of the firsts WEEE Assessment Study to develop a sound methodology for estimation the volume of WEEE produced in India (limited to computers, television, and mobile phones). This study aimed at developing methodology for calculating WEEE in India, including – (i) projections of e-waste over next five years, (ii) disposal behaviour and recycling practices, (iii) identify stakeholders in e-waste trade value chain, (iv) assess capacities of existing recyclers, and (v) recommend a national action plan for major stakeholders to ensure proper handling and disposal of e-waste (Khattar et al. 2007: 9). The methodology adopted for e-waste assessment and quantification study was 'Funnel Approach' for accuracy and better understanding of the e-Waste production in India; WEEE was estimated at three levels: (i) potential annual e-waste;[14] (ii) e-waste available for recycling;[15] and (iii) e-waste recycled.[16] Based on this method,

> ...the total annual e-waste generated in India in the year 2007 is 3,82,979 MT,[17] including 50,000 MT of imports in India...the amount available for recycling was 1,44,143 MT but due to the presence of considerable refurbishment market only 19,000 MT of e-waste has been recycled in the year 2007.'
> (Khattar et al. 2007: 9)

Another survey was carried out in Mumbai and Pune cities by an expert group appointed by Maharashtra Pollution Control Board (MPCB) in 2006–2007. The report (2007: 28) has described conceptual methodology for mapping of e-waste in Mumbai and Pune cities in a layered manner. The four layers are: identifying e-waste streams as layer 1; value added [chain] as layer 2; labour input as layer 3; and hazards as layer 4. It stresses on primary survey method for estimation of WEEE quantity – material flow, input quantities/import, reuse, disposal, recycling technology, and hazardous processes – these are the stages of estimation; this is similar to UNEP Manual (2007). Based on survey, MPCB informed that total e-waste generation in Maharashtra was 20,270.6 tonnes, out of which Navi Mumbai contributed 646.48 tonnes, Greater Mumbai 11,017.06 tonnes, Pune 2,584.21 tonnes and Pimpri-Chinchwad 1,032.37 tonnes (MPCB 2007).

Until almost 2010, e-waste related estimates included computers, cell phones, and TVs. Different projections were made about generation of e-waste during 2005–2009. For example, ELCINA (2007) estimated 4.84 lakh tonnes (0.48 Mt) e-waste by 2009; CPCB (2008) estimated 8.0 lakh tonnes (0.80 Mt) by 2012 (quoted in LARRDIS 2011: 5); while Dwivedy and Mittal (2012) projected e-waste around 2.49 million MT during 2007–2011 based on a study conducted in 2010. Thus, recognising a range of e-products for preparing a list of e-waste became a point of policy/regulatory framework in India, which was reflected in the *Rules, 2011*. The need for preparing inventory of e-waste in the country has been an agenda for almost 15 years.

The UNEP (2007: 12) data mentioned that 'total e-waste generated in the EU is about 14–15 kg per capita or 5 MT to 7 MT per annum while in countries like India and China, annual generation per capita is less than one kg.'

After the *Rules, 2011* were notified and enforced in 2012, *GEM 2014* reported that India generated 1.7 Mt every year. This shows that increase of almost 1.4 Mt in seven years, that is, 0.37 Mt e-waste in 2007, jumped to 1.7 Mt in 2017; about one kg/inh to 1.3 kg/inh (1,641 kt). In *GEM 2017*, India was ranked fifth with 2.0 Mt (about 2.0 kg/inh) e-waste generated annually (Baldé et al. 2017).

Details about imported e-waste

Along with e-waste generation in India, imported e-waste was also talked about; figures were available in 'truckloads', estimating in tonnes until 2009. For example, 'Old Seelampur[18] acquires about 15–20 truckloads of e-waste, amounting to 1.5–1.8 tonnes of e-waste every day' (Basu 2019: 57), thus, 45–50 tonnes a month.

> About 300 days of the year, two truckloads of scrap PCs arrive daily in Delhi…about 133,000 units and 3,600 tonnes arriving per year (PC weighs about 27 kg). For an assumed obsolescence time of 7 years, the quantity of locally produced PC scrap is almost doubled by imports (+ 89%).
>
> (Quoted in Babu 2007: 316)

One of the official figures of imported e-waste is available through a newspaper report, which mentioned, 'the environment and forest ministry has approved the import of 8,000 tonnes of e-waste by Attero Recycling, a company that has set up an integrated recycling plant for safe extraction of metals near Roorkee.' (Mudur, 22 September 2009.)

Sinha (2019a: 32) mentioned that, 'estimates suggest that import of e-waste accounts for an amount almost equal to that being generated in the country.' He further provided details, 'the waste follows a very circuitous route, originating from developed or OECD countries or through many intermediaries before landing up at one of the India ports.' (ibid.: 33). The reason for importing e-waste at India, China, and Pakistan was, 'the cost of recycling a single computer in the United States is $20, while the same could be recycled in India for $2, a gross saving of $18 if the computer is exported to India' (ibid.: 33). This reason also became a point of advocacy, arguing that

> even though the import of e-waste is legally banned in India, there are many reports of such landing at Indian ports…these goods are brought in under different nomenclature, like mixed metal scrap, or as goods meant for charity, by exploiting and finding loopholes in the current regulation.
>
> (ibid.: 33)

(ILO 2014:17) provided more details about imported items and why illegal e-waste is difficult to track. Importers bring in huge quantities of e-waste including used and obsolete monitors, printers, keyboards, central processing units (CPUs), typewriters, projectors, mobile phones, polyvinyl chloride (PVC) wires, etc. These items exist in all ranges, models and sizes, and are functional as well as unsellable and non-reusable materials.

> Often, illegal shipments of e-waste are labelled as donations or imports of second-hand EEE, to cross borders as a legal trade transaction. These illegal transactions are difficult to track as they are both hidden and controlled by criminal groups that profit from informal e-waste recycling practices.
>
> (ibid.)

Reasons for huge amount of imported e-waste were identified after studying Customs Act, 1962[19] and confusing related to this Act; also, loopholes in the *Basel Convention* were referred to. Simultaneously, information and knowledge base include existence and functioning of informal sector, which had dominant presence for collection, crude methods applied for recycling of e-waste, and selling of recovered materials in the existing market (Toxics Link 2003; Inagaki 2008). Second-hand computer could be received as donation for some charitable institutions, anomaly of the EXIM (export-import) code for both old and new computers are the ways to importing e-waste (Sinha 2019b). To bring about clarity and required changes in the *Customs Act* became a point of awareness raising as well as a policy issue – amendments in the existing Act in consonance with the *Basel Convention*.

The Southern Asia statistics on exports showed that 'an average of 0.9 kt/year for the period of 2008 to 2013, with a total value of EUR 2.8 million. The exports show a rapid increase trend from 2008 to 2012, but a rapid decrease after 2012' (Baldé et al. 2016: 23). This led to believe that flow of imported e-waste is reduced; however, not stopped, and no further statistics are available for India.

Recycling scenario

Regarding e-waste recycling, several authors noted that it was gaining currency as a lucrative business from early 2000s, as larger quantities of electronics are coming into the waste stream and e-waste as an abundant source of metals. Also, that recycling is known to be a complex task, especially in terms of special logistics requirement of its collection, cost, release of toxins, and its environmental impact (Toxics Link 2004; Arora 2019b; Basu 2019; Jain 2019; Sinha 2019b). In India, 'environmental concerns among manufacturers as well as the awareness of consumers regarding environmental issues are not very high. While the government has passed several environmental protection laws, their enforcement remains questionable' (Sinha-Khetriwal et al. 2005: 498). Parallel to these processes, a couple of recycling units were established and recognised by the SPCBs across India, who showcased recovery of precious metals through formal way of functioning, that is, by installing proper infrastructure, technology, and scientific methods by 2005 (www.attero.in; www.ewasteindia.com).

'The informal recycling sector has a vast network of collection, storage, segregation, and material recovery facilities' (Sinha 2019a: 34); a large number of women, children, and migrant unskilled labourers are engaged in different stages of recycling. Inagaki (2008: 21) mentioned,

> Only 5% of the total e-waste recycled in India is handled by four formal recycling companies who have recently emerged in the recycling market; and apart from large corporate, some of formal recyclers are now under the negotiation with informal recyclers in specific stages of the chain on benefit sharing from PC components collected by them. The same formal recycler repeated that this scheme would create the win–win effect on both of the informal and formal sides.

Attero, a recycling enterprise, officially informed in the same newspaper report that, 'We have a capacity of processing 36,000 tonnes of e-waste each year,' (Mudur, 22 September 2009), which indicated capacity of formal recycling in India, that is, of 400,000 tonnes of domestic waste generated in India. However, the CPCB reported in 2011 that 'there are 23 registered e-waste recycling units in operation having recycling capacity of about 90,000 MT per annum,' (quoted in LARRDIS 2011: 99). By 2013, there were 'over 2,000 informal recyclers in India, and Gujarat ranks among the top states for this practice,' (Shah 2014: 9). He further noted about Ahmedabad based authorised recycler 'receives a total of 6–7 tons/month, far below its e-waste facility's capacity of 500 tonnes/month. Thus, it operates at a meagre 1.5% of its capacity, far below AMC estimates of recyclers operating at 30% capacity' (ibid.: 26).

Jain (2010: 6) has provided an overview of scrap industry, not specific to e-waste and resource recovery, as follows:

> At sector level, the recycling industry is organized into paper, plastic, ferrous, and non-ferrous sectors. In the non-ferrous sector, the majority of recycling industry is involved in zinc, copper, and lead production. Recycling industry meets 40 to 50% of the total demand of the metals, plastic, and paper in the country.

Trade chain and informal sector

In India,

> the informal sector has a historic role in waste management and recycling, partly because of the notion of waste being a fringe commodity, rather than being a waste. As a result, historically the fringe commodity was left to be handled by the fringes of society – the informal sector.
>
> (Chaturvedi et al. 2010: 2)

As waste management is primarily a responsibility of local governments, every government agency needs to manage huge quantities of waste generated in large cities. As traditionally, the existing informal sector has been contributing to reduce the burden of formal waste management agencies with their manual skills, widespread and active network, recycling of waste, especially e-waste makes a profitable business venture. Khattar et al. (2007) mentioned that 94% of manufacturers were not aware of IT disposal policy and were disposing e-waste to the informal sector.

As part of understanding the network for e-waste management, functioning of the informal sector, particularly material flow, trade value chain, recycling methods and recovered materials were studied, and alongside, hazardous emissions, residues/metal precipitates and landfills, leaching of toxins into soil and water, etc. during recycling techniques related concerns were highlighted.

> The existing recycling methods used are helpful only in the recovery of merely a few metals and non-metals, namely Cu, Au, Ag, Al, Fe, Pb and plastics. The present technology is of no use for the recovery of other elements, e.g. Pt, Pd and Ni, or glass.
>
> (Dimitrakakis et al. 2006: 3)

'Primary survey by the Greenpeace found high concentrations of Sb, Cu, Pb, Ni, Sn and Zn,' (Brigden et al. 2005: 7). Some data was generated on toxicity and its impact through a primary field study (Brigden et al. 2005; Dimitrakakis et al. 2006; Manda 2008; Wath et al. 2011). The recycling techniques of the informal sector has mainly been studied from Delhi[20] and surrounding areas, and a few from Chennai and Bangalore; most media reports were Delhi centric (Manda 2008).

Most observers of informal sector agree upon that this sector survives in the country because it externalises different costs including recycling infrastructure, recycling materials, labour cost, and logistics related costs (Sinha-Khetriwal et al. 2005; Raghupathy et al. 2010; Skinner et al. 2010; Sinha 2019b).

> The cost of labour, the structure of the economy including the important informal sector, the existing regulatory framework and the possibilities and limits of law enforcement have to be taken into account in order to find

solutions that can improve the situation with regard to environmental impacts, occupational hazards and economic revenue.

(Sinha-Khetriwal et al. 2005: 503)

Some observers also confirmed that the informal sector focuses on cherry picking of the precious components for metal recovery and the non-recoverable are disposed off in landfills (Chaturvedi et al. 2010; Khetriwal-Sinha 2019).

The study conducted in Bangalore on precious metal recovery by the informal sector states that the efficiency of the processes adopted by the sector is around 28–30% whereas the gold extraction efficiency is around 99.99% by the smelting companies in developed countries.

(Chaturvedi et al. 2010: 2)

Inagaki (2008: 23) had studied PC-waste in Delhi and described five stages of trade value chain as follow, which is applicable to all types of e-waste even after a decade:

In the first stage, big traders purchase bulk PC-waste through domestic auctions and from importers, and then re-sell the PC-waste to small traders. In the second stage, small traders purchase PC-waste from big traders, store the waste, segregate it into working and non-working PCs and parts. The working PCs are sold to the secondary market and the non-working PCs are sold to dismantlers. In the third stage, dismantlers purchase non-working PCs from small traders through tender or from middlemen or household waste scrap collectors and dismantle them...sell dismantled components to extractors. In the fourth stage, extractors purchase scrap components constituting specific raw materials and extract these materials but not in a pure form. In the final stage, smelters recover specific raw materials.

Inagaki (2008: 25–31) has studied spatial organisation of the chain, social structure.[21] how upper part of trade chain – traders have huge economic gain because they are equipped with large financial and spatial assets, and bottom part of the chain – dismantlers and extractors, who seem to gain profit at the expense of payment of safe equipment to workers and utility. Due to the difference in financial and social status between trading and recycling parts, a structure of dependency of recyclers on traders have been established. Economic benefits and environmental health costs are structured differently between the trading and recycling parts; environmental health costs are mainly burdened on workers and local residents in and around the recycling units, affected through exposure to toxic materials emitted during the recycling process.

As against structural analysis of the informal sector's functioning, Sinha (2019: 34–35) opined that

the e-waste trade chain, though informal in nature, is a very well-oiled machine – well-networked adapting itself to an excellent hierarchy of control and distribution...excellent outreach points, its ability to access materials from the most remote points and then getting back to mainstream trade is highly efficient...the sector has deeper understanding of materials involved and financial benefits associated with it.

He further argued bringing the state in the picture,

> the real cause of concern is not the informal trade chain, but the process involved in segregation and metal recovery from the waste...the state has not made any effort either educate people involved or bring in that kind of awareness among them so that practices are improved.
>
> (ibid.)

This argument is supported by different actors, focusing on dignity of workers, improving their quality of life, recycling facility, low rate to recovery of materials, and need for transparency about sourcing of raw materials an operation of this sector (Babu 2007; Manda 2008; Subramanian 2014; Sinha 2019b).

Sinha (2019a) presented trade chain from the below,[22] from collection to recycle, unlike Inagaki (2008).

> The first players in this sequence of collection are the individual waste dealers or kabadiwallahs...then linked to large waste dealers or traders...these large traders also acquire waste from the large offices...through auctions... from the scrap dealer, the waste moves to he dismantler...each component is dismantled and cannibalises the useable components like ICs, capacitors...dismantlers are finally linked to the recyclers...who are engaged in final recovery of materials. The metals extracted are usually sold to smelters that purify the metals and sell them in the market for reuse.
>
> (Sinha 2019a: 36–38)

The recycling trade provides livelihoods to a significant number of urban poor; recovery of materials from this waste and ploughing them back into the supply chain process are some of the advantages of the sector. The flipside of the recycling sector is the hazardous practices and processes (Basu 2019; Sinha 2019a). As per a study conducted by the Centre for Science and Environment, it mentioned that as informed by the district administration, around 100,000–150,000 persons are engaged in informal e-waste recycling in Moradabad (Uttar Pradesh) alone. Workers are paid around INR 200 per day for working in the e-waste recycling sector with women and children earning far less (CSE 2015). 'The situation is likely to worsen if there is an exclusive environmental focus while implementing the e-waste rules with scant attention paid to livelihoods of the informal sector,' (Chaturvedi and Gaurav 2016: 5). Three goals are considered, 'closing' the recycling loop, optimising the value added, and sustainability of recycling (Wath et al. 2011; ILO 2014).

EPR and take-back campaign

Nokia organised take-back campaign for mobile phones in 2009 and continued till 2012, in different phases. The details of this campaign are presented in detail in Chapter 2. In the context of EPR, based on Nokia experience about take-back system, Singhal (2010) said that EPR is effective when there is a shift from 'Brand Environmental Responsibility,' (BER) to 'ecosystem approach' takes place; adopted by every producer. Implementation of EPR based regulations, material flow chain for each e-waste item, and channelisation of material at the levels of country state, and city; internal/external leakage prevention; local and cheap solutions for E-waste dismantling/recycling; and integration of informal sector to formal sector; etc. are the challenges and the regulatory framework should effectively address these challenges (Jain 2010; Sinha 2019b).

Formal-informal partnerships fostered

Informal sector's employment presents a challenge in extending the reach of the state to sections of the population that are often very large. The challenges are of social and economic types that call upon much more than labour or social policy, which include macroeconomic policies, fiscal policies, generally the structural composition of value added and wealth creation, and job creation. Among them, macroeconomic policies are the key drivers, structural and sector policies provide right incentives including improving governance and fighting corruption, and social protection and risk management policies recognise voice and role of non-state actor (Jutting and de Laigesia 2009). In this context, Indian informal sector managing e-waste has remained unnoticed in macroeconomics, and structural and sectoral policies; the protection and risk management (pollution, informal economy, etc.) related concerns have been raised by non-state actors. Job creation, resource recovery and secondary material management aspects of macroeconomics in relation to e-waste recycling have not been duly addressed in India.

ILO (2014) has introduced 'decent work deficit' with reference to e-waste sector. Due to bulk of e-waste recycling being carried out in the informal economy, which is labour-intensive activities. Workers get 'low earnings, long working hours and exposure to hazardous substances, leading to a serious of decent work deficits. The potential mismanagement of e-waste by informal workers can have damaging consequences on entire communities, including children.' (Ibid.: 18.)

As more formal recyclers entered in the sector for recycling of e-waste after 2005, the discourse on role of informal sector is fashioned around environment (harmful to environment); and social, and economic (poverty centric/economic disadvantages) challenges. This discourse discusses the following points: first, can formal-informal co-exist, especially when the focus of environment is shifting to economy (CE); second, what would be the impact on environment of partnership between formal and informal; and third, whether the existing legal actions/ regulatory provisions would lead towards formal economy in India.

As part of fostering formal-informal partnership, organising workshops and training programmes for exchange of information, along with a 'study tour' to appropriate industrial sites in Europe as part of Indo-European training workshop on efficient e-waste management, and detailing of e-waste flow and quantum, strengthening knowledge base, and creating consensus on policy issues. An awareness campaign was also launched, which led to knowledge and technology transfer between the major European and Indian stakeholders and contributed to the training of the project target groups in optimum management practices and technologies (Dimitrakakis et al. 2006). These workshops provided space for dialogue between various non-government actors, such as, CSOs, bi-lateral agencies, industrial associations, and recyclers (Dimitrakakis et al. 2006; Manda 2008).

A group of observers said that there is a need for the formal-informal partnership, referring to the *National Environmental Policy, 2006* (NEP) stressed upon a point that there is a need to identify the activities and contributions of the informal sector and provide them with a legal status. They believed that both, formal and informal together can gain from trading material, social welfare can also be enhanced, reduction in pollution, better resource management, and creation of 'green' jobs can take place with formal-informal partnership. Social opportunities include raising awareness of communities, engagement of citizens and the mainstreaming of the informal sector; economic benefits including job creation, tax revenues for the government, and recycling and resource recovery; and improvement in environment. (Chaturvedi et al. 2010; Raghupathy et al. 2010). Accordingly, the roles and responsibilities of the informal and formal sector in the recycling chain should be clearly specified ensuring socially acceptable, economically feasible, and environmentally responsible workable models – overcoming the problems related the environmental, health and safety hazards (Chaturvedi and Gaurav 2016).

A roadmap was prepared by Chaturvedi et al. (2010: 4–5) saying that the path to formalisation of the informal sector units would require a number of stages. First, to identify the major clusters of activity within the informal sector. Second, to federate the disparate members within the cluster and also identify the various processes within these groups. Third, efforts to create awareness and build capacities among the groups of informal sector workers on environmentally sound processes, and economics of recycling using efficient technologies for processing e-waste. Fourth, hands-on trainings on skills upgradation, process efficiency, and dos and don'ts, etc. as step towards formalisation process. Fifth, specific allocation of funds for integration of the activities of the informal and formal sectors, and environmental surveillance by the formalised informal sector units. Further, the cost structure of the informal sector would change radically with the introduction of certain processes which were not a part of their value chain. Sixte, this would require the support of the government in terms of provision of financial aid, easing access to credit and provision of financial incentives such as subsidies and introduction of insurance schemes. The formal recyclers could also support this integration process by building the capacity of informal sector associations as well as jointly developing the norms for trade of material between the two sectors.

146 Strategies and initiatives for dealing

Skinner et al. (2010) specified the role of legislation, in the context of reducing the environmental hazards of e-waste recycling in India, which needs to address the ability of informal recyclers to outbid formal and state-of-the-art recyclers (Figure 6.1).

Legislation must either prevent informal recyclers from accessing e-waste in the same markets as formal recyclers or prevent them from externalizing their

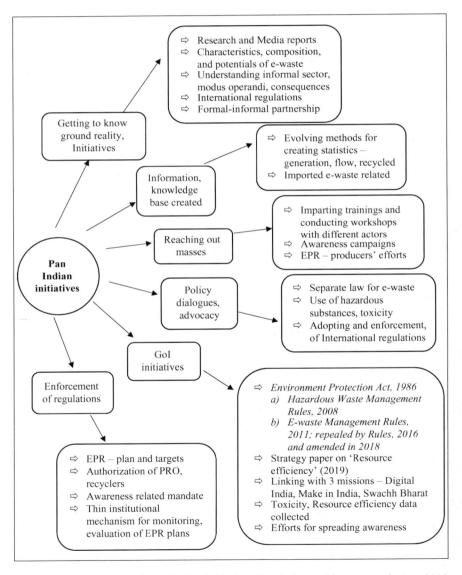

FIGURE 6.1 Overview of pan-Indian initiatives for dealing with e-waste during 2000 and 2020

costs. Ideally, this would be done in such a way that the informal sector would be integrated into the formal one.

(Skinner et al. 2010: 11)

Policy dialogue and advocacy for legislation on e-waste

The consortium formed after the workshop in 2004 continued working on identifying various aspects of e-waste management. A workshop was jointly organised by GTZ, Toxics Link, MAIT (Manufacturers Association of Information Technology) and EMPA in 2009, in which 'many stakeholders have argued that the absence of legislation is one of the biggest stumbling blocks in implementing an e-waste management system,' (quoted in Skinner et al. 2010: 19). Dimitrakakis et al. (2006: 8) mentioned that there is no policy or regulations for handling and disposal of e-waste in the country out of the existing 14 laws for governing the environment[23]. Though the GoI has signed the *Basel Convention* on the control of transboundary movement of hazardous wastes and their disposal from developed countries, India needs to ensure that wastes do not flow from the countries that are not members of the agreement convention.

Wath et al. (2011: 260) had prepared an overarching map of different types of challenges including scientific (eco-friendly recovery solutions for base and precious metals, value addition to recyclables for reuse, such as, plastics, glass and others, and disposal of process waste and residues – reduction in toxins and its extent); engineering (scientific collection, transport, handling, segregation, and disposal of e-waste, integrated/distributed processing facilities – informal to formal, and engagement of NGOs and small and medium enterprises (SMEs), feasible techno-economic solutions – processing, recycling, and recovery); and institutional challenges (appropriate definition for e-waste in Indian context, inventorisation of e-waste generation, import, and its characterisation, organisation and structuring e-waste management system, and training and awareness on safety, health, and environment). This map has been enhanced with many other social actors' studies (comparing India with other countries – EU countries, USA, etc.), experiences and suggestions on management of e-waste; legal framework and compliance; and formal-informal partnership, which are actually cross-cutting concerns (Figure 6.2).

There was only one study conducted by ELCINA on consumer's behaviour for e-waste (Jain 2010). The key findings of this study include: at household level, 65% of the individuals while at corporate/ business level, 60% of the companies/ offices look for best monetary or exchange value for their old e-products; of them, 2% of individuals and 6% of the organisations think of the impact on environment while disposing off their old EEE respectively. Of total respondents, 48% replaced computers under 'exchange and buy back scheme,' 21% through second-hand market, and 11% enter e-waste stream through scrap dealers.

Most social actors expressed concern about imported e-waste and need for complying with international legislations (Puckett et al. 2002; Jain 2010); and amendments in the existing *Customs Act* in consonance with the *Basel Convention* (Toxics

148 Strategies and initiatives for dealing

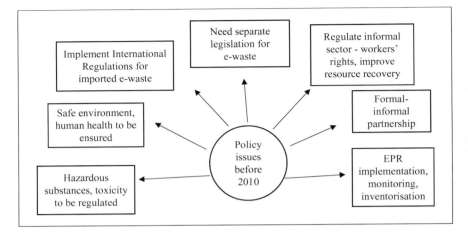

FIGURE 6.2 Policy issues for e-waste management before 2010

Link 2003; 2004). Initial workshops, meeting, and studies on e-waste generation and flow stressed upon two policy issues – production and consumption pattern and need for inventorisation; and product design improvement for increased life-span of an e-product, reduction in RoHS, and introduction of newer technology (Toxics Link 2004; Khattar et al. 2007).

ILO (2014: 19) has articulated policy issues with respect to informal sector, suggesting that the regulation and formalisation of the sector will be required to tackle negative employment indicators and improve working conditions. As profits in this sector are high and growing, and many view e-waste as an opportunity for business ventures and income generation. The contrasts within the sector vis-à-vis income needs to be recognised. Informal collectors, who are at the bottom of the value chain, live on survival incomes while the incomes of traders, scrap dealers, and dismantlers can vary greatly depending on how low or high they are in the value chain.

The recycling scenario in the country was studied by several actors, and they stressed upon the following policy issues: poor working conditions in informal units dealing with e-waste, employment of child labour and casual labour, rudimentary methods applied for recycling of e-waste, landfills, and leaching of toxins, formal-informal partnership for creating win-win situation, etc. resource efficiency, resource recovery, reuse/dealing with secondary materials – improved technology, scientific methods, and infrastructure; legal framework to ensure safe environment and protection from health hazards; designing system and its institutionalisation related to collection, transport, economic instrument, roles, and responsibilities of every stakeholder, monitoring); and creating data on level of toxicity, level of emission and pollutants, and their impact on workers as well as on environment and human health from different parts of India (Toxics Link 2004; Khetriwal-Sinha 2005; Jain 2010; Skinner 2010; Arora 2019b; Basu 2019; Jain 2019; Sinha 2019b).

Multi-pronged strategy, specific fund allocation, and necessary action with reference to the *NEP, 2006* for fostering formal-informal partnership. WEEE management related activities and outcomes cover a wide range of sectors, thus affecting the whole chain of industry, trade, academia, community, and environment. Therefore, with regard to environmental protection and the quality of life of the people involved in the recycling chain need special attention; knowledge and technical expertise transfer, sensitisation, and dissemination, etc. need to be addressed by the legislation (Dimitrakakis et al. 2006; Chaturvedi et al. 2010; Skinner 2010).

Refurbishment has specifically not mentioned by the existing studies, rather it has been considered as part of reuse/recycling. In response to the 'Draft E-waste Management Rules' in 2010 (Skinner et al. 2010: 22) mentioned 'Given the role of the refurbishment market in India, it may take considerable time for the benefits of this provision to become evident in recycling facilities.'

All these policy issues have been articulated from a sectoral perspective as well as e-waste as hazardous waste (keeping safe environment and human health as a context), with a greater emphasis on enacting a legislation. They envisaged the State at the centre-stage along with assigning responsibilities to producers; the State to take up responsibilities of creating inventorisation, streamlining recycling activities through monitoring and follow up necessary action by the regulatory bodies while producers to take responsibilities for activating and managing entire value chain – from e-waste collection to recycling; and dealing with informal sector in such a way that its skills, value, and trade chain, etc. create win-win situation for different actors in the sector. In between this space three issues have been put forth: fostering formal-informal partnership; need for studying EPR models and modify according to Indian scenario; and awareness leading to behavioural changes (disposing e-waste responsibly and accepting 3Rs).

What was not thought about in the policy dialogue and advocacy before 2010

In this scheme of 'role of awareness,' aspects, such as, the consumer/user of an e-product is the producer of e-waste; repair and refurbishing are ways to lengthen life of e-products; management of secondary materials in the globalised era and global market; etc. were not thought thoroughly and put forth extensively.

The economics of recycling (technology, infrastructure, cost of reverse logistics, etc.); potentials of recycling – resource recovery and organising secondary material management; economics of EPR functions and performance; economics of informal sector's functions and performance, violation of worker's rights, etc; issues of governance and institutionalisation (engagement of various ministries and centre-state government agencies) in federal structure and linkage of e-waste with international regulations, Customs, Science and Technology, Trade and Commerce, Environment, Health ministries, etc. were not articulated expansively based on almost a decade's experience regarding e-waste and its management.

Due to non-recognition of informal nature of e-waste work by the authorities, the workers remained excluded from the social and policy dialogue as well as from gaining full awareness of the sectoral dynamics (risks involved in their occupation) and from forming organisations and securing representation in sectoral dialogues with other stakeholders in the value chain. Thus, workers' collective concerns, needs and challenges among other industry players and public authorities, and improving their working conditions, including skills development and better income remained away from policy dialogue (ILO 2014).

In order to respond to policy dialogue and advocacy measures, the most important step by the GoI was to prepare a research paper (titled *E-waste in India*) by the Research Unit (LARRDIS) of Rajya Sabha Secretariat in 2011. This report has covered country's e-waste management scenario very comprehensively and with minute details. The knowledge base created by all the civil society actors is wisely used in the report; describing legal nitty-gritties, policy requirements, different department/ministry's data and performance, media reports, and people's perception, etc. are substantial value addition to the existing literature on the e-waste management in India.

II: Law-driven e-waste management – initiatives by the government, non-government agencies, and judiciary

This section covers pan-Indian initiatives post-2012; almost all initiatives appeared to be associated or driven by the existing regulations. The actors are – government, industry actors, non-government agencies, and the judiciary. The initiatives include awareness measures; educational initiatives; conducting research on various topics, such as, formal-informal partnership, gap analysis in e-waste management based on multi-stakeholder views, etc; preparing roadmap for the Agenda 2030; experimentation for resource efficiency and working out its economics as part of CE; and launching courses on e-waste management.

Initiatives by government agencies and industry actors post-2012

The first set of initiatives, taken by various government agencies, such as, state government/ department (IT, Science & Technology, etc.) issuing Executive Orders,[24] mandating the government agencies for the proper disposal of e-waste and its mechanism during 2012 and 2016; strategy papers on 'resource efficiency in EEE sector', and on 'resource efficiency and circular economy' by the GoI in 2019; expression of intention to link three missions (Digital India, Clean India, and Make in India) for economic betterment of EEE sector; actions taken by regulatory agencies – CPCB and SPCBs at centre and state levels respectively including inventorisation, creating database on e-waste generation; state run academic institutions/ portal (e.g. SWAYAM,[25] Skill Council for Green Jobs (SCGJ),[26] and National Skill Development Corporation (NSDC)[27]) launching a course on e-waste management, and providing hand on experience; a training manual for training of trainers on *E-waste awareness for bulk consumers*[28] published by the MeitY under Digital India Mission (Chaturvedi et al. 2016b); initiatives on SDGs/Agenda 2030; and so on.

The second set of initiatives cover industry actors (associated in the chain of EPR implementation), including PROs, dismantlers and recyclers, repairers, refurbishers, etc. contributing to the sector as part of legal compliance and strengthening formal economy. Some corporate entities (e.g. YES Bank and TERI report) have attempted to capture corporate perspective, bringing in newer ideas as future action plan. The third set is of civil society organisations (CSOs) including academic and research institutions, international (e.g. International Finance Corporation (IFC), a World Bank Group and its five year long 'e-waste management program') and bilateral agencies (e.g. GTZ). Their initiatives include awareness measures; fostering formal-informal partnership; furthering research; and teaching e-waste management at various places, in different ways. The fourth set of initiatives came from the judiciary. This section is covered s part of 'evolving jurisprudence on e-waste management' in Chapter 5. Few observations about the profile of litigants, judiciary's way of dealing with the legality, etc. are presented very briefly.

Awareness related efforts, research, and materials created

One of the firsts awareness raising on e-waste by the GoI is the Environmental Information System (ENVIS).[29] The centres are active in installation of e-waste bins or e-bins and are motivating and providing the subsidised infrastructural facilities and other necessary things to the private players for management and disposal of collected e-waste through these bins. Chandigarh administration, in companionship with the CII and Attero Recycling Private Ltd., collected approximately 800 kg of e-waste from the city of Chandigarh alone (Yadav and Bandopadhyay 2015).

Awareness aspect of e-waste and its management were explored by a few studies in the 2010s, more so, after the regulatory framework was enforced capturing ground reality. Most studies are micro level, city specific like Ahmedabad[30] (Shah 2014), Bengaluru[31] (Iyer 2014; Botharkur and Govind 2017), Delhi[32] (Kwatra et al. 2014), Srinagar, Uttarakhand (Nath et al. 2018);[33] Pune[34] (Bhat and Patil 2014; Shivathanu 2016), etc. while a study by Toxics Link (2016) is a multi-city study, with the largest number of respondents from different parts of India. All these studies are carried out studying *Rules, 2011* but the findings are relevant in the present time. These studies considered 'awareness about e-waste' as a critical part of e-wate management, as awareness can lead to enhancement of e-waste collection, to increase in recycling, and consequently reduction in hazards for environment as well as human health. They have focused on different aspects related to e-waste, such as, awareness about 'what is e-waste'; about *Rules, 2011*; as hazardous waste; disposal related – perception, attitude, behaviour, and the existing mechanism; about recycling – methods, hazards, etc. Among these studies, the most common findings among different cities, reflecting ground reality are awareness about e-waste varies; e-waste as hazardous waste is known among almost 80% respondents; not more 50% know about channel of disposal; and not more than 40% know about the *Rules, 2011*. Wipro has its take-back channel which reported 100% recycling against the collection. Most banks and IT companies prefer to dispose of e-waste through auction.

Pan India Awareness Programme (PIAP) was organised by MeitY, GoI in 2015. It was identified that lack of awareness about the safe disposal of e-waste amongst stakeholders is a key challenge in enforcement of the *Rules, 2016* (Chatterjee and Porwal 2019). The author duo has shared key findings of the programme.[35] First, informal sector has low awareness about the health and environmental impacts as well as safety precautions associated with the recycling of e-waste. Second, informal sector workers have very low literacy and awareness regarding hazards related to the unsafe handling of e-waste. Third, awareness amongst consumers regarding e-waste management is inadequate; consumers expect some return from end-of-life products and do not contribute anything towards the safe recycling of products and thereby further promoting unsafe recycling. Fourth, limited information and guideline on responsibility for inventorisation of e-waste, getting authorisation for EPR and renewal, recycler registration, monitoring compliance and action against violations of these rules. With this context, they have described a few suggestions, which include awareness and capacity-building content based on the local need and in local languages, on social media, on platforms for massive open online courses (MOOC) are made available; different media to be used for reaching out to each stakeholder; and effective implementation of EPR, wherein producers' websites and awareness programmes are necessary (Chatterjee and Porwal 2019: 59–63). Three manuals have been prepared under the Digital India, sponsored by MeitY, GoI (Chaturvedi et al. 2016b, 2016c, 2016d).

Recently, Delhi based study by Malhotra (2020), covering 100 respondents is another effort to know about awareness after *Rules, 2016*. Major findings are: nearly 90% replace their mobile phones every 4–6 years; 60% were aware of e-waste's hazardous impact on environment and health. Around 51% of the respondents were not aware about the existing policy for e-waste. 79% did not come across any advertisements, campaigns, or any other related initiatives of the government on e-waste disposal. 41% respondents shared that they had rarely come across advertisements by any manufacturing or producer entity; this finding corroborates Toxics Link (2019b) study on EPR compliance by producers – low level of compliance by most of the producers, have not reached the consumers, at large. 33% respondents sold their electronics to *Kabaadiwala*; 75.6% respondents were willing to trade off e-scrap to recycler provided they were paid for it. 81.63% did not know of any other collection mechanism for the purpose; 14% could identify formal recycling companies. The study observed that 'the responses of consumers point towards "lack of information" on formal collection services rather than "lack of willingness" as a barrier to safe waste disposal.' (Toxics Link 2019b: 33.)

Regarding attitude of consumers towards e-waste, Ahmedabad based study has quoted a government official of Gujarat state, which has been repeatedly been corroborated by micro studies:

> Indian consumers are not willing to part with electronic goods without some monetary compensation…buyers and sellers do not know the definitive value of an unused electronic. Without set prices, a trust deficit arises between the

buyer and seller...both buyers and sellers are discouraged from operating in the formal system, in turn encouraging informal exchanges.

(Shah 2014: 23)

Preparing inventory on e-waste

Post-2012, inventorisation of e-waste is stressed upon, as there is no clarity about its composition, method for calculation, and tracking e-waste that is collected and recycled. Two states, Chhattisgarh and Telangana prepared inventory after 2015 (IRG 2016).[36]

Telangana state reported that 39.11 MT e-waste generated by three government registered producers during the year 2016–2017. Of them,

> M/s. Electronics Corporation of India Limited (ECIL), (Dept. of Atomic Energy) produced 24.500 MT; M/s. Apple India Pvt., Limited, 5-132/B, Sy.No.97/C, Near Kompally Railway Bridge, Secunderabad produced 13.585 MT, and M/s. Bharat Electronics Ltd., (A Govt. of India Enterprises), IDA Mallapur produced 1.0227 MT e-waste.

(TSPCB 2016: 102)

The projected district wise E-waste inventory estimates both in numbers and weights for Raipur division starting from 2011 till 2020. In 2016, 78,004 cellular phones with 11.70 tonnes, 13,213 fixed line telephones with 13.21 tonnes, 6,092 computers with 127.54 tonnes, 2,798 printers with 19.59, 289 washing machines with 15.87 tonnes, 51,243 TV with 1,584.17, 431 refrigerators with 15.07, and 200 air conditioners with 11.02 tonnes are listed (IRG 2016: 58–59).

Formal-informal partnership roadmap based on work experience, research

The informal sector has a historic role in waste management and recycling in India, and have strong linkages with secondary material market. Some theoretical considerations are developed for formal-informal partnership. They are: first, the existing reality in India since more than a decade is – although formal recycling units ensured recycling in environmentally sound manner and increased recovery, they were unable to access large volumes of feed material owing to the activities of informal collectors, scrap dealers, and recyclers who operate on a door-to-door basis and pay a good price for e-waste compared to formal recyclers. This situation asked for striking a balance between two sectors (Wath et al. 2011; Chaturvedi and Gaurav 2016). Second, the existence of an informal is enabled with a widespread and active network, considerable manual skills, and economics of recycling; the SMEs are infrastructure based entrepreneurial units that permit a profitable e-waste management business. As most of the informal SMEs concentrate on one or two recycling stages (collection, segregation, dismantling) with well established relationships to other informal e-waste recycling SMEs up or down the recycling chain, some value is added at each stage creating employment at different levels, which may contribute to sustain the system. Third, among the informal sector recyclers, social bond is an important factor, which could be used as a cohesion factor to bring them closer and provide a platform for them to share their thoughts. Once the informal recyclers create a bond among themselves, a ground is prepared for their interactions with formal sector actors. Fourth, though the formal recyclers are equipped with best available technologies, they face dual challenges – investment in machinery along with more cost-intensive working standards, and competition with informal sector recyclers vis-à-vis flow of e-waste and on cost factor. Hence, the complementarity is thought of. Fifth, recycling *per se* is considered as a secondary enterprise; its ability to create employment is considered to be lesser than the primary/informal sector with its value chain. The move towards formalisation of the informal sector can begin through integration of mainstream recycling of e-waste, making them registered units, forming associations, and professionalising their businesses. (Raghupathy et al. 2010; Wath et al. 2011.)

GTZ/GIZ started forming partnership of formal-informal sectors for waste management in developing countries (Brazil, Egypt, and India) by late 2000s. One of the reasons given was informal recycling economy in solid waste management financially supplements the formal system in many ways (GTZ 2010, 2011). Learning from SWM experiences, GTZ started articulating similar concept for e-waste management. For example, forming and registering member based organisations of informal sector workers after creating common grounds for organising (trust building and a shared vision); strengthening capacities of the informal sector (making informal sector workers as stable entrepreneurs and reliable partners); technical specialisation; feeding experiences into national policies and legislation; and so on (ibid.).

The Indian e-waste sector is characterised by highly dynamic market environment and high degree of fragmentation. As of now, linkages between formal and informal actors in India are scarce and have not been implemented on a large scale. After a ten-month project financed by GIZ, a study was conducted in 2017 to advise public and private institutions on approaches to sustainable management of WEEE regarding options for producers and formal recyclers to partner with informal collectors under the *Rules, 2011*. Six case studies were investigated – green e-waste recyclers, Delhi; SWaCH, Pune; Saahas Zero Waste, Bengaluru; E-WaRDD, Bengaluru; GIZ-Microsoft, Delhi, Kolkata and Ahmedabad; and Chintan, Delhi – which succeeded or failed in maintaining formal-informal partnerships across the Indian e-waste management system (GIZ 2017). In 2018, similar study was initiated to complement the study of 2017, aimed at providing practical guidance under the recast policy framework of the *Rules, 2016* (GIZ 2018).

Before sharing the findings, the report clarified that 'at times, the research team was confronted with contradictory information and needed to cross-check various sources in order to verify findings and produce warranted results. Therefore, the findings presented in this paper should be interpreted carefully' (GIZ 2017: 5). As part of recommendations, the report focused on design of partnerships, agreements and incentives, longevity of partnerships, and scale up and replication. The report GIZ (2018) complements the report GIZ (2017) and provides practical guidance under the recast policy framework of the *Rules, 2016*.

After the *Rules, 2011*, it was found important that the entrepreneurial character of informal collectors is to be recognised and respected in a way that the organisational structure of partnerships should avoid strict top-down hierarchies. After the *Rules, 2016*, focus shifted to how producers fulfil their responsibility. In principle, they can opt to do so either individually or collectively; through self or through a PRO. In the given scenario, two options were suggested – an assessment of stakeholders should cover all relevant parties of the informal economy (collectors, dismantlers, aggregators and recyclers) and analyse their willingness to formalise; and producers and/or PROs shall cooperate with local interface agencies, possibly represented by CSOs/NGOs or cooperatives of waste pickers operating in the e-waste sector. Because trust is an important factor, in fact, a pre-condition for the creation of formal-informal relationships and should be seen as a valuable resource when connecting to informal collectors. The CSOs can offer additional benefits to informal collectors in form of trainings, educational activities or advocacy of workers' rights and have the ability of raising awareness for proper handling of e-waste among the informal sector. For true partnership, if producer provide additional information on the company's view on the informal sector, it can strengthen the credibility of EPR plans (GIZ 2017, 2018).

After the *Rules, 2011*, it was suggested that should be some degree of flexibility in agreements between formal and informal, in order to adapt to changing local conditions. The *Rules, 2016*, neither address the informal sector *per se* nor specific prescription is provided to producer for channelisation e-waste – collection to recycling. Here is a scope for collaboration for formalisation in qualitative manner, offering long-term support and technical assistance to partnering informal sector players. Fostering an incremental approach also has been suggested; frequent interactions and close monitoring by producers or PROs should determine reporting frequencies for the amount of e-waste collected together, also to assess the quality of materials, recommend changes in organisational set-ups and prevent leakages of collected e-waste towards informal channels producers. Such protocols need to include occupational aspects, such as decent health and safety standards in collection, dismantling and recycling, transparency and reliability of prices paid to informal workers and strict exclusion of child labour (ibid.).

Institutionalising partnership include a few important aspects, such as, designing an implementation schedule as a monitoring tool for producers and PROs, conduct periodic audits at the partnering organisation, data from audits needs to be thoroughly documented in coordination with the partnering organisation, reporting to public domain if both partners agree, sealing leakage as much as possible with mutual commitment, and so on. For such partnership and interactions, necessary resources should be provided, along with direct support in form of granting access to in-house communication channels, establishing contacts to bulk consumers or offering tailor-made capacity-building measures (ibid.).

Corporate sector's perspective and performance

A report written by Agarwal and Mullick (2014), published by YES Bank and TERI-BCSD provides corporate sector's perspective on e-waste management including decision making about e-waste disposal, whether any policy exists in the company, awareness about the Rules, channelisation of e-waste for recycling, and filing annual return.

This study has surveyed 150 respondents from various sectors including BFSI (Banking, Financial services, and Insurance), IT & ITES (Information technology and outsourcing services), education, automotive, EEE manufacture, and miscellaneous such as consulting, aviation and hospitality. In order to present corporate perspective, the survey has looked into how companies comply with the *Rules, 2011*. Of total 150, 52 (37%) respondents/companies were not aware of the Rules; in corporations, 28% IT department takes care of compliance but 16% did not know who complies with the Rules; 43% companies do not have any policy to manage e-waste; 60% of them have authorisation from SPCB to handle e-waste in their facility, however, 100% comply by filing return (Form 2); 32% bulk consumers channelise their e-waste to authorised vendors and recyclers and 30% maintain records (Form 1) and submit to SPCB. These findings show that the companies lack awareness, have taken half-hearted measures for implementation of the Rules and compliance related actions. The results corroborate with Toxics Link reports (2014b, 2019a) regarding performance of producers (Agarwal and Mullick 2014).

Regarding the recent environmental laws, the report observed that, the corporates aimed at

> products rather than end-of-pipe pollution focus on new product design mandates, substance restrictions, energy efficiency, and take-back mandates. Such emerging trends of legislation is identified as a risk and creator of challenges for the industry: functioning of EPR systems hampered due to unbranded and counterfeit products, original components often get replaced with those of other brands during repair, by the lack of knowhow regarding collection systems for recyclables, etc; transparency in downstream of recycling industry in terms of data loss, data leakage, and data security; and limited success of take-back policies.
>
> (Agarwal and Mullick 2014: 12–13)

The report stressed on collection system as a crucial leverage for the success of the overall system, and suggested that conventional market-based collection system is to be utilised, if it is appropriate; in case, a new collection system is evolved, the stakeholders should be made aware of that. The government needs to provide incentives to the actors in collection system; the cost and responsibility (primarily transportation and recycling) should be shared by three primary stakeholders – the producer, the generator (households and bulk consumers), and the local regulatory body (municipality).

Regarding collection and recycling model, multiple modes of collection are required for achieving the closed-loop flow for e-waste recycling; producers to pay for this. The entire setup can be accomplished through strong mass public awareness programmes to operationalise the system in the region, which can be the mandate of PROs (setting up collection agents, aggregation, and transport system). Manufacturers should bear the part of the financial responsibility by contributing to a 'Producer Responsibility Fund' that would finance the cost of establishing and operating PROs. The collection agents could be the local bodies, NGOs or private entities, and may engage *kabaadiwalas* for door-to-door collection.

The model of integration of the activities between the informal and formal sectors is portrayed as an ideal requirement, for e-waste collection, segregating, and dismantling. For consumers and bulk consumers, recommendations include robust policy by bulk consumers, empanelling authorised recycler, and sensitisation of their employees about hazards of e-waste. For manufacturers, various action complying the Rules, including RoHS related, collection and recycling related policy, communication related, etc. for policy makers and regulators, recommendations include establishing strict monitoring mechanisms, inclusion of informal sector, organising awareness raising programmes, and creating schemes to encourage entrepreneurs to establish dismantling and recycling facilities in the state.

Gap analysis in e-waste management representing multi-stakeholder views

A report written by Verena Radulovic (2018), published CRB (Centre for Responsible Business) and GEC (Green Electronics Council) has undertaken gap analysis in the context of the given challenges in implementing the *Rules, 2016*. This report was prepared based on survey of 20 stakeholders (producers, authorised PROs, and recyclers, NGOs and Waste-picker Collectives, Trade Associations, Government, Multilateral organisations, academics, and general waste management provider), and their work experience since May 2017. This report aimed to assess current priorities of the government and industry practices pertaining to EoL management of electronics in India, and what kinds of capacity-building criteria would most effectively ESM.

The report has presented a synopsis of e-waste management efforts during 2008 and 2017, covering regulatory overview, producers' collection and recycling programmes, bulk consumers', and households' pattern of disposing e-waste, operations of informal sector, and flow of e-waste. The report introduced 'voluntary consensus sustainability standard' (VCSS) to build capacity.

> Over the past decade, voluntary ecolabels for electronics have given purchasers a mechanism to demand more sustainable products that exceed product-centred environmental regulations, namely ones that are even more energy efficient, made with fewer harmful substances, and recycled responsibly at end-of-life.
>
> (Radulovic 2018: 12)

The findings highlight current gaps and posit ideas for how capacity-building[37] criteria in a voluntary standard (to which producers would certify and that purchasers would use) could help ameliorate them.

(ibid.: 13)

Major findings include the following: (i) poor e-waste collection by producers and inadequate supply of e-waste to the authorised recyclers; (ii) lack of metals extraction capability among formal recyclers and leakage of e-waste to informal, local recycling markets; informal collectors, dismantlers, and aggregators continue to generate higher profits selling material to informal recyclers instead of formal recyclers; (iii) any NGOs with whom producers, PROs or recyclers partner to reach informal workers may need initial training to understand India's e-waste trading markets;[38] (iv) consumers and bulk consumers lack awareness of their responsibilities under the current Rules, and of collection and recycling opportunities; (v) CPCB and SPCBs lack technical capacity and resources to screen and enforce registrations of recyclers and PROs; and (vi) only a few stakeholders are in the early stages of considering linkages between e-waste management, SDGs, and CSR (corporate social responsibility) requirements under the *Companies Act* (ibid.).

This report has described opportunities for future research areas for e-waste management in India; they are: (i) Audits for financial and mass balance traceability claims; (ii) Formal processing (metal processing capabilities and reasons for why smelters have not been established); (iii) Small Scale processing for current informal recyclers (evaluate feasibility of mobile processing small scale factories); (iv) Organising the informal sector (what lessons from other industries, such as, tanning, electroplating, fruit selling, etc. could apply to informal communities for e-waste management); and (v) Material downstream flows (examine end markets for materials in electronics within India).

IFC's e-waste programme in India: multiple agenda achieved

This programme was started in 2012 with a pilot study in three cities – Ahmedabad, Delhi, and Hyderabad. The baseline collected information from consumers and last mile collectors (LMC). One of the achievements reported was – increased income of LMCs, from USD7/month (INR 6,500) to estimated USD 36/month (approx. INR 25,000). The Bhubaneshwar project demonstrated public-private partnership model. Several multi-stakeholder dialogues on business, environment, health and social policy, and technology; celebration of E-waste Day; etc. were organised during 2017 and 2019.

IFC and Karo Sambhav, Pvt. Ltd. a PRO, jointly developed an ecosystem, aligned partnership with multiple stakeholders and civil society actors. Five major programmes were developed – with schools for awareness raising and e-waste collection; with bulk consumers for channelising e-waste and creating awareness; with repair shops for capacity-building of repairers; with waste pickers for engaging

LMCs and increase in their income; and with waste aggregators for moving towards formalisation/formal economy.

Roadmap India – vision 2030 documents experiences and views of stakeholders

A published compilation titled, *E-waste roadmap 2030 for India: A compilation of thought pieces by sector experts*[39] by IFC and Karo Sambhav Pvt. Ltd. (2019) has captured Indian scenario and has shared a roadmap for e-waste sector. Some important thoughts, initiatives, etc. are shared here as potential area for future action – EPR, PRO, formal-informal integration, recycling technology and infrastructure, inventorisation of e-waste, monitoring for implementation of the Rules, public awareness, etc. Only newer thoughts, which have not been covered until now/in the previous chapters are mentioned here.

Tsuyoshi Kawakami (2019) reminded of ILO (International Labour Organization) Safety and Health Convention (No. 155, 1981) that defines the responsibilities of the government and employers in OSH (occupational safety and health) and also the duties and rights of workers. He stressed upon implementation of ILO Guidelines on OSH Management Systems (known as ILO-OSH 2001) offer systematic approaches (training and coordinating government policy) for continuous improvements of OSH at the workplace/e-waste recycling units.

Bernd Kopacek (2019: 74–76) has identified similarities and differences regarding e-waste in India and Europe. His observations have been shared in the Chapter 5.

Shift in discourse and necessary actions for e-waste management by the GoI

Most important shift observed in the discourse of e-waste management is the focus on CE. In the initial phase of public policy dialogue, safe environment and human health under EPR were the focus. Now after almost a decade, CE has become a focal point along with EPR as a core strategy to achieve SDGs too. Initiatives by the GoI, such as, skill building initiatives under SCGJ and NSDC 2015 onwards, experiments by C-MET, strategy paper (MeitY and NITI Aayog 2019), etc. are directed toward enhancement of resource efficiency, in turn, strengthening the CE through e-waste management. The regulatory provisions, especially covered under the EPR and guidelines for its implementation clearly show that these efforts are directed to strengthen CE.

However, the financial arrangements, and economics is yet to be worked out for by the GoI, that is, fund allocation by the concerned ministries/state department (e.g. MoEFCC, MeitY, Science and Technology), by three different missions, and other sources. Two policies – *New Environment Policy, 2006*, and *National Policy on Electronics, 2012* under which newer programmes/schemes could be launched by the GoI for the e-waste management. Such possibilities and potentials are on the way.

Monitoring (data based, field inspection) by the regulatory bodies has been stressed upon in most write ups/dialogue. The CPCB took action based on inspection in Uttar Pradesh and has served a notice to three authorised dismantlers/recyclers on 12 March 2020. It has been intimated to the concerned stakeholders that

> during inspection, the above-mentioned dismantlers/recyclers were found to be in violation with E-Waste (Management) Rules, 2016 and the amendments thereof. All the producers and PROs are hereby informed not to have interaction/agreement related to EPR of producers under the E-Waste Rules with the above-mentioned dismantlers/recyclers.

The Goa SPCB has withdrawn authorisation of a collection centre with immediate effect in 2018.[40] An engineer, in charge on e-waste at the Gujarat Pollution Control Board (GPCB) informed on 4 August 2020 that he had served 'intent notice' to every authorised dismantler/recycler unit in Gujarat state in the month of March/April 2020, stating that there exists a gap between recycling capacity and amount of e-waste recycled reported in last one year. This means that each the unit is not functioning to its full capacity. The notice seek explanation from each unit. Consequently, there has been an increase of about 10–25% in dismantling/recycling of e-waste in a quarter (during May to July 2020). He has also started a dialogue with all the authorised dismantlers/recyclers in order to understand challenges they face. He has suggested to form an association of all authorised dismantling/recycling units; thus, dealing with the existing challenges of dismantling/ recycling, such as, improve quantum of inflow of e-waste, sharing of facilities, reducing leakage, dealing with cherry picking, and so on. The formation of an association of the authorised dismantlers/recyclers is under progress, as reported by the engineer of the GPCB.

Effective implementation of the *Rules, 2016* and *Amendment Rules, 2018* have begun to bear results in terms of legal compliance by the PROs, filing annual returns by the bulk consumers, etc. based on figures available from the website of the respective SPCBs, the latest annual reports of 2017–2018.

Indian e-waste sector is expanding

Throughout the chapter, role played by different Indian actors – government agencies, industry actors, non-government agencies, research institutions, and the regulatory bodies – and how each one interacted with bi-lateral, multilateral and international actors/agencies on individual or collective basis is mapped out. The initiatives include measures awareness raising; educational initiatives; conducting research on various topics, such as, formal-informal partnership, gap analysis in e-waste management based on multi-stakeholder views, etc; preparing roadmap for the Agenda 2030; experimentation for resource efficiency, and working out its economics as part of CE and bringing in standardisation; and launching courses on e-waste management.

The e-waste sector needs to deal with a couple of chronic, inherent problems of e-waste management, which have not been addressed by the existing legal framework, for example, dominant presence of informal sector and workers engaged in various operations; need for evolving standardisation for collection and segregation, and dismantling/recycling of e-waste; preparing inventory of e-waste so that cherry picking for recycling could be prevented; provision for funding to develop recycling infrastructure and technology, which could enhance resource recovery and efficiency. The process for developing 'voluntary consensus sustainability standard' could be operationalised. Market development for sale of secondary development is need of the hour so that not only metals but also different type and grade plastics and glass also could be reused; access to this market for the recyclers/dismantlers could be established and enhanced.

Notes

1 It is estimated that the volume of cell phone handsets will surge to over 100 million and PCs to 25.5 million by 2007 (Mehra 2004). Of nearly 5 million PCs, 1.35 million were likely to become obsolete in India in 2003, and in terms of weight it was equivalent to 414,000 tonnes (Toxics Link 2003: 13); these figures were revised – of nearly 8 million PCs, 2 million were likely to become obsolete in India (Toxics Link 2004a). For more details, refer LARRDIS 2011.
2 For example, about 30 MT of e-waste was imported and landed at Ahmedabad port. Out of this, 20 MT was pure scrap and 10 MT was in reusable condition (Toxics Link 2003: 14). 'According to a study conducted by the Central Pollution Control Board (CPCB), 7,200 tonnes of imported e-waste arrive daily in the city [Delhi] for 300 days a year' (quoted in Dimitrakakis et al. 2006: 6).
3 Toxics Link from India, SCOPE (Society for Conservation and Protection of the Environment) from Pakistan, and Greenpeace from China.
4 This report provided details about composition of a PC, sedimentation related details of 18 metals and its impact on human health – allowable limits and increased pollution, etc. as annexures.
5 This programme was planned in three phase: first phase (2003–2004) was to identify and document the current e-waste handling situation in three urban areas – Delhi (India), Beijing (China) and Johannesburg (South Africa); second phase (2004–2005) was planned for improving the prevailing situation were jointly developed with the local partners in the same three countries; and third phase (2005–2008) the programme is instrumental in supporting the various involved stakeholders to implement the planned activities (Widmer et al. 2008: 466).
6 Swiss Federal Laboratories for Materials Testing and Research also named as Swiss Federal Institute for Materials Science and Technology. In 2003, Switzerland had initiated a knowledge partnership programme with industrialising countries, including India, China, and South Africa. This was funded by Seco (Swiss State Secretariat for Economic Affairs) and implemented by EMPA in cooperation with local partners and authorities.
7 GTZ (Deutsche Gesellschaft für Technische Zusammenarbeit) has been active in India on behalf of the German Federal Ministry for Economic Cooperation and Development (BMZ), a cabinet level ministry of the Federal Republic of Germany. GTZ works with the Central Government and various State agencies with its priority areas; e-waste is one of them as part of environmental policy and conservation,

and sustainable use of natural resources. Renamed as GIZ (Deutsche Gesellschaft für Internationale Zusammenarbeit) in 2011.
8 The Ministry of Environment and Forests (MoEF) was renamed in 2014 as Ministry of Environment, Forests and Climate Change (MoEFCC).
9 MoEF, MoIT, CPCB, SPCBs, and PCCs
10 CETMA (Consumer Electronics and Television Manufacturers Association), MAIT (Manufacturers Association of Information Technology), NASSCOM (National Association of Software and Service Companies), CII (Confederation of Indian Industries), ELCINA (Electronic Industries Association of India), and Telecom Equipment Manufacturers Association of India (TEMA), and others.
11 This included Development Alternatives, TERI (The Energy and Resources Institute), and Toxics Link.
12 IRGSSA (IRG System South Asia Pvt. Ltd.). 2005. *Country level WEEE assessment study.* Delhi: Central Pollution Control Board. The e-copy or physical copy of this report is not available.
13 For more details, refer Arora et al. 2019b: 69–87.
14 It typically includes products at the end of active life which either gets stacked inside warehouses/store rooms or products that are not sold by consumers because of inappropriate resale value or are used for lower level application.
15 It includes the products that have been exchanged/ sold by their owners. Large quantities of the Waste Electrical and Electronic Equipment get refurbished, reused or relocated to smaller towns or villages.
16 This includes the disposed electronic products which are actually recycled and would include the dismantled parts and components of EEE.
17 Of total 382,979 MT e-waste, 50,000 MT was imported, 56,324 MT was of computers, 27,5000 MT was of TVs, and 1,655 MT of mobile phones. Of total 144,143 MT e-waste available for recycling, 50,000 MT was imported, 24,000 MT was of computers, 70,000 MT was of TVs, and 143 MT was of mobile phones. Of total 19,000 MT e-waste recycled, 12,000 MT was of computers and 7,000 MT was of TVs.
18 Old Seelampur and Shastri Park in Delhi are the hubs for dismantling and recycling of e-waste since early 2000s.
19 For example, 'scrap of electrical items and copper wire, including jelly filled telephone cables were imported under Chapters 85 and 74 of the Customs Act, respectively, during financial year 2000–2001.
20 'Nearly 25,000 workers are employed at scrap yards in Delhi alone, where 10,000 to 20,000 tonnes of e-waste are handled every year' (quoted in Dimitrakakis et al. 2006: 7). Delhi had become well-known for two processes – receiving and channelising imported e-waste for treatment, and housing several recycling units.
21 The informal recycling chain is embedded with unique social structure with high ratio of Muslim population involved. Starting from big traders, the deeply connected Muslim community penetrates along the chain of recycling activities. The recycling part of the chain is mainly dominated by poor Muslim migrants.
22 For the sequence of events in a recycling chain, see Sinha 2019a: 38 – a flow chart.
23 The MoEF has issued the following notifications related to hazardous waste until 2006: *HWM Rules, 1989/ 2000/ 2002*; *MoEF Guidelines for Management and Handling of Hazardous Wastes, 1991*; *Guidelines for Safe Road Transport of Hazardous Chemicals, 1995*; *The Public Liability Act, 1991*; *Batteries (Management and Handling) Rules, 2001*; *The National Environmental Tribunal Act, 1995*; *Bio-Medical Wastes (Management and Handling) Rules, 1998*; *Municipal Solid Wastes (Management and Handling) Rules, 2000//2002*;

Strategies and initiatives for dealing 163

The Recycled Plastic Manufacture and Usage (Amendment) Rules 2003; and *The National Environment Policy, 2006.*

24 Department of Science & Technology, GR no. COB-2004-394-DST, Gandhinagar, Dated 24/12/2014 by the Government of Gujarat. Circular No. MPCB/RO(HQ)/B-1980, Dated 20.04.2013 by the member secretary of the Maharashtra Pollution Control Board, State of Maharashtra. State of Kerala, State of Goa and many other state governments have issued notifications.

25 SWAYAM is a programme initiated by Government of India and designed to achieve the three cardinal principles of Education Policy viz., access, equity and quality. The objective of this effort is to take the best teaching learning resources to all, including the most disadvantaged. SWAYAM seeks to bridge the digital divide for students who have hitherto remained untouched by the digital revolution and have not been able to join the mainstream of the knowledge economy (https://swayam.gov.in).

26 SCGJ promoted by the Ministry of New and Renewable Energy (MNRE) and CII, established as a not-for-profit, autonomous, industry-led society under the *Societies Registration Act XXI, 1860* on 1 October, 2015.

27 NSDC acts as a catalyst in skill development by providing funding to enterprises, companies and organizations that provide skill training. It also develops appropriate models to enhance, support and coordinate private sector initiatives. The differentiated focus on 21 sectors under NSDC's purview and its understanding of their viability will make every sector attractive to private investment (https://nsdcindia.org).

28 This manual aimed at covering 10 states Madhya Pradesh, Uttar Pradesh, Jharkhand, Orissa, Goa, Bihar, Pondicherry, West Bengal, Assam and Manipur. The activities include organising awareness workshops for RWAs (resident welfare association)/localities, schools, colleges, bulk consumers (including corporate & Govt. sectors), informal sector, dealers, refurbishers, manufacturers, etc. so as to build capacities of the target groups to channelize e-waste in a manner that the rules are effectively implemented (Chaturvedi et al. 2016b).

29 ENVIS was introduced in 1983, as a part of the Sixth Five-Year Plan. This is a government's computerised database system which facilitates qualitative and quantitative information to policy makers, research organisations, decision makers, scientists, etc. There were 68 nodes known as ENVIS centres existed in 2012.

30 A survey covering 55 respondents in Ahmedabad city in 2014 shared that 40 respondents did not know about formal collection channel/system; 18 respondents could name specific hazard of e-waste while 37 knew about hazards but could not name any; six knew about government body or policy for e-waste management but none of them knew particularly about the *Rules, 2011*.

31 Iyer (2014) conducted a study regarding e-waste collection and safe management in academic institutions in Bangalore based on 37 respondents (students and teaching faculty); Faculty is more concerned towards e-waste generation, collection and disposal, compared to student community. Botharkur and Govind (2017) conducted an empirical study with the 'bulk consumers' – Banks, educational institutions, an IT sector companies – to evaluate the existing E-waste management structures, consumers' disposal behaviour and associated awareness. IT companies like Wipro adopts a 'take-back system;' most of the banks and educational institutes take 'auction' as the measure by calling tenders from authorised e-waste recyclers; one bank embracing an 'e-waste exchange system,' or complying through PROs; they were unaware of recycling practices.

32 Kawatra et al. (2014) covered 400 respondents in Delhi. Major findings: very low awareness level; most were totally unaware about correct ways of its recycling and management;

less than a fourth replaced their consumer e-products and PCs within the first three years of purchase; some users expressed willingness to pay extra cost for proper management of e-waste provided that there is proper cost sharing between consumers and producers; stressed upon producer take-back channel.

33 This was a community based cross sectional (consumers and scrap dealers) study in Srinagar city of Uttarakhand state on knowledge about e-waste, its types and disposal practices. 6.7% respondents heard the term e-waste; 77% of the respondents did not know about the ways of disposal; 45.7% were totally unaware of hazardous effects of improper disposal. Knowledge among scrap dealers about e-waste was altogether absent.

34 Bhat and Patil (2014) conducted a survey of 100 respondents of Pune city. Of them, 65% were unaware of e-waste policy; 80% know about its hazardousness, collection facility, and presence of metals; 57% disposed e-waste along with MSW. Shivathanu (2016) conducted a survey of total of 600 consumers from Pune city. 58.5% of the consumers are aware of e-waste management, and of them 91.45% of the show preference for proper disposal of e-waste.

35 The manual of ToT (Chaturvedi et al. 2016b) was used to reach out to different stakeholders

36 Both reports have mentioned about five models, mentioned in UNEP Manual (2007). Chhattisgarh state has adopted Carnegie Mellon method for inventory assessment; two approaches were adopted for required data – (i) combination of primary and secondary data, and (ii) e-waste tracker tracking. The required data were: (a) information about stakeholders i.e. recycler/dismantler, scrap dealer, consumer etc; (b) stock and generation of e-waste; (c) origin of new electrical and electronic equipment i.e. mode of procurement; (d) lifetime of electrical and electronic equipment; (e) EoL management of EEE; (f) process involved during dismantling; and (g) final destination of e-waste fractions. A combination of Carnegie Mellon method and tracer tracking has led to inventory assessment, covering all the aspects of material flow chain (IRG 2016: 50–51).

37 'Capacity building' need not be limited to the informal sector, but also applies to formal market and regulatory actors to foster systems better equipped to deliver environmentally sound EoL management of e-waste.

38 PRO's work with informal collectors, dismantlers, and aggregators, specific interventions can begin to shift selling behaviour into formal channels; and interventions should be tailored to the informal worker's role in the e-waste management hierarchy and the geographic market in which he or she operates.

39 Most of the written pieces are also published in the 'Colloquium – E-waste management in India: Issues and strategies' in the journal Vikalpa, 44(3).

40 No. 1/20/18-PCB Lab/10785 Dated 31/08/2018.

7
MOVING TOWARDS HORIZONS

Traditionally, India has had a longstanding culture of circularity, which was pushed in the early 1990s to a linear system of production which was more compatible with global trade, global supply chains, and economies of scale. This was resulted in to downscaling of traditional values of reuse and repair, and the jobs associated with the end of the value chain being transferred to the informal economy where they exist today. However, in recent years, the return of circular economy principles has brought these traditional Indian values back into the mainstream, mainly through a route of policy making in India. Businesses have begun to adopt resource efficiency and circular production in their operations, creating opportunities for the formal waste management sector (MeitY and NITI Aayog 2019).

The way ahead could be consolidated on four domains of the e-waste management as illustrated in the Figure 7.1. They are: legal and judicial domain; economic concerns; recycling culture/ society; and environment concerns. These domains are organised based on the 'e-waste management thinking' matrix, presented in the Chapter 6. This chapter is organised around these four domains.

I: Legal and judicial domain

As the e-waste and its management is largely law/regulation driven with EPR as a strategy, it is very important to comprehend the architecture of the regulation; how it offers opportunities and identifies challenges for its enforcement thorough institutional mechanism, processes, and action by the stakeholders; role of monitoring ensuring legal compliance; what happens in case of non-compliance; understanding jurisprudence; and how regulatory body plays its role – in monitoring, enforcement, and legal compliance after the Court/Tribunals' order.

DOI: 10.4324/9780429285424-7

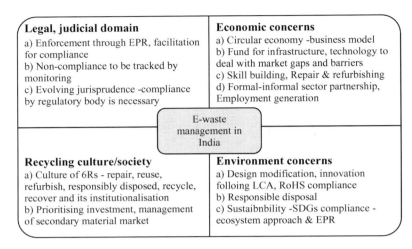

FIGURE 7.1 Way ahead for e-waste management in India

Architecture of the regulation, EPR, and outcomes

The architecture of the regulation shows clear equation, in line with EPR, as follow: classification of the e-waste according to its various components and compositions (Schedules I and II), and emphasising on preparing inventory, role of stakeholders defined including collection to treatment mechanism creating awareness raising, reporting, and filing annual returns, etc., and this database becomes an instrument for monitoring and evaluation. This would lead in increase in e-waste collection and recycling, and thus a step forward for the resource recovery, resource efficiency, and the CE. The CE is important, especially in terms of making life longer of e-products, reducing quantum of e-waste, and contributing to economy.

In such a straightforward equation, several nodes, and legal loopholes remained untied or unaddressed, which have become challenges. The challenges are articulated from wider context of environment, economics, human health, dominance of informal sector, and of governance. This domain covers mainly the following aspects that have created opportunities and challenges: (i) statistics related; (ii) legal compliance by producer, through PRO; (iii) regulatory body related; (iv) monitoring import of e-waste; (v) awareness raising among various stakeholders related; and (vi) coordination with/among different ministries/government agencies/missions (government programmes).

Role and scope of statistics and data driven actions

Almost all countries have expressed concerns for either not having database or difficulties in creating database, mainly due to absence of standards and methods for calculating e-waste – generation, collection, flow, treatment and/or recycling as well as data on resource recovery based formal economy (ISWA 2014).

With mandate for all the stakeholders of maintaining records and updating time to time, and filing annual returns, have created a huge opportunity and a possibility of a strong database, inventory of the e-waste. As against this, the first challenge is, if the required information is not provided by the stakeholders, what action would be taken by the regulatory authority?

With collection of these data, every stakeholder's performance could be monitored and evaluated, as and when required, based on the available database. However, as these reporting items on e-waste are limited, some essential data would not be created/available on other important aspects of e-waste management, such as, extent of resource recovery and improvement in efficiency, secondary market scenario, jobs/employment created and other economic benefits, how the CE is enhanced, impacts on human health, and impact on environment (CO_2 emission, BFR related, mercury level, use of fossils, carbon and natural resources, levels of contamination of different metals and POPs, etc.), and cost saving through refurbishing of EEE.

Though refurbishers are key players as per the *Rules, 2016*, their contribution to e-waste management, in terms of repair and reuse of EEE, also may remain undocumented. Whether authorised units could employ skilled labour or the unauthorised units/informally operating units for dismantling/recycling e-waste earning livelihood – such broader concern of unemployment/development agenda would remain largely unanswered. Empirically, such concerns may remain open to question (Gaikwad 2019).

A few challenges are also foreseen with regard to informal sector's functioning that has not been covered under the *Rules, 2016*. For example, informal collection and unscientific recycling of e-waste would be continued by unauthorised dismantlers/recyclers, and consequently would remain unreported. How would CPCB and SPCBs would collect data that has remained unreported, out of the legal purview. 'To what extent e-waste has been dealt by unauthorized agencies,' may not be answered with the existing database. In this case, some damage to environment and human health takes place by unauthorised dismantler/recyclers, how would CBPB or SPCB find out. What actions would be taken against them?

Data may be collected on collection, dismantling, and recycling but in absence of due processing the collected data, the monitoring by regulatory authority may not take place or remain weaker. For example, data on 'awareness measures taken by producers and its impacts' may not be available in form of whether awareness led to the desired extent of disposal of e-waste. If awareness of consumers/bulk consumers, and other stakeholders leads to some positive environmental impacts (reduction in toxicity, use of energy, reduction in emission, etc.), the desired/required statistics may not get generated/available due to greater emphasis on EPR enforcement strategy.

A couple of questions are raised, which may turn out to be a challenge related to statistics and e-waste management through meaningful statistics. For example, can wholesome inventory be prepared based on available data, and whether CPCB is equipped with methods and technology to process the available data?

Thus, selective set of data would be collected as part of regulatory measures; effective use of datasets would depend upon the enforcement agency, leading to achievement of e-waste management. The scope for data driven actions remain limited, for example, awareness raising, employment generation, CE related.

Legal compliance by producer, through PRO

Under EPR, producers pay for entire reverse supply chain, clarity on funding mechanism is required. However, ambiguity about 'who is a producer' further complicate the matters; and becomes a barrier for new business models. For example, along with material flow and financial flow analysis, who pays to whom for what and how are critical, as these matters are technical and political in nature (Khetriwal 2019; Sharma 2019).

If producer cannot implement all the responsibilities mandated under the Rules, performing these duties through an authorised (capacitated) PRO[1] is an opportunity to achieve objectives of the Rules, as it sets up entire value chain (from collection to recycling e-waste)/ecosystem. However, this provision has its own implications and challenges.

Though the concept of PRO as an entity is an integral part of EPR, which is mainstreamed across the world; Indian stakeholders covered under these Rules are still not well aware of it. Further, masses know lesser about the PRO as an entity. The partnership between a PRO and a producer is critically based on principle of cooperation, on long term basis; generally speaking, this also is a lesser-known fact. A couple of PROs, dealing with e-waste in the country have started sharing their work experiences, and are articulating challenges based on their work experience.

A PRO has to build a holistic system/ecosystem that goes beyond 'compliance' in its simplistic form. Building up ecosystem aims to collaborate and develop partnerships with all the concerned stakeholders from the entire value chain for varied tasks – large number of informal waste pickers and aggregators from various locations, 'bulk consumers' including central and state government authorities, civil society actors and organisations, research and academic institutions, and so on. PRO's varied tasks include quality of e-waste collected, ensuring safety measures for storage and transportation, fair pricing, recycling and recovery, etc. Creating and maintaining database for such varied tasks and activities become necessary for a PRO (Sinha 2019b), which demands commitment and efficiency.

Given objectives of the *Rules, 2016*, reduction in illegal e-waste collection and recycling requires due diligence in such long-term processes. Usually, a producer engages a PRO on annual, contractual basis. This situation creates a sort of gap between the two entities on the count of commitment – the process-oriented targets become physical target on short term basis. This situation creates potential scope for 'paper trading, malpractices,[2] multiple accounting practices,[3] misreporting' (Singhal 2019b: 152), and age-old problem of leakage of e-waste – from a PRO/recycler to informally functioning recycling unit, back to the waste aggregators and again marketed as e-waste to be recycled. Though such problems defeat the objectives of these Rules, they have not been taken into consideration.

In order to enhance e-waste collection, it is important that bulk consumers dispose their e-waste and legally comply by filing annual returns. Most bulk consumers are not aware of PROs and their role in e-waste management; those who are aware about PROs, have not started disposing e-waste through PROs, mainly because of lack of coordination and gap of communication between government entities. For example, a platform like Metal Scrap Trading Corporation (MSTC) which is used for selling scrap material, including e-waste, by most public institutions. At present, MSTC does not allow PROs to use its platform. On one hand, the CPCB authorises the PROs, and the government run unit like MSTC does not recognise the authorised entity like PRO, on the other hand. 'However, it has not been communicated to the MSTC,' (ibid.).[4]

Regulatory body – institutional mechanism, capacity, and effectiveness

The CPCB is an autonomous regulatory body, which is an advantage. CPCB and SPCBs perform several functions, such as assessment of pollution – air, waste, soil; monitoring of source specific pollution of air, water, soil; monitoring of ambient air and water quality; development and enforcement of standards; hazardous waste management and dissemination of information; and conducting mass-awareness programmes (IIML 2010); and improving quality of air and water, disposal of different types of wastes (hazardous, electronic, bio-medical, municipal solid, etc.). These bodies have been engaged in monitoring of pollution levels, contamination, etc.; thus, they would be able to monitor e-waste as per *the Rules*.

Building capacity of these bodies is an opportunity. Thomas Lindhqvist in his interview in 2019, reflecting on EPR implementation, shared his observations and views. Regarding EPR monitoring, he said, 'we need to raise the competence of these organizations (CPCB and SPCBs). They really have to learn how to do this efficiently.' While answering the question, 'what is not working regarding EPR implementation in India,' he said, 'you have to try to make people understand why it's important and understand what consumers want... you also have to make companies understand why this is important and that people might not reward you every time they are buying something, but they (companies) have to build an image of a responsible actor, of someone consumers can believe in.' Quoting EU countries as examples, he also stressed the need to think beyond guidelines (rules), and interpreting them to fulfil. Such intention is to be replicated in India (Kapil 2019).

As against these responsibilities, there exists very thin mechanism for enforcement at the CPCB and SPCB, with a staff small in number. This creates huge challenges for their effective functioning, especially monitoring, reporting non-compliance, taking necessary punitive actions as per the legal provisions, ensuring compliance ordered by the Court/Tribunal, and so on. The Centre for Science and Environment (CSE) has shared their experiences regarding regulating e-waste as an environmental policy issue, its report highlights that the approach of regulatory agency is geared towards giving multiple clearances, consents and authorisations, and with poor monitoring and enforcement (CSE 2014: 6–10). By giving an example, the report reinstated that most SPCBs suffer from severe deficit of manpower, infrastructure, and competence in addition to the challenge of transparency and accountability. Describing MPCB in 2014, the report illustrated that a technical officer is responsible for monitoring more than 250 factories; 30% of the sanctioned posts have been filled in the Pollution Control Boards of Haryana, Andhra Pradesh, and Odisha states).

As such, the formalisation (registration, authorisation, and monitoring) of producers and dismantlers/recyclers may be effective under EPR, yet several loopholes and implementation related challenges are highlighted by the practitioners of e-waste management. A couple of suggestions[5] for improvements in performance of SPCBs in dearth of human resources and multiple functioning are under consideration by the CPCB.

First, there are several unauthorised units are functional for e-waste collection, channelisation, and dismantling/recycling. Without authorisation, selling or placing of EEE in the market by any producer is not legal, penal provisions are not mentioned in *The Rules*. How would CPCB find out functioning of non-authorised units? For continuity of such illegal activities, what role regulatory authority can play for achieving the objectives of the *Rules, 2016*?

Every producer is expected to achieve the target every year; in case, the target is not achieved by a producer – how would CPCB verify? What penal action will be taken by whom – the CPCB or MoEFCC – is not mentioned in *The Rules*. The process of maintaining records for compliance with the regulation's requirements would be expensive in addition to the administrative costs to every key player. The authorised producers and dismantlers/recyclers are already struggling to compete with informal sector players. There is a likelihood of weak compliance on the count of maintaining records of different types; the regulatory authority would have difficulty in monitoring with thin mechanism, without putting IT solution in place.

In this context, the third challenge is, if data on RoHS compliance is not provided – what action will be taken by whom (CPCB or MoEFCC) is not mentioned in the Rules; the CPCB Guidelines too is silent on this point. If no data provided by a PRO on awareness measures undertaken, what action will be taken by whom (CPCB or MoEFCC) is not mentioned in the Rules.

An e-portal for monitoring by the CPCB has been in process, as mandated by the NGT. However, it is argued that instead of centralised database, the process needs to be state-centric for better performance at state level. In light of dearth of human resources, it is suggested that third party audit and verification of local/state data of vendors, aggregators, recyclers, etc. could be done by the IT solutions, in place of every SPCB office. Thus, human burden could be reduced, and monitoring could be effective with technology enabled solutions. The problem of leakage of e-waste is closely linked to this issue. One of the ways to deal with this problem is: an association of recyclers/dismantlers could be promoted so that every SPCB office deal with the association. At present, every SPCB deals with each authorised recycler/dismantler on one-to-one basis. If there is a platform on which common issues are discussed (e.g. auction of e-waste by every bulk consumer, collection and transportation of e-waste within state, minimum quantum of e-waste to be recycled per annum, etc.), solutions could be sought and implemented affectively, and generalised solutions rather than a piece-meal solution, by building the bridge between the different stakeholders/ implementors and the regulators.

The attitude of the existing rules and regulations is 'to eradicate' informal players, which is not possible in the current scenario. Regarding leakage and e-waste entering grey market, revision in the existing provision is required as well as role of municipal corporations/urban local bodies (ULBs) to be operationalised. For example, every waste collector needs to be registered with an authorised recycler. At present, every authorised recycler is required to recycle a maintain a minimum quantum of (300–500 tonnes e-waste) per annum. Instead, if small scale recycling/dismantling units are authorised, the informal sector units could be formalised this way, and transportation of collected e-waste would reach state-based recycler. Tracking e-waste within a state by the regulator would be easier, small scale unit (becoming informal to formal unit) would be able to treat e-waste in small quantities and reported, and consequently, how much e-waste residues (plastic, glass, etc.) other than the metals recovered go to the landfill could be quantified. Further, if market linkages are established for selling of secondary materials, landfills and consequent contamination could be controlled to great extent along with stoppage of leakage of e-waste. Thus, overall monitoring by the regulators improves at state level, in decentralised manner, along with participation of different stakeholders.

Tracking of recovered materials needs to be done on two counts – RE and CE, and toxicity; thus, along with economic value of recovered materials, data is availed on toxic materials recovered, leading to effective environment protection. This is an opportunity, and a challenge, too.

Monitoring import of e-waste – not duly addressed

Skinner et al. (2010) commented on the Draft Rules, 2010, based on a research on monitoring efforts in the EU and USA. This observation has come true and is still applicable, even after a decade. 'The draft rules are unlikely to stop e-waste imports, illegal or legal, as the complex mechanisms involved with monitoring imports, exports and domestically generated e-waste are all extremely resource-intensive,' (Skinner et al. 2010: 23). Monitoring in India could be 'hampered by a lack of international customs codes differentiating between new computers, old computers and e-waste, and a large number of entry and exit points for e-waste in each country.' (Ibid.) Further,

> the states possess the main responsibility for determining methods of monitoring and compliance may lead to additional administrative and compliance costs as well as differing degrees of enforcement...Unnecessary administrative

costs caused by legislative and monitoring contradictions and overlaps further add to the financial burden of enforcement activities.

(Ibid.)

Awareness raising responsibility of different stakeholders and their performance – producers, state governments, regulatory body

It is believed that if consumers are aware of e-waste, its composition with hazardous and non-hazardous substances, its potential for resource recovery and responsible use of e-products and disposal of e-waste could be enhanced; and in turn strengthen the formal or circular economy. Awareness can lead to behavioural changes, customers' commitment to 6Rs could be translated into practice. Thus, awareness is seen as a critical component of e-waste management; the Rules have mandated different stakeholders to spread awareness, which is considered to be promising opportunity.

Toxics Link report (2014b, 2015) showcased that limited awareness measures have been undertaken by producers. Toxics Link (2016) revealed that 66% of consumers (including bulk consumers) remained unaware of e-waste and the Rules, after five years of its implementation. These revelations articulate the challenges regarding awareness, implementation of EPR, and e-waste management, especially, the continuation of informal sector's operations, such as collection and unscientific recycling of e-waste, employing children as workers, and so on.

Different aspects of awareness on e-waste were discovered with studies carried out in different cities (see Chapter 6). The state governments and ULBs are made responsible for undertaking initiatives for e-waste management. With a special reference to Ahmedabad Municipal Corporation (AMC), a study has observed that most ULBs have no financial mechanism in place, which hinders e-waste collection activity. This makes producer compliance ever more vital (Shah 2014). The AMC had a tie up with an authorised recycler in 2017; however, the recycler did not get anticipated quantum of e-waste. 'Ahmedabad procures around 400 tonnes of electronic waste [every month]. Of this, only 13% is recycled,' (Patel 2017). A study on Pune city reported that its solid waste management system has to bear an extra 30% of load of e-waste not being separated, collected of recycled by the government institutions (Takale et al. 2015: 4241).

The challenges are as follow: various stakeholders – producers, state governments, SPCBs, etc. are responsible for spreading awareness on different aspects of e-waste management. However, in absence of availability of macro data, it is not clear – who has done what, how many initiatives, with which stakeholders, etc. awareness spreading, and impacts of awareness measures.

Coordination among different government agencies and missions

E-waste is complex. Different ministries are involved in e-waste management; for example, MoEFCC is a nodal ministry, MeitY has taken up various measures including awareness related, resource recovery related (through C-MET), role of Ministry of Science & Technology in innovation, etc. The strategy paper by MeitY and NITI Aayog (2019) on resource efficiency has mentioned involvement of three missions (Clean India, Digital India, and Make in India) – these are opportunities for e-waste management. However, concrete actions like budget/fund allocation, launch of a specific programme for e-waste management, upscaling C-MET experiment – from laboratory to commercial scale for recycling unit, etc. awaited. Some cities (e.g. Ahmedabad, Pune) have entered into association with an NGO for waste collection, including e-waste, and have created a channel from e-waste collection to recycling.

Disposal of e-waste by bulk consumers, specifically government agencies require changes in General Finance Rules (GFR). There are practical problems as against the Ahmedabad and Pune city is, a commissioner, in charge of waste management, faces issues of e-waste disposal and the revenue earned. It is observed[6] that if a municipal corporation ties up with a PRO for e-waste disposal, the revenue earned and associated financial auditing ask for changes in the present set up. It is also observed that the District Collector asks for an Executive Order/guidelines for e-waste disposal. For example, the Department of Science and Technology, Government of Gujarat has issued a notification in 2014 regarding e-waste disposal by the government agencies. This notification could be considered valid even after the *Rules, 2016* were enacted. However, the ULBs expressed a need for specific guidelines. Thus, such opportunities become challenges.

Scope for legal review, institutional feedback mechanism, grievance redressal mechanism needs to be built in

The existing regulation is as such in form of rules and not legislation in itself, thus the scope for implementation is restricted. While looking at from governance perspective, i.e. accountability, people's participation, and transparency, it becomes clear that it does not provide a scope for institutional feedback mechanism and grievance redressal mechanism. When any regulation directly deals with industrial matters, opportunity for its review is essential, as it can incorporate experience-based leaning and modification-based performance. The regulation thus evolves simultaneously with industrial development. Two mechanisms – institutional and grievance redressal – provide opportunities to plug the gaps identified during implementation of *the Rules*.

II: Economic concerns

Economic concerns include opportunities for CE through the existing/newer business model; building up infrastructure supported with a cadre of skilled workers; using green technology; dealing with market gaps and barriers; need for employment and skill building for repair and refurbishing units; and by fostering formal-informal sector partnership.

Business opportunities

E-waste is a value creating waste, mainly through the process of recovery of materials, and selling of recovered/secondary materials. Two opportunities created through the Rules – first, start-up for dismantling/recycling of e-waste; and second, being PRO and creating ecosystem for upscaling innovative and cohesive initiatives for e-waste management. There is a huge potential for job creation in the value chain of e-waste, including waste collectors, aggregators, repair shops, refurbishers, warehouse keepers, and transportation business. The e-waste sector has the potential to create around 6 million jobs, perhaps in just a few years. The opportunity for a start-up is linked to the legal provision – all state governments are made responsible for facilitating e-waste management related various activities including creating eco-parks, providing infrastructure, capacity and skill building of dismantling/recycling units, and workers engaged in e-waste collection and recycling for start-ups. 'Hub and Spoke model'[7] for infrastructure and viable recycling businesses is suggested (Chaturvedi and Gaurav 2016).

Financing for start-ups is a challenge. Recycling, its infrastructure, capital investment, inflow of e-waste, circular value creation across downstream and upstream, etc. challenges have been mentioned in the preceding chapters. Another set of challenges is whether or not a state government would be able to maintain e-waste focus in every infrastructure created for industrial purpose is to be seen, a challenge in itself.

Refurbishers occupy an important position in the emerging circular economy for electronics, as they extend the lifetime of both new and used EEE. However, in doing so, they invariably generate residues from the e-waste from the used EEE. Due to a lack of infrastructure and waste management systems, this e-waste is not always disposed of in a safe and environmentally sound manner (Shevchenko 2019).

Fostering formal-informal partnerships

In the existing set up, informal sector has a very organised network for collection to recycling of e-waste as well as selling of secondary materials. This sector has flourished on market-driven requirements and strategies, especially the entire value and trade chain, subsidising the cost of formal operations across the chain. Studying functioning of the informal sector players, their functioning, skills, management abilities, infrastructure, sustaining and expanding the network of various players in the entire value and trade chains, etc. and learning from them could be a value addition. This is a huge opportunity for moving towards formal economy, and away from the informal economy, and making the formal and circular economy sustainable. The informal sector has been recycling e-waste, and trading the secondary materials for more than four decades, and expanding exponentially. Building up formal-informal partnership can bring in more transparency, accountability, and auditability.

While focusing on collection and treatment (refurbish/dismantle/recycle) of e-waste, the existing regulatory framework has not taken cognisance of the informal sector in the country, dealing with e-waste and controlling entire value chain – from collection to recycling. As the regulation has not taken cognisance of unorganised sector, it does not entail measures for rehabilitating those persons who are engaged in the e-waste management operations in unorganised manner.

By not recognising existence of informal sector players, these Rules are also overlooking critical aspects of the objectives, 'how informal operations – collection to dismantling/recycling activities would be reduced.' Making informal sector and its range of activities for the trade chain as 'illegal' through regulatory measures would not deal with problem of dominance of informal sector in e-waste management (Agarwal 2016; Gaikwad 2019). Consequently, not paying adequate attention to health hazards, damage to environment, working conditions, wages, and social security of workers, etc. also would be continued until a suitable business model is developed. The existing Rules also need to harmonise with Labour Laws on this regard.

Employment and skills related concerns

There are a few persistent challenges for e-waste management, 'including but not limited to, employment opportunities for youth and women, re-skilling and up-skilling, establishing sustainable enterprises, green jobs and transitioning from informal to the informal economy.' (ILO 2019a: 9.)

No learnings from the informal sector regarding such skills, ability to trade recovered material in the domestic market, need for recycling infrastructure, and related projects that can help in building up small scale industrial units, etc. are not taking place. These are identified as barriers for moving towards formal economy, and resulting in losses to the formal economy. The Skill India promoting institutions and initiatives (such as NSDC, SWAYAM) can play trend-setting roles in this scenario. With skill upgradation and job creation processes, this sector can be very promising for economic growth, fulfilling requirements of safe environment as well as OSH, and rights of workers.

III: Environment concerns

Environment concerns include a range of issues from design, production to recycling (lifecycle to end-of-life cycle) and resource use (e.g. of carbon, fossils, water, energy, etc.); reduction of RoHS or totally substituting the use of hazardous substances; adopting green technology; safe disposal and alternatives to landfilling; techniques to identify and reuse components and materials (e.g. plastics, glass) as integral part of e-waste management. Such envisioning indicates potentials for safe environment and human health.

Adopting green technology

Green technology focuses on minimisation of energy, and use of natural resources, right from the design stage to the recycling stage. In terms of environment protection, two very important concerns – green technology and alternatives to landfill (as this is the only option for disposal of e-waste) – have remained underused in the existing regulatory framework.

Improvement in product design unheeded

One of most important policy principles of the EPR for e-products is to promote environment improvements, especially in the area of design of the products, production systems, and final disposal. The area of products includes factors such as product material, design, and expected life. The product design for environment/sustainable development (DfE/DfD), for instance, reducing or totally substituting the use of hazardous substances, adopting environment friendly technology, techniques to identify smooth dismantling/recycling, and reuse components and materials, including plastics and measures to promote the use of recycled plastics in new products, etc. This is an opportunity to promote improvements, if included in the regulatory framework; eventually, varied concerns of entrepreneurship/start-ups/business, viable technological solutions, and benefits of capitalist economy could be well elaborated, and their direct linkages could be established vis-à-vis CE as well as environment and health protection.

The 'E-Waste: From Toxic to Green initiative' by Chintan organisation could serve as a model to help other countries recycle e-waste and fight poverty. This model of handling e-waste is claimed to be highly replicable due to its low cost, it can be adopted by other cities, and countries where e-waste involves significant risk to workers, communities and the environment.[8]

Standardisation related

Standards have a harmonising effect and can remove trade barriers and enhance economic growth (CENELEC 2017) and ensure safety of all. The Rules have mandated the stakeholders to follow standards for storage, dismantling, recycling, and transportation; however, standardisation in the entire e-waste value chain is not conceived and not mentioned in the guidelines of the Rules. There is a need for developing India specific standards on the following: inventorisation of e-waste data; recycling and rate of resource recovery; depolluting standard – limit value for concentrations of hazardous substances during EoL treatment processes; and quality of secondary materials and cost.

These standards shall be aligned with global practices and methods, such as, WEEELabex, E-Stewards, R2 (responsible recycling) and CENELEC – this is an opportunity for harmonizing effect and removing trade barriers, as promoted by various stakeholders; they have suggested that these standards could be developed by the Bureau of Indian Standards in collaboration with CPCB, and in consultation with NITI Aayog and MoEFCC (Bhaskar 2019; Singhal 2019b). Recently, a bi-lateral agency, a couple of industry actors, and a research organisation have started working on standardisation; their consolidated efforts would build a step forward, encashing the opportunity.

Treatment facilities require to follow the defined standards. It is important to monitor downstream fractions, which provides a verifiable and accurate basis for the calculation of the recycling and recovery rates, and it provides a clear insight into the hazardous waste streams processed by downstream operators, with the state-of-art-technologies (ibid.).

Recycling and disposal of residues related issues partially addressed

Recycling capacity has been increasing through increase in number of formal units since 2011. This is seen as an opportunity for greater resource recovery/efficiency, building database on recycling processes, etc. Though the number of authorised recycling units have increased, final disposal of e-waste in environmentally sound manner is a significant challenge for India, especially in the context of dominant presence of informal sector for e-waste collection to the recycling, selling of secondary materials, and limited availability state-of-art technology and infrastructure for recycling (capacity of recycling), and its sustainability.

The *Rules, 2016* assume that greater e-waste collection would lead to greater recycling and recovery of resources; in this context, mandating 'recycling target' shall be useful. As number of authorised recycling units have increased manifold under the Rules, opportunity is created for scientific way of recycling, increasing resource efficiency, reducing adverse impact on human health and environment, and so on. As against this opportunity, a couple of problems/ challenges are elaborated for low rate of recycling of e-waste in India.

> recycling charge is dependent on multiple factors including but not limited to the cost of procurement from multiple channels, cost of development of channels, logistics cost, ecosystem development costs as well as returns from recycling which could be positive or negative.
>
> (Sinha 2019b: 142)

Such situations mostly results into 'cherry picking – whereby only the positive value fractions are recycled – is rife. Negative value fractions, such as CRT TVs or lamps, are not found attractive, and therefore not accepted by many recyclers,' (Sinha 2019b: 142).

1. Material composition of electronics is changing with technological advances, over time, resulting into lesser amount of recovery and intrinsic value of recovered materials after recycling of e-products/e-waste, thus affecting economics of recycling.

   > Recyclers and producers agree that monitoring and control are essential. Recyclers want monitoring to ensure more producers are financing formal recycling, and there is a crackdown on informal recycling; producers want

monitoring to ensure recyclers meet standards and are not engaged in paper trading.

(ibid: 143)

2. Recycling facility cannot be generalized, as composition of every e-product is different from the other. Many Indian recycling units have witnessed failure, as they started recycling unit with latest technology and huge investment; as against that, the e-waste flow and economics of recovered material was skewed.
3. 'Employing effective recycling technologies for e-waste may require significant upfront capital expenditures, which may not be justified for private entities in the absence of certainty around sourcing of enough quantities of e-waste. Also, these markets suffer from information barriers.' (Turaga 2019: 130.) For example, learning from the informal sector is not taking place, low awareness and lack of reliable information affect functioning of recycling activities.
4. Some critical aspects of recycling/micro-management of recycling to be addressed, such as, optimising recovery and product specific method for optimum recovery; infrastructure and technology required for product specific dismantling/recycling and capital required for a start-up; sustainability of a dismantling/recycling unit based on quality and quantum of e-waste received, resources recovered, and selling of recovered/secondary material, and so on.

While comparing the *WEEE Directive* and the *Rules, 2016*, Kopacek (2019) has articulated two major challenges for treating e-waste – first, rapid technological advances (including 3D printing) make it necessary to keep up with the fast progress and develop constantly new recycling processes. Second, more and more chemical processes may take over because the e-products become a more and more complex mix of materials. These points require proper guidelines, suitable infrastructure, future planning and readiness to bring about necessary changes in different ways of e-waste management.

IV: Recycling culture/recycling society

The recycling culture is a civil society centric concept and a requirement, beyond the regulatory framework, wherein all the stakeholders remain the same/not distinctly categorised. Role of awareness in enhancement of e-waste collection, recycling, and resource recovery has been well established. Realisation of the 6Rs is an opportunity that can change the existing scenario of e-waste. Academic courses started on SWAYAM and upscaling through many more educational institutions engaging in academic courses, research, and activities would be highly appreciative effort towards realising this concept among the audience, especially students/youngsters who believed to be in large number as users of e-products.

The present vicious cycle of 'Consume–Collect–Recover–Dispose' is considered as a model in practice. This is found to be inadequate based on the argument that it results in unbridled accumulation of e-waste in the environment. As awareness and knowledge on the subject tends to determine their recycling behaviour (Malhotra 2020), 'recycling culture' requires deeper thinking including role of different social actors, and how to mainstream the concept of recycling society.

The dust is yet to settle

One of the major learnings for e-waste management is that there cannot be one-fits-to-all approach; neither within a nation nor any comparison between nations. Three most common concerns about e-waste – transboundary movements, dominant presence of informal sector and small portion of e-waste being collected and recycled, and need for legislation or regulatory framework in every country have been stressed upon. Ghana reported high levels of imported e-waste, and severe impacts of e-waste recycling by the informal sector on human health a decade ago. Now,

> *Technical Guidelines on Environmentally Sound E-Waste Management for Collectors, Collection Centers, Transporters, Treatment Facilities, and Final Disposal* have been developed and are being enforced. In Nigeria, the EPR took off with formation of the E-waste Producer Responsibility Organization of Nigeria (EPRON), a non-profit organization set up by electrical and electronic producers.
>
> (Forti et al. 2020: 69)

Once, Agbogbloshie in Ghana was considered to be an e-waste dumpsite; now, 'it can be described as well-organized scrapyard,' (ibid.). Ghana, Nigeria, and Kenya in Africa are still the countries where informal sector is still dominant in the entire trade value chain. Guiyu in China once was known as an e-waste dumpsite; now it is a hub in the global e-waste trade. A vast complex of large industrial hangars, rooms, and multi-storied houses, each filled to the brim with e-waste. The workers are mechanically disassembling with simple tools and wearing basic protective gear. Necessary infrastructure and market linkages are organised in Guiyu (Mujezinovic 2019). It is expected that India, too, will evolve on the counts of market access, Eco-park development, formal-informal partnership for dealing with e-waste, and creating level playing fields for different actors.

Key learnings of EU countries, especially enforcement of regulations; several policy considerations including futuristic estimation about e-waste generation and treatment related processes to be undertaken; smart city concept to be operationalized from environment (toxic free environment) and sustainability (zero waste policy) perspective; driving the transition through research, innovation, and digitisation; sustainable finance – taxonomy, corporate governance framework; developing EU green bond standards; and so on. Referring to India-EU Resource Efficiency and Circular Economy Partnership, declared in July 2020, operationalising such partnership is certainly an opportunity for e-waste management in India; incorporating of human and social costs in the RE, CE enhancing model would turn the opportunity into long term benefits for India.

Continuing enforcement of the Rules and innovative initiatives

The regulation driven business initiatives have started showing results as indicative of enforcement of *the Rules*, such as, increase in number of authorised PROs and development of their ecosystems as well as formalization of informal waste collection, increase in number of dismantlers/recyclers, resulting into recycling capacity, compliance by the bulk consumers, discussions on etc. These initiatives show a shift in the discourse of e-waste management, i.e. from WHY e-waste management to HOW e-waste management. Newer topics of discussions have begun, such as, resource efficiency and circular economy, newer technology, methods of recovery are tried out by the GoI at laboratory level, infrastructure have to be set up accordingly on industrial scale, and standardisation across value chain. The RoHS has been largely complied by the producers. Such beginning for e-waste management is encouraging.

Challenges have been identified, such as, waste aggregation is not discussed much despite being an important concern, cherry picking of e-waste for recycling, paper trading and leakage of e-waste make several players feel 'lack of level playing field;' document submission related compliance is low and how to increase it through regular monitoring; cost of compliance for every producer and every product needs to be worked out; tie up of bulk consumers, producers, and PROs with government run platform like MSTC and streamlining process of metal scrap auctioning; need for sectoral 'should cost analysis' including procurement, logistics, recycling and recovery, and administrative, etc. need for initiating processes of dialogues and networking among different stakeholders, especially the recyclers and PROs rather increasing competitive and conflicting areas of interests; need for fostering informal-formal partnerships; and so on. Regarding recycling/treatment of e-waste, standardisation of depollution practices is required; along with collection of e-waste, resource recovery targets need to be specified; how to finance recycling infrastructure and technology, and creating market access for sale of secondary materials are challenges that are to be addressed.

Areas for further action and research have been identified: several micro studies are required on different components of e-waste management. For example, to quantify the impact of e-waste (exposure to metals, small particulate matter, POPs, and PAHs); environmental risk assessment; economics and sustainability of small/medium scale processing for current informal recyclers; upstream and downstream flows of e-waste and secondary materials; 'voluntary consensus sustainability standard'; and so on.

Chaurvedi and Gaurav (2016) have suggested a few initiatives, such as the State–civic–business alliances – ULB or SPCB – could play lead roles in such formation; strengthening links between ULBs and SPCB in every state; 'Hub and Spoke model' for infrastructure and viable recycling businesses. Other ideas for action include creation of a knowledgebase, developing a strategy for raw materials and secondary resource, market for sale of recovered/secondary material and linkages to be developed, capacity building of regulators, debate and engagement with informality, deepening engagement of SPCB with OEMs and formal recyclers, cross-ministry collaboration for developing effective policies and programme on e-waste.

The *Rules, 2016* are yet to be studied from different perspectives in depth, for example, 'environmental justice,' 'recycling culture' or 'recycling society,' 'sustainability' and 'voluntary sustainability standards,' and 'circular economy with human ad social costs.' When e-waste regulations would be studied from these perspectives, they would be able to articulate opportunities and challenges.

The environment justice perspective draws attention on uneven distribution of economic benefits and environmental health costs. The 'producer' focused policy (EPR) encourages the private companies to take profit-oriented strategies and hence leads to involvement of the formal recycling companies. This equation is the most suitable to the concept of CE, and intent of safe environment and human health but does not enter policy debates showcasing the existing inequality, that is, environmental health hazards faced by socially and economically powerless workers and local residents or its potential root cause. This set of stakeholders is yet to be engaged with and to be recognised in the policy-making in India.

Notes

1 Karo Sambhav Pvt. Ltd., an authorised PRO has mentioned their focus areas: inclusion, fairness, convergence & scalability, traceability, transparency, and auditability as part of e-waste management. To ensure transparency and auditability, Karo has developed tech-platform, which is also used to create a database.
2 Issuance of certificates of recycling for materials that have not even been sent to recycling by the recyclers to the concerned part (PRO/producer). Aggregators of e-waste have shared that some PROs have offered to pay them 5% GST and 10% commission for making an invoice without physical transaction and collection of e-waste.
3 E-waste which has been collected and recycled is allocated to multiple brands leading to a situation where a collection/recycling of 100 tons is shown as allocated to five different brands with targets of 100 tons each.
4 This portion was discussed in the conference on 'A circular economy in E-waste for an Atmanirbhar Bharat conference' on 14 October 2020 as part of celebration of 'International E-waste Day' organized by Karo Sambhav Pvt. Ltd. Recording of the conference is available at https://www.youtube.com/watch?v=MKb0aETylYE&t=1s
5 In a personal interview with Shri Devang Thakar, engineer, in charge of e-waste management, Gujarat State Pollution Control Board (GSPCB), dated 10 April 2021.
6 Based on the author's personal experience during 2018. Municipal Commissioners of Bikaner and Nagpur cities shared this problem. The then District Collector of Kachchh district insisted for the Executive Order for disposal of e-waste through ULBs.
7 A hub and spoke model for recycling (for solid waste) – a hub is established to shoulder the financial burden of operating a recycling centre. The spokes, which are typically located in very rural areas, provide the hubs with recyclable materials. The hubs process the material and benefit from capturing the value of the material that they market. The spokes don't benefit from the sale of the recyclables, and they are not liable for any of the

expenses that come with operating the facility (https://www.waste360.com/business/benefits-hub-and-spoke-recycling-system accessed on 2 August 2020). For e-waste recycling, CPCB or MeitY can provide strategic orientation for development of adequate and appropriate infrastructure.

8 Accessed from https://unfccc.int/climate-action/momentum-for-change/lighthouse-activities/e-waste-from-toxic-to-green on 26 August 2020.

BIBLIOGRAPHY

Agarwal, Arpit. 2016. 'E-waste management in India: New rules, old problems'. *Sustainability outlook*, April 29. Retrieved from http://www.sustainabilityoutlook.in/content/e-waste-management-india-new-rules-old-problems-756361 accessed on 4 July 2020.

Agarwal, Richa, and Arupendra Nath Mullick. 2014. *E-waste management in India – The corporate imperative*. Mumbai: YES Bank Ltd. and New Delhi: TERI-BCSD (Business Council for Sustainable Development). Retrieved from http://cbs.teriin.org/pdf/researchreports/EWasteManagementReport.pdf accessed on 23 April 2020.

Ali, Lafir, and Y.C. Chan. 2008. 'Impact of RoHS/WEEE- on effective recycling- electronics system integration'. *2008 2nd Electronics System integration Technology Conference*. DOI: 10.1109/estc.2008.4684403.

Anand, Kumar. 2019. 'Implementation experience of current Indian legislation – E-waste (Management) Rules, 2016'. Presented at Electronic Waste Policy Awareness Workshop. New Delhi: Central Pollution Control Board. Retrieved from https://www.itu.int/en/ITU-D/Regional-Presence/AsiaPacific/SiteAssets/Pages/Events/2019/Policy-awareness-workshop-on-E-waste/27-11-2019%20Implementation%20experience%20of%20current%20%20Indian%20Legislation.pdf accessed on 28 April 2020.

Arora, Rachna, Ulrike Killguss, Ashish Chaturvedi, and David Rochat. 2019b. 'Wither e-waste in India – the Indo-Germen-Swiss initiative'. In Johri Rakesh (ed.). *E-Waste: Implications, regulations, and management in India and current global best practices* (pp. 69–87). New Delhi: TERI press (second reprint).

Arora, Rachna, Katharina Paterok, Abhijit Banerjee, and Manjeet Singh Saluja. 2017. 'Potential and relevance of urban mining in the context of sustainable cities'. *IIMB Management Review*, xx: 1–15. DOI: 10.1016/j.iimb.2017.06.001.

Arora, Rachna, Reva Prakash, Pranav Sinha, and Gautam Mehra. 2019a. 'Resource efficiency and circular economy paradigms towards e-waste management'. In Neeta Mishra, Sarina Bolla, and Kalyan Bhaskar (eds.). *E-waste roadmap 2030 for India: A compilation of thought pieces by sector experts* (pp. 68–73), Delhi: IFC and Karo Sambhav Pvt. Ltd.

Bibliography

ASSOCHAM-cKinetics. 2017. 'Electronic waste management in India'. *Associated Chambers of Commerce and Industry of India* (ASSOCHAM). Retrieved from https://www.assocham.org/newsdetail.php?id=5725 accessed on 8 August 2019.

ASSOCHAM-NEC. 4 June 2018a. 'India among the top five countries in e-waste generation: ASSOCHAM-NEC study'. Retrieved from https://www.assocham.org/newsdetail.php?id=6850 accessed on 4 September 2019.

ASSOCHAM-NEC. 2018b. *Electricals and electronics manufacturing in India.* Retrieved from https://in.nec.com/en_IN/pdf/ElectricalsandElectronicsManufacturingInIndia2018.pdf accessed on 6 July 2020.

Awasthi, Abhishek Kumar, Xianlai Zeng, and Jinhui Li. 2016. 'Environmental pollution of electronic waste in India: A critical review'. *Environmental Pollution*, 211: 259–270. DOI:10.1016/j.envpol.2015.11.027.

Babu, Balakrishnan Ramesh, Anand Kuber Parande, and Chiya Ahmed Basha. 2007. 'Electrical and electronics waste: A global environment problem'. *Waste Management Research*, 25: 307–318. DOI: 10.1177/0734242X07076941.

Baldé, C.P., V. Forti, V. Gray, R. Kuehr, and P. Stegmann. 2017. *The global e-waste monitor: Quantities, flows, and resources.* United Nations University-Institute for the Advanced Study of Sustainability. Retrieved from https://www.itu.int/en/ITU-D/Climate-Change/Documents/GEM%202017/Global-E-waste%20Monitor%202017%20.pdf accessed on 20 November 2018.

Baldé, C.P., F. Wang, and R. Kuehr, 2016. *Transboundary movements of used and waste electronic and electrical equipment.* United Nations University, Vice Rectorate in Europe – Sustainable Cycles Programme (SCYCLE). Bonn, Germany. Retrieved from http://www.step-initiative.org/files/_documents/other_publications/UNU-Transboundary-Movement-of-Used-EEE.pdf accessed on 9 April 2020.

Baldé, C.P., F. Wang, R. Kuehr, and J. Huisman. 2015. *The global e-waste monitor – 2014.* Bonn, Germany: United Nations University, IAS – SCYCLE. Retrieved from https://i.unu.edu/media/unu.edu/news/52624/UNU-1stGlobal-E-Waste-Monitor-2014-small.pdf accessed on 20 November 2018.

Bastein, Ton, Elsbeth Roelofs, Elmer Rietveld, and Alwin Hoogendoorn. 2013. *Opportunities for circular economy in the Netherlands.* Netherlands: TNO Innovation for life. Retrieved from https://www.tno.nl/media/8551/tno-circular-economy-for-ienm.pdf accessed on 21 June 2020.

Basu, Shubhankar. 2019. 'E-waste generation, mitigation, and a case study, Delhi'. In Johri Rakesh (ed.). *E-Waste: Implications, regulations, and management in India and current global best practices* (pp. 45–68), New Delhi: TERI press (second reprint).

Berners-Lee, Mike. 2010. 'What's the carbon footprint of…using a mobile phone?'. *The Guardian*, 9 June. Retrieved from https://www.theguardian.com/environment/green-living-blog/2010/jun/09/carbon-footprint-mobile-phone accessed on 10 August 2020.

Bharadwaj Rai, Shruti. 2016. 'Extended producer responsibility in e-waste perspective: Indian perspective'. *International Workshop on Extended Producer Responsibility in India: Opportunities, challenges and lessons from international experience*, May 12–13, 2016. Retrieved from https://www.oecd.org/environment/waste/Session_1-EPR-in-E-waste-management-Indian-Prospective-Shruti_Rai.pdf accessed on 20 November 2018.

Bhaskar, Kalyan. 2019. 'E-waste management and business in India – What Lied ahead?: Colloquium – E-waste management in India: Issues and strategies'. *VIKALPA*, 44(3): 154–157. DOI: 10.1177/0256090919880655.

Bhaskar, Kalyan, and Ram Mohan Turaga. 2017. 'India's e-waste rules and their impact on e-waste management practices: A case study'. *Journal of Industrial Ecology*, 22(4): 930–942. DOI: 10.1111/jiec.12619.

Bhat, Viraja, and Yogesh Patil. 2014. 'E-waste consciousness and disposal practices among residents of Pune city'. *Procedia – Social and Behavioral Sciences*, 133(2014): 491–498. DOI:10.1016/j.sbspro.2014.04.216.

Borthakur, Anwesha, and Madhav Govind. 2017. 'How well are we managing E-waste in India: Evidences from the city of Bangalore'. *Energy, Ecology, and Environment*, 2(4): 225–235. DOI: 10.1007/s40974-017-0060-0.

Brandl, H., R. Bosshard, and M. Wegmann. 2001. 'Computer-munching microbes: Metal leaching from electronic scrap by bacteria and fungi'. *Hydrometallurgy*, 59(2): 319–326. DOI: 10.1016/S0304-386X(00)00188-2.

Brigden, Kevin. 2008. *Waste recycling and disposal sites in Accra and Korfuridua, Ghana*. Amsterdam: Greenpeace Research Laboratories, Technical note 10/2008.

Brigden, K., I. Labunska, D. Santillo, and M. Allsopp. 2005. 'Recycling of electronic wastes in China and India'. *Work Place & Environmental Contamination*, pp. 1–56. Amsterdam: Greenpeace. Retrieved from https://www.greenpeace.to/publications/chemical-contamination-at-e-wa.pdf accessed on 23 February 2020.

Buchert, Matthias, Andreas Manhart, Daniel Bleher, and Detlef Pingel. 2012. *Recycling critical raw materials from waste electronic equipment*. Freiburg, Germany: Öeko-Institute. Retrieved from https://www.oeko.de/oekodoc/1375/2012-010-en.pdf accessed on 12 May 2020.

CAG (Comptroller and Auditor General). 2015. 'Chapter 7, Ministry of Environment and Forests, Compliance Scientific department report'. Report no. 30 of 2015. New Delhi: Government of India. Retrieved from https://cag.gov.in/sites/default/files/audit_report_files/Union_Compliance_Scientific_Departmen_Report_30_2015_chap_7.pdf accessed on 23 July 2020.

Cao, Jian, Bo Lu, Yangyang Chen, Xuemei Zhang, Guangshu Zhai, Gengui Zhou, Boxin Jiang, and Jerald L. Schnoor. 2016. 'Extended producer responsibility system in China improves e-waste recycling: Government policies, enterprise, and public awareness'. *Renew Sustainable Energy Reviews*, 62: 882–894. DOI:10.1016/j.rser.2016.04.078.

CENELEC. 2017. *European standards for waste electrical and electronic equipment (WEEE): Collection, transport, re-use, treatment*. Brussels: CENELEC. Retrieved from https://www.cencenelec.eu/news/publications/publications/weee-brochure.pdf accessed on 23 June 2020.

Central Pollution Control Board (CPCB). 2004. *Report of the national workshop on Electronic Waste Management*. Retrieved from https://www.mpcb.gov.in/sites/default/files/electronic-waste/related-documents/archives/weee.pdf accessed on 10 July 2020.

Central Pollution Control Board (CPCB). 2016. *Implementation guidelines for E-waste (Management) Rules, 2016*. New Delhi: Government of India. Retrieved from http://www.wbpcb.gov.in/writereaddata/files/GUIDELINES_E%20WASTE_RULES_2016.pdf accessed on 17 November 2017.

Central Pollution Control Board (CPCB). 2019. *List of authorised e-waste dismantler /recycler as on 27.06.2019*. Retrieved from http://greene.gov.in/wp-content/uploads/2019/09/2019091881.pdf accessed on 28 April 2020.

Centre for Science and Environment (CSE). 2014. *Strengthen institutions, reform laws and streamline processes*. New Delhi: Centre for Science and Environment. Retrieved from http://www.indiaenvironmentportal.org.in/files/file/strengthen-institutions-reform-laws-and-streamline-processes_0.pdf (accessed on 20 July 2020).

Centre for Science and Environment (CSE). 2015. *Recommendations to address the issue of informal sector involved in e-waste handling: Moradabad, Uttar Pradesh*. New Delhi: Centre for Science and Environment. Retrieved from https://cdn.downtoearth.org.in/pdf/moradabad%20-e-waste.pdf accessed on 26 May 2020.

Chatterjee, S., and Krishna Kumar. 2009. 'Effective electronic waste management and recycling process involving formal and non-formal sectors'. *International Journal of Physical Sciences*, 4(13): 893–905. Retrieved from https://academicjournals.org/article/article1380705620_Chatterjee%20and%20Kumar.pdf accessed on 25 May 2020.

Chatterjee, Sandip, and Priyanka Porwal. 2019. 'Awareness about electronic waste in India'. In Neeta Mishra, Sarina Bolla, and Kalyan Bhaskar (eds.). *E-waste roadmap 2030 for India: A compilation of thought pieces by sector experts* (pp. 58–63). Delhi: IFC and Karo Sambhav Pvt. Ltd.

Chaturvedi, Ashish, Rachna Arora, and Sharon Ahmad. 2010. 'Mainstreaming the informal sector in e-waste management'. *Paper presented for Workshop on Urban, Industrial and Hospital Waste Management* on 7–8 May 2010. Ahmedabad: Saket Projects and Gujarat Pollution Control Board. Retrieved from http://nswai.com/docs/Mainstreaming%20the%20Informal%20Sector%20in%20E-Waste%20Management%20(1).pdf accessed on 25 June 2020.

Chaturvedi, Ashish, and Jay Kumar Gaurav. 2016. 'E-waste management in India: Key issues and recommendations', paper presented at symposium on *E-waste to no waste*, Mumbai: Bombay Chamber of Commerce & Industry. Retrieved from http://bombaychamber.com/admin/uploaded/Reference%20Material/Paper%20on%20E-Waste%20Management%20in%20India.pdf accessed on 4 May 2020.

Chaturvedi, Ashish, Gautam Mehra, Sonal Chaturvedi, and Jai Kumar Gaurav. 2016b. *E-waste awareness for bulk consumers: Manual for training of trainers*. New Delhi: Ministry of Electronics and Information Technology, Government of India. Retrieved from http://greene.gov.in/wp-content/uploads/2018/01/Day-1_manual_final-ilovepdf-compressed-ilovepdf-compressed.pdf accessed on 21 January 2020.

Chaturvedi, Ashish, Gautam Mehra, Sonal Chaturvedi, and Jai Kumar Gaurav. 2016c. *E-waste awareness for manufacturers: Manual for training of trainers*. New Delhi: Ministry of Electronics and Information Technology, Government of India. Retrieved from http://greene.gov.in/wp-content/uploads/2018/01/Manufacturers_Manual_v8-2-1.pdf accessed on 23 July 2020.

Chaturvedi, Ashish, Gautam Mehra, Sonal Chaturvedi, and Jai Kumar Gaurav. 2016d. *E-waste awareness for government officials: Manual for training of trainers/1 Day*. New Delhi: Ministry of Electronics and Information Technology, Government of India. Retrieved from http://greene.gov.in/wp-content/uploads/2018/01/Day-1_manual_final-ilovepdf-compressed-ilovepdf-compressed.pdf accessed on 21 June 2020.

Chaudhary, Nivedita. 2018. 'Electronic waste in India: A study of penal issues'. *ILI Law Review*, II (Winter Issue): 1–25. Retrieved from http://ili.ac.in/pdf/env.pdf accessed on 8 July 2020.

Chen, Yu, Chen Mengjun, Li Yungui, Wang, Bin, Chen Shu, and Zhonghui Xu. 2018. 'Impact of technological innovation and regulation development on e-waste toxicity: A case study of waste mobile phones'. *Scientific Reports*, pp. 1–9. Retrieved from www.nature.com/scientificreports

Committee on Subordinate Legislation (2015–2016). *Rules on e-waste management (Presented to Lok Sabha on 10.8.2-16) (Sixteenth Lok Sabha) Fifteenth report*. New Delhi: Lok Sabha Secretariat. Retrieved from http://www.indiaenvironmentportal.org.in/files/file/RULES%20ON%20E-WASTE%20MANAGEMENT.pdf accessed on 3 April 2020.

Darnall D.W., B. Greene, M.T. Henzl, J.M. Hosea, R.A. McPherson, J. Sneddon, and M.D. Alexander 1986. 'Selective recovery of gold and other metal ions from an algal biomass'. *Environment Science Technology*, 20(2): 206–208. DOI: 10.1021/es00144a018.

Bibliography

Darshan, P.C., and S.Vidhya Lakshmi. 2016. 'Global and Indian e-waste management – methods & effects'. Retrieved from https://www.researchgate.net/publication/310442485 accessed on 3 April 2020.

Debnath, Biswajit, Ranjana Chowdhury, and Sadhan Kumar Ghosh. 2018. 'Sustainability of metal recovery from e-waste'. *Frontiers of Environmental Science & Engineering*, 12(6): 1–13. DOI: 10.1007/s11783-018-1044-9.

Dimitrakakis, Emmanouil Evangelos Gidarakos, Subhankar Basu, K.V. Rajeshwari, Rakesh Johri, Bernd Bilitewski, and Matthias Schirmer. 2006. 'Creation of optimum knowledge bank on e-waste management in India'. Retrieved from https://www.iswa.org/uploads/tx_iswaknowledgebase/3b_-_1145_-_P_-_Gidarakos_et_al_-_Uni_GR.pdf accessed on 28 June 2020.

Down To Earth. 28 June 2015. 'Tricks of the e-waste trade'. *Down To Earth*. Retrieved from https://www.downtoearth.org.in/coverage/tricks-of-the-ewaste-trade--325 accessed on 24 December 2019.

Duan, H. Miller, T.R. Gregory, J. and Kirchain, R. 2013. *Quantitative Characterization of Domestic and Transboundary Flows of Used Electronics, Analysis of Generation, Collection, and Export in the United States*. Massachusetts: Massachusetts Institute of Technology. Retrieved from http://www.step-initiative.org/files/_documents/other_publications/MIT-NCER%20 US%20Used%20Electronics%20Flows%20Report%20-%20December%202013.pdf accessed on 9 April 2020

Dwivedy, Maheshwar, and R.K. Mittal. 2010a. 'Estimation of future outflows of e-waste in India'. *Waste Management*, 30(3): 483–491. DOI:10.1016/j.wasman.2009.09.024.

Dwivedy, Maheshwar, and R.K. Mittal. 2010b. 'Future trends in computer waste generation in India'. *Waste Management*, 30(11): 2265–2277. DOI:10.1016/j.wasman.2010.06.025.

Dwivedy, Maheshwar, and R.K. Mittal. 2012. 'An investigation into e-waste flows in India'. *Journal of Cleaner Production*, 37 (2012): 229–242. DOI:10.1016/j.jclepro.2012.07.017.

ELCINA Electronic Industries Association of India. 2007. *Country report on the Indian electronic sector: Issues and capacity building needs in relation to international and national product-related environmental regulations and other requirements*. EuropeAid Cooperation Office. Retrieved from https://cfsd.org.uk/Indian_AEDE_Report.pdf accessed on 13 April 2020.

Elia, Valerio, and Maria Grazia Gnoni. 2015. 'How to design and manage WEEE systems: A multi-level analysis'. *International Journal of Environment and Waste Management*, 15(3): 271–294. DOI:10.1504/ijewm.2015.069165.

Ellen Macarthur Foundation. 2013. *Towards the circular economy: Economy and business rationale for an accelerate transition*. United Kingdom: Ellen Macarthur Foundation. Retrieved from https://www.ellenmacarthurfoundation.org/assets/downloads/publications/Ellen-MacArthur-Foundation-Towards-the-Circular-Economy-vol.1.pdf accessed on 31 March 2020.

'Joint statement – 15th EU-India Summit, 15 July 2020', European Commission News, 15 July 2020. Available at https://www.consilium.europa.eu/en/press/press-releases/2020/07/15/joint-statement-15th-eu-india-summit-15-july-2020/

European Union (EU). 2018. *Report on critical materials and circular economy*, Brussels 16.1.2018 SWD (2018) 36 final PART 1/3. Brussels: European Union. Retrieved from https://ec.europa.eu/docsroom/documents/27327/attachments/1/translations/en/renditions/native accessed on 16 December 2019.

EXPRA. (2013). *Extended Producer Responsibility at a glance*. Retrieved from www.expra.eu:www.expra.eu/uploads/downloads/EXPRA%20EPR%20Paper_March_2016.pdf accessed on 23 December 2019.

Ffact, Recupel, and UNU-ISP (United Nations University-Institute for Sustainability and Peace). 2013. *(W)EEE mass balance and market structure in Belgium*, Delft: Ffact and UNU-ISP. Retrieved from http://i.unu.edu/media/unu.edu/news/39523/Recupel-Report-FINAL.pdf accessed on 12 May 2020.

Forti, Vanessa, Baldé Cornelis Peter, Kuehr Ruediger, and Bel Garam. 2020. *The Global E-waste Monitor 2020: Quantities, flows and the circular economy potential*. Bonn/Geneva/Rotterdam: United Nations University (UNU)/United Nations Institute for Training and Research (UNITAR) – co-hosted SCYCLE Programme, International Telecommunication Union (ITU) & International Solid Waste Association (ISWA). Retrieved from http://ewaste-monitor.info/wp-content/uploads/2020/07/GEM_2020_def_july1_low.pdf# accessed on 7 July 2020.

Gaikwad, Vaibhav. 2019. *A very short policy brief: Improving e-waste management in India*, Vol. 11 (January). Australia: Australia India Institute. Retrieved from https://www.aii.unimelb.edu.au/wp-content/uploads/2019/01/26912-AII-Very-Short-Policy-Brief-VOL-11-p2.pdf accessed on 23 April 2020.

GIZ. 2017. *Building the link: Leveraging formal-informal partnerships in the Indian e-waste sector*. Bonn and Eschborn, Germany: Deutsche Gesellschaft für Internationale Zusammenarbeit (GIZ) GmbH. Retrieved from https://www.giz.de/en/downloads/giz2017-en-formal-informal-partnerships-e-waste-india.pdf accessed on 3 April 2020.

GIZ. 2018. *Creating successful formal-informal partnerships in the Indian e-waste sector: Practical guidance for implementation under the Indian E-waste Rules*. Bonn and Eschborn, Germany: Deutsche Gesellschaft für Internationale Zusammenarbeit (GIZ) GmbH.

GIZ and MESTI (Ministry of Environment, Science, Technology and Innovation). 2019. *E-waste training manual*. Bonn and Eschborn, Germany: Deutsche Gesellschaft für Internationale Zusammenarbeit (GIZ) GmbH. Retrieved from https://www.giz.de/en/downloads/giz2019-e-waste-management.pdf accessed on 20 February 2020.

Greenpeace. 2005. *Recycling of electronic wastes in China & India: Workplace & environmental contamination*. UK: Greenpeace International.

GTZ. 2010. *The waste experts: Enabling conditions for informal sector integration in solid waste management*. Germany: GTZ.

GTZ. 2011. *Recovering resources, creating opportunities: Integrating the informal sector into solid waste management*. Germany: GTZ.

Gui, Luyi, Atalay Atasu, Özlem Ergun, and L. Beril Toktay. 2013. 'Implementing extended producer responsibility legislation'. *Journal of Industrial Ecology*, DOI: 10.1111/j.1530-9290.2012.00574.x.

Ha, Nguyen Ngoc, Tetsuro Agusa, Karri Ramu, Nguyen Phuc Cam Tu, Satoko Murata, Keshav A. Bulbule, Peethmbaram Parthasaraty, Shin Takahashi, Annamalai Subramanian, and Shinsuke Tanabe. 2009. 'Contamination by trace elements at e-waste recycling sites in Bangalore, India'. *Chemosphere*, 76(1): 9–15. DOI:10.1016/j.chemosphere.2009.02.056.

Haldar, P. C. 2020. 'Foreword'. In Manika Malhotra (ed.). *E-waste management: Policy analysis and implementation* (p. vii). New Delhi: The PPF – Centre for Cohesive Society Studies. Retrieved from https://www.ppf.org.in/wp-content/uploads/2020/02/Final-E-Waste-Management_Feb-2020-PPF.pdf accessed on 23 July 2020.

Henam, Sonia. 23 March 2018. 'Centre amends e-waste management rules 2016 yet again'. *Down to Earth*. Retrieved from https://www.downtoearth.org.in/news/waste/centre-amends-e-waste-management-rules-2017-yet-again-60021 accessed on 24 December 2019.

Honda, Shunichi, Deepali Sinha Khetriwal, and Ruediger Kuehr. 2016. *Regional E-waste Monitor: East and Southeast Asia*. Bonn, Germany: United Nations University and Tokyo:

Japanese Ministry of the Environment. Retrieved from http://ewastemonitor.info/pdf/Regional-E-Waste-Monitor.pdf accessed on 7 April 2020.

Inagaki, Hiromi. 2008. *The myth of 'Environmentally Sound' management of e-waste: A case study from computer recycling activities in Delhi, India. Research paper for partial fulfilment of Masters of Arts in Development Studies*, The Hague: Institute of Social Studies. Retrieved from https://thesis.eur.nl/pub/7117/Hiromi%20Inagaki%20ESD.pdf accessed on 11 April 2020.

Institute for Global Environmental Strategies (IGES). 2012. 'Applying EPR in developing countries'. *Rio+20 towards and beyond*, Vol 3, March, UN conference on Sustainable Development. Retrieved from http://www.iges.or.jp/en/rio20/ accessed on 25 May 2020.

IIML (Indian Institute of Management, Lucknow). 2010. *Evaluation of Central Pollution Control Board (CPCB)*, New Delhi: Ministry of Environment and Forest, Government of India. Retrieved from http://www.indiaenvironmentportal.org.in/files/Rpt_CPCB.pdf accessed on 1 May 2020.

International Labour Organisation (ILO). 2014. *Tackling informality in e-waste: The potential of cooperative enterprises in the management of e-waste*. Sectoral Activities Department (SECTOR), Cooperatives Unit (COOP) – Geneva: ILO. Retrieved from https://www.ilo.org/public/libdoc/ilo/2014/114B09_165_engl.pdf accessed on 12 January 2020.

International Labour Organisation (ILO). 2019a. *Decent work in the management of electrical and electronic waste (e-waste)*, Issue paper for the Global Dialogue Forum on Decent Work in the management of Electrical and Electronics Waste (E-Waste), 11–12, April. Geneva: ILO. Retrieved from https://www.ilo.org/wcmsp5/groups/public/---ed_dialogue/---sector/documents/publication/wcms_673662.pdf accessed on 18 June 2020.

International Labour Organisation (ILO). 2019b. *From waste to jobs: Decent work challenges and opportunities in the management of e-waste in India, Working Paper No. 323, International Labour Office, Sectoral Policies Department*, Geneva: ILO. Retrieved from https://www.ilo.org/wcmsp5/groups/public/---ed_dialogue/---sector/documents/publication/wcms_732426.pdf accessed on 3 April 2020.

International Solid Waste Association (ISWA). 2014. *Extended producer responsibility*, Vienna, Austria: ISWA. Retrieved from https://www.iswa.org/index.php?eID=tx_bee4memem-berships_download&fileUid=235 accessed on 28 April 2020.

IRG Systems South Asia Pvt. Ltd. (IRG) 2016. *E-waste inventorisation of Bastar Division*, New Delhi: IRG Systems South Asia Pvt. Ltd. Retrieved from http://enviscecb.org/Reports/Technical%20Report/E-Waste%20Inventorization%20Report.pdf accessed on 25 May 2020.

Isernia, Raffaele, Renato Passaro, Ivana Quinto, and Antonio Thomas. 2019. 'The reverse supply chain of the e-waste management processes in circular economy framework: Evidence from Italy'. *Sustainability*, 11: 2430: 1–19; doi:10.3390/su11082430

Islam, Md Tasbirul, and Nazmul Huda. 2019. 'Material flow analysis (MFA) as a strategic tool in E-waste management: Applications, trends and future directions'. *Journal of Environmental Management*, 244: 344–361. doi:10.1016/j.jenvman.2019.05.062.

Iyer, Lakshmi Shankar. 2014. 'A study on the attitude towards e-waste collection and safe management in academic institutions in Bangalore'. (January 1): 1–15. DOI: 10.2139/ssrn.2480323.

Jain, Amit. 2010. 'E-waste management in India: Current status, emerging drivers & challenges'. *Presented at regional workshop on E-waste/WEEE management*, July 8, Osaka, Japan. Retrieved from https://gec.jp/gec/jp/Activities/ietc/fy2010/e-waste/ew_1-2.pdf accessed on 9 July 2020.

Jain, Amit. 2019. 'Global e-waste growth'. In Johri Rakesh (ed.). *E-Waste: Implications, regulations, and management in India and current global best practices* (pp. 3–22), New Delhi: TERI press (second reprint).

Jutting, Johannes, and Juan R. de Laiglesia. 2009. 'Dealing with informal employment: Towards a three-pronged strategy'. In Johannes Jutting and Juan R. de Laiglesia (eds.). *Is informal normal?: Towards more and better jobs in developing countries* (pp. 143–163). Development Centre of the Organisation for Economic Co-operation and Development. DOI: 10.1787/9789264059245-8-en.

Kawakami, Tsuyoshi. 2019a. 'Improving safety, health and working conditions of e-waste workers'. In Mishra, Neeta, Sarina Bolla, and Kalyan Bhaskar (eds.). *E-waste roadmap 2030 for India: A compilation of thought pieces by sector experts* (pp. 49–73), Delhi: IFC and Karo Sambhav Pvt. Ltd.

Kapil, Shagun. April 05, 2019. 'Recycling e-waste: 'CPCB' competence must be raised'. *Down to Earth*. Retrieved from https://www.downtoearth.org.in/interviews/waste/recycling-e-waste-cpcb-s-competence-must-be-raised--63853 accessed on 29 April 2019.

Karo Sambhav Pvt. Ltd. 2019. 'Planning 2020–2022'. unpublished. Gurugram: Karo Sambhav Pvt. Ltd.

Kaur, Banjot. 16 July 2018. 'Can India manage its toxic e-waste?'. *Down To Earth*, 16–30 Jun 2018, Retrievd from https://www.downtoearth.org.in/news/waste/can-india-manage-its-toxic-e-waste--60891 accessed on 24 December 2019.

Kawakami, Tsuyoshi. 2019b. 'Improving safety, health and working conditions of e-waste workers'. In Mishra, Neeta, Sarina Bolla, and Kalyan Bhaskar (eds.). *E-waste roadmap 2030 for India: A compilation of thought pieces by sector experts* (pp. 49–73). Delhi: IFC and Karo Sambhav Pvt. Ltd.

Khan, Anish, Inamuddin, and Abdulla M. Asiri (eds.). 2020. *E-waste recycling and management: Present scenarios and environmental issues.* Switzerland: Springer.

Khattar, Vivek, Jaspreet Kaur, Ashish Chaturvedi, and Rachna Arora. 2007. *E-Waste assessment in India: Specific focus on Delhi.* New Delhi: GTZ. Retrieved from http://www.nswai.com/docs/e-Waste%20Assessment%20in%20India%20-%20Specific%20Focus%20on%20Delhi.pdf accessed on 16 February 2020.

Khetriwal Sinha, Deepali. 2019a. 'Financing e-waste management: A producer perspective: Colloquium – E-waste management in India: Issues and strategies'. *VIKALPA*, 44(3): 142–145. DOI: 10.1177/0256090919880655.

Kopacek, Bernd. 2019. 'A Note on Best Practices and the European Experience'. In Neeta Mishra, Sarina Bolla, and Kalyan Bhaskar (eds.). *E-waste roadmap 2030 for India: A compilation of thought pieces by sector experts* (pp. 74–76). Delhi: IFC and Karo Sambhav Pvt. Ltd.

Kuehr Ruediger, Velasquez German T., and Eric Williams. 2003. 'Computers and the Environment – An Introduction to Understanding and Managing their Impacts'. In R. Kuehr and E. Williams (eds.). *Computers and the Environment: Understanding and Managing their Impacts (Vol. 14, pp. 1–15).* Eco-Efficiency in Industry and Science. Dordrecht: Springer. DOI:10.1007/978-94-010-0033-8_1.

Kuntz, Valerie. 7 April 2020. 'What is "EU RoHS3?"' Retrieved from https://help.assent-compliance.com/hc/en-us/articles/360001203047-What-is-EU-RoHS-3 – accessed on 21 February 2020.

Kuyucak, N., and B. Volesky. 1988. 'Biosorbents for recovery of metals from industrial solutions'. *Biotechnology Letters*, 10(2): 137–142. DOI: 10.1007/BF01024641.

Kwatra, Swati, Suneel Pandey, and Sumit Sharma. 2014. 'Understanding public knowledge and awareness on e-waste in an urban setting in India'. *Management of Environmental Quality: An International Journal*, 25(6): 752–765. DOI:10.1108/meq-12-2013-0139.

LARRDIS. 2011. *E-Waste in India*. New Delhi: Rajya Sabha Secretariat. Retrieved from https://rajyasabha.nic.in/rsnew/publication_electronic/E-Waste_in_india.pdf accessed on 20 November 2018.

Ledwaba, Pontsho, and Ndabenhle Sosibo. 2017. 'Cathode ray tube recycling in South Africa'. *Recycling*, 2(1): 4. DOI: 10.3390/recycling2010004.

Lepawsky, Josh. 2015. 'The changing geography of global trade in electronic discards: Time to rethink the e-waste problem'. *The Geographical Journal*, 181(2): 147–159. DOI: 10.1111/geoj.12077.

Lepawsky, Josh, and Chris McNabb. 2010. 'Mapping international flows of electronic waste'. *The Canadian Geographer*, 54(2): 177–195. DOI: 10.1111/j.1541-0064.2009.00279.x

Levinson, Tzvi, Christina Folman, and Julia Lietzmann. 2019. 'E-waste legislation in the European Union and the Basel Convention'. In Johri Rakesh (ed.). *E-Waste: Implications, regulations, and management in India and current global best practices* (pp. 151–168), New Delhi: TERI press (second reprint).

Lindhqvist, Thomas. 2000. *Extended Producer Responsibility in Cleaner Production: Policy Principle to Promote Environmental Improvements of Product Systems*. Lund, Sweden: IIIEE (The International Institute for Industrial Environmental Economics), Lund University. Retrieved from https://lup.lub.lu.se/search/ws/files/4433708/1002025.pdf accessed on 28 April 2020.

Lundgren, Karin. 2012. *The global impact of e-waste: Addressing the challenge*. Geneva: International Labour Organisation Office, Programme on Safety and Health at Work and the Environment (SafeWork), Sectoral Activities Department (SECTOR). Retrieved from http://www.saicm.org/Portals/12/Documents/EPI/ewastesafework.pdf accessed on 11 April 2020.

Magazine Monitor. 2014. 'Who what why: How much gold can we get from mobile phones?'. 16 August. Retrieved from https://www.bbc.com/news/blogs-magazine-monitor-28802646 accessed on 10 August 2020.

Mahesh, Priti. 2007. *EPR: Sustainable solution to electronic waste*. Toxics Link. Retrieved from http://toxicslink.org/docs/06167_EPR_Sustainable_solution_to_ewaste.pdf accessed on 6 June 2019.

Malhotra, Manika. 2020. *E-waste management: Policy analysis and implementation*. New Delhi: The PPF – Centre for Cohesive Society Studies. Retrieved from https://www.ppf.org.in/wp-content/uploads/2020/02/Final-E-Waste-Management_Feb-2020-PPF.pdf accessed on 23 July 2020.

Manda, Krishna B.K. 2008. *E-waste management policy in India: Stake holders' perceptions and media attention, thesis for Master of Science in Environmental Sciences, Policy & Management*. Sweden: Lund University. Retrieved from https://lup.lub.lu.se/luur/download?func=downloadFile&recordOId=1413818&fileOId=1413825 accessed on 25 June 2020.

Manomaivibool, Panate. 2011. *Advancing the frontier of extended producer responsibility: The management of waste electrical and electronic equipment in non-OECD countries* (doctoral dissertation). Sweden: International Institute for Industrial Environmental Economics, Lund University. Retrieved from https://portal.research.lu.se/ws/files/3115417/2156616.pdf accessed on 1 July 2020.

Manomaivibool, Panate, and Jong Ho Hong. 2014. 'Two decades, three WEEE systems: How far did EPR evolve in Korea's resource circulation policy?'. *Resources, Conservation and Recycling*, 83: 202–212. DOI:10.1016/j.resconrec.2013.10.011.

McCann, Duncan, and Annelaure Wittmann. 2015. *E-waste prevention, take-back system design and policy approaches (Solving the e-waste problem (Step) Green paper)*. United Nations University – Institute for the Advanced Study of Sustainability (UNU-IAS). Retrieved from http://www.step-initiative.org/files/_documents/green_papers/Step%20Green%20Paper_Prevention%26Take-backy%20System.pdf accessed on 7 April 2020.

Mehra, Harish C. 2004. 'PC wastes leaves toxic taste'. *The Tribune*, March 22. Retrieved from https://www.tribuneindia.com/2004/20040322/login/main1.htm accessed on 28 June 2020.

MeitY and NITI Aayog. 2019. *Strategy on resource efficiency in electrical and electronic equipment sector*. New Delhi: Government of India.

Miliute-Plepiene, Jurate, and Lena Youhanan. 2019. *E-waste and raw materials: From environmental issues to business models*. Stockholm, Sweden: IVS Swedish Environmental Research Institute. Retrieved from https://www.ivl.se/download/18.2299af4c16c6c7485d0c39/1567678533720/E-waste_190905.pdf accessed on 7 June 2020.

Ministry of Electronics and Information Technology (MeitY) and NITI Aayog. 2019. *Strategy on resource efficiency in electrical and electronic equipment sector*. New Delhi: Government of India.

Ministry of Environment and Forests. 2006. *National Environment Policy*. New Delhi: Government of India. Retrieved from https://ibkp.dbtindia.gov.in/DBT_Content_Test/CMS/Guidelines/20190411103521431_National%20Environment%20Policy,%202006.pdf accessed on 1 July 2020.

Ministry of Environment and Forests (MoEF) and Central Pollution Control Board (CPCB). 2008. *Guidelines for environmentally sound management of e-waste*, Delhi: Government of India. Retrieved from https://www.yumpu.com/en/document/read/6274477/guidelines-for-environmentally-sound-management-of-e-waste accessed on 7 April 2020.

Ministry of Environment and Forests (MoEF) and Central Pollution Control Board (CPCB). 2011. *Implementation of E-waste Rules, 2011 – Guidelines*, New Delhi: Government of India. Retrieved from http://toxicslink.org/docs/rulesansregulation/E-waste-rule-guidelines.pdf accessed on 20 April 2020.

MPCB (Maharashtra Pollution Control Board). 2007. *Report on assessment of electronic waste in Mumbai-Pune area*. Mumbai: Maharashtra Pollution Control Board.

Mudur, G.S. 22 September 2009. 'Not rubbish! India buys e-garbage – Centre allows e-waste imports for recycling, activists cry foul'. *The Telegraph*. Retrieved from https://www.telegraphindia.com/india/not-rubbish-india-buys-e-garbage-centre-allows-e-waste-imports-for-recycling-activists-cry-foul/cid/591946 accessed on 11 July 2020.

Mujezinovic, Davor. 2019. 'Electronic waste in Guiyu: A city under change?' *Environment & Society Portal, Arcadia*, no. 29. Rachel Carson Center for Environment and Society. doi.org/10.5282/rcc/8805.

Nath, Bhola, Ranjeeta Kumari, Valendu Gupta, N.D. Vaswani, and Seema Lekhwani. 2018. 'A community based study on e-waste disposal in Srinagar, Uttarakhand: Assessment of awareness and practices'. *International Journal of Community Medicine and Public Health*, 5(8): 3429–3434.

NITI Aayog and EU. 2017. *Strategy on resource efficiency*. New Delhi: Government of India.

Niu, H., and B. Volesky. 1999. 'Characteristics of gold biosorption from cyanide solution'. *Journal of Chemical Technology and Biotechnology*, 74(8): 778–784. DOI:10.1002/(SICI)1097-4660(199908)74:8<778::AID-JCTB99>3.0.CO;2-Q.

OECD. 2001. *Extended Producer Responsibility: A guidance manual for governments*. Paris, France: OECD. Retrieved from https://www.wastenet.net.au/assets/documents/content/information/epr-guide_for_govt-2001.pdf accessed on 14 April 2019.

OECD. 2016. *Extended Producer Responsibility: Updated Guidance for Efficient Waste Management*. Paris: OECD Publishing. DOI: 10.1787/9789264256385-en.

Oers, Lauran Van and Arnold Tukker. 2016. *Development of a resource efficiency index of nations*. Illustrative calculations, Switzerland: World Resources Forum WRF. Retrieved from http://www.wrforum.org/wp-content/uploads/2016/04/Resource-efficiency-indicators-WRF-calculations_FINAL.pdf accessed on 8 July 2020.

Ogushi, Yasuhiko, and Milind Kandlikar. 2007. 'Assessing extended producer responsibility laws in Japan'. *Environmental Science & Technology*, 41(13): 4502–4508. DOI:10.1021/es072561x.

Oteng-Ababio, Martin. 2012. 'Electronic Waste Management in Ghana – Issues and Practices'. In Sime Curkovic (ed.). *Sustainable development: Authoritative and leading edge content for environmental management* (pp. 149–166). Kalamazoo: Western Michigan University. DOI: 10.5772/2562

PACE (Platform for Accelerating the Circular Economy) and WEF (World Economic Forum). 2019. *A circular vision for electronics: Time for a global reboot*. Switzerland: PACE and The E-waste Coalition. Retrieved from http://www3.weforum.org/docs/WEF_A_New_Circular_Vision_for_Electronics.pdf accessed on 3 April 2020.

Parajuly, K., R. Kuehr; A.K. Awasthi, C. Fitzpatrick, J. Lepawsky, E. Smith, R. Widmer, and X. Zeng. 2019. *Future e-waste scenarios*. Bonn, Germany: StEP Initiative, Bonn: UNU ViE-SCYCLE, and Osaka: UNEP IETC. Retrieved from http://www.step-initiative.org/files/_documents/publications/FUTURE%20E-WASTE%20SCENARIOS_UNU_190829_low_screen.pdf accessed on 11 April 2020.

Patel, Lakshmi. November 24, 2017. *Electronic waste collection: AMC, why don't you fix your digital dump first? Times of India*. Retrieved from https://ahmedabadmirror.indiatimes.com/ahmedabad/cover-story/electronic-waste-collection-amc-why-dont-you-fix-your-digital-dump-first/articleshow/61774594.cms accessed on 15 July 2020.

Patil, Rashmi Anoop, and Seeram Ramakrishna. 2020. A comprehensive analysis of e-waste legislation worldwide. *Environmental Science and Pollution Research*. DOI:10.1007/s11356-020-07992-1.

Pont, Ana, Antonio Robles, and Jose A. Gil. 2019. 'e-waste: Everything an ICT scientist and developer should know'. *IEEE Access*, 7: 1–22. DOI: 10.1109/ACCESS.2019.2955008.

Puckett, Jim, Leslie Byster, Sarah Westervelt, Richard Gutierrez, Sheila Davis, Asma Hussain, and Madhumitta Dutta. 2002. *Exporting harm: The high-tech trashing of Asia*. The Basel Action Network (BAN) and Silicon Valley Toxics Coalition (SVTC). Retrieved from http://svtc.org/wp-content/uploads/technotrash.pdf accessed on 20 May 2020.

Radulovic, Verena. 2018. *Gap analysis on responsible e-waste management efforts in India: Institutional, economic, and technological and the potential role of a sustainability standard to build capacity and help foster solutions*. Centre for Responsible Business and Green Electronics Council. Retrieved from https://greenelectronicscouncil.org/wp-content/uploads/2018/11/GEC-CRB-Gap-Analysis-Report-FINAL-Oct-2018.pdf accessed on 25 July 2020.

Raghupathy, Laxmi, Ashish Chaturvedi, Rachna Arora, and Vinnie Mehta. 2010. 'E-waste management in India'. *E-Scrap*, May.

Rajya Sabha Secretariat. 2008. *Department related parliamentary standing committee on science and technology, environment and forests – Hundred and ninety second report on functioning of Central Pollution Control Board*. New Delhi: Parliament of India, Rajya Sabha. Retrieved from http://wwfenvis.nic.in/files/Environment,%20Forest%20and%20Climate%20Change/192.pdf accessed on 23 April 2020.

Ram Mohan M P, Iti Garg, and Gayatri Kumar. 2019. 'Regulating e-waste: A review of the international and national legal framework on e-waste'. In Johri Rakesh (ed.). *E-Waste: Implications, regulations, and management in India and current global best practices* (169–188). New Delhi: TERI press (second reprint).

Rohrig, Brian. 2015. Smartphones: Smart chemistry. Retrieved from https://www.acs.org/content/acs/en/education/resources/highschool/chemmatters/past-issues/archive-2014-2015/smartphones.html accessed on 12 April 2020.

Sander, Knut, Naoko Tojo, and Jan Vernon. 2007. *The producer responsibility principle of WEEE Directive*. Germany: Ökopol GmbH Institute for Environmental Strategies, Sweden: The International Institute for Industrial Environmental Economics Lund University, and United Kingdom: Risk & Policy Analysts. Retrieved from https://ec.europa.eu/environment/waste/weee/pdf/final_rep_okopol.pdf accessed on 8 June 2020.

Schinner, F., and W. Burgstaller. 1989. 'Extraction of zinc from industrial waste by a Penicillium sp'. *Applied Environment Microbiology*, 55(5): 1153–1156. DOI: 10.1128/aem.55.5.1153-1156.1989.

Shamsuddin, M. 1986. 'Metal Recovery from Scrap and Waste'. *Journal of Metals*, 38(2): 24–31. doi:10.1007/bf03257917.

Shah, Anuj. 2014. *An assessment of public awareness regarding e-waste hazards and management strategies*. Independent Study Project (ISP) Collection, 1820. Retrieved from https://digitalcollections.sit.edu/isp_collection/1820 accessed on 12 November 2020.

Sharma, Hitesh. 2019. 'EPR for e-waste management in India: A producer perspective: Colloquium – E-waste management in India: Issues and strategies'. *VIKALPA*, 44(3) 158–160. DOI: 10.1177/0256090919880655.

Shevchenko, Tetiana, Kirsi Laitala, and Yuriy Danko. 2019. 'Understanding consumer e-waste recycling behavior: Introducing a new economic incentive to increase the collection rates'. *Sustainability*, 11(9), 2656: 1–20. DOI: 10.3390/su11092656.

Shivathanu, Brijesh. 2016. 'User's perspective: Knowledge and attitude towards e-waste'. *International Journal of Applied Environmental Sciences*, 11(2): 413–423. Retrieved from https://www.ripublication.com/ijaes16/ijaesv11n2_06.pdf accessed on 13 June 2020.

Singh, Narendra, Huabo Duan, Oladele A. Ogunseitan, Jinhui Li, and Yuanyuan Tang. 2019. 'Toxicity trends in e-waste: A comparative analysis of metals in discarded mobile phones'. *Journal of Hazardous Materials* 380: 1–9. DOI: 10.1016/j.jhazmat.2019.120898

Singh, Pooja and Shanu Thomas. 2016. 'E-waste management and environment protection: A critical legal analysis'. *Bharti Law Review*, January–March: 27–35. Retrieved from http://elibrary.azimpremjifoundation.org:2103/pers/Personalized.aspx accessed on 15 August 2020.

Singhal, Pranshu. 2010. 'Shaping consumers' behaviour for responsible recycling'. Paper presented at the Going Green – Care Innovation 2010, Vienna.

Singhal, Pranshu. 2012. 'Crafting environmental change agents: An ecosystem approach'. Paper presented at the Electronics Going Green, Berlin.

Singhal, Pranshu. 2019a. 'Disrupting the status quo via systematic transformation-PROs and e-waste'. In Neeta Mishra, Sarina Bolla, and Kalyan Bhaskar (eds.). *E-waste roadmap 2030 for India: A compilation of thought pieces by sector experts* (pp. 15–25). Delhi: IFC and Karo Sambhav Pvt. Ltd.

Singhal, Pranshu. 2019b. 'Disrupting the status quo via systematic transformation-PROs and e-waste: Colloquium – E-waste management in India: Issues and strategies'. *VIKALPA*, 44(3) 151–153. DOI: 10.1177/0256090919880655.

Sinha-Khetriwal, D., P. Kraeuchi, and M. Schwaninger. 2005. A comparison of electronic waste recycling in Switzerland and in India. *Environmental Impact Assessment Review*, 25(5): 492–504. doi:10.1016/j.eiar.2005.04.006.

Sinha Khetriwal Deepali. 2019b. 'The informal sector in e-waste management: Colloquium – E-waste management in India: Issues and strategies'. *VIKALPA*, 44(3) 142–145. DOI: 10.1177/0256090919880655.

Sinha, Satish. 2019a. 'Dark shadows of digitization on India horizon'. In Johri Rakesh (ed.). *E-Waste: Implications, regulations, and management in India and current global best practices* (23–44). New Delhi: TERI press (second reprint).

Bibliography

Sinha, Satish. 2019b. 'The informal sector in e-waste management'. *VIKALPA*, 44(3) 133–135. DOI: 10.1177/0256090919880655.

Sjödin, Andreas, Carlsson Hakan, Thuresson Kaj, Sjölin Sverker, Bergman, Åke, and Conny Östman. 2001.'Flame retardants in indoor air at an electronics recycling plant and at other work environments'. *Environmental Science & Technology*, 35(3): 448–454. DOI:10.1021/es000077n.

Sjödin, Andreas, Patterson Donald Jr., and Åke Bergman. 2003.'A review on human exposure to brominated flame retardants?particularly polybrominated diphenyl ethers'. *Environment International*, 29(6): 829–839. doi:10.1016/s0160-4120(03)00108-9.

Skinner, Alexandra, Dinter Yvonne, Lloyd Alex, and Philip Strothmann. 2010.'The Challenges of E-Waste Management in India: Can India draw lessons from the EU and the USA?'. *ASIEN*, 117:S. 7–26. Retrieved from http://asien.asienforschung.de/wp-content/uploads/sites/6/2014/04/ASIEN_117_Skinner-Dinter-Llyod-Strothmann.pdf accessed on 28 April 2020.

Socolof, Maria Leet, Jonathan G. Overly, and Jack R. Geibig. 2005.'Environmental life-cycle impacts of CRT and LCD desktop computer displays'. *Journal of Cleaner Production*, 13(13-14): 1281–1294. DOI:10.1016/j.jclepro.2005.05.014.

Sohail, Sadia. July 04, 2015. 'E-waste management: Nokia sets example'. *Down to Earth*. Retrieved from https://www.downtoearth.org.in/news/ewaste-management-nokia-sets-example--41799 accessed on 26 November 2019.

Statista.com. 2020. 'Number of smartphones sold to end users worldwide from 2007 to 2020'. February 28. Retrieved from https://www.statista.com/statistics/263437/global-smartphone-sales-to-end-users-since-2007/ accessed on 27 September 2019.

Steger, Manfred B. and Ravi K. Roy. 2010. *Neoliberalism: A very short introduction*. Oxford: Oxford University Press.

Stewart R., 2012. 'EU legislation relating to electronic waste: The WEEE and RoHS Directives and the REACH regulations'. In Vannessa Goodship and Ab Stevels (ed.). *Waste electrical and electronic equipment (WEEE) handbook* (pp. 17–51), Woodhead Publishing (eBook). DOI: 10.1533/9780857096333.1.17.

Subramanian, Logakanthi. 2014. *Management of electronic waste by bulk consumers: The case of India's IT service sector*. Doctoral thesis, Faculty of Humanities. North Manchester: University of Manchester. Retrieved from https://www.research.manchester.ac.uk/portal/files/54553713/FULL_TEXT.PDF accessed on 13 July 2020.

Takale, K.R., S.M. Gawande, and P.J. Rangari. 2015. 'Electronic waste & its present scenario for Pune city'. *International Journal of Innovative Research in Science, Engineering and Technology*, 4(6): 4238–4244. DOI:10.15680/IJIRSET.2015.0406089.

Telangana Sate Pollution Control Board (TSPCB). 2016. *Inventorisation of e-waste for Telangana state: The inception report*. Hyderabad: Telangana Sate Pollution Board. Retrieved from http://tspcb.cgg.gov.in/CBIPMP/Consultancy%20Services/E-waste/Inception_Repot.pdf accessed on 27 May 2020.

The Gazette of India. 2011. *E-waste (Management and Handling) Rules, 2011*. Retrieved from https://www.ecsenvironment.com/images/rules/E-waste(M&H)Rules,2011.pdf accessed on 2 July 2020.

Toxics Link. 2003. *Scrapping the high-tech myth: Computer waste in India*. New Delhi: Toxics Link. Retrieved from http://toxicslink.org/docs/Scrapping_The_Hitech_Myth_Computer_Waste_in_India_mail.pdf accessed on 4 July 2019.

Toxics Link. 2004a. *E-waste in India: System failure – Take action NOW!*. New Delhi: Toxics Link. Retrieved from http://toxicslink.org/docs/06040_repsumry.pdf accessed on 25 June 2020.

Toxics Link. 2004b. *E-waste in Chennai: Time is running out*. New Delhi: Toxics Link. Retrieved from http://toxicslink.org/docs/06033_reptchen.pdf accessed on 25 November 2019.

Bibliography

Toxics Link. 2014a. *Impact of e-waste recycling on water and soil*. Delhi: Toxics Link. Retrieved from http://toxicslink.org/docs/Impact-of-E-waste-recycling-on-Soil-and-Water.pdf accessed on 2 February 2020.

Toxics Link. 2014b. *Time to reboot*. New Delhi: Toxics Link. Retrieved from http://toxicslink.org/docs/Time-to-Reboot.pdf accessed on 4 September 2019.

Toxics Link. 2015. *Time to reboot II*. New Delhi: Toxics Link. Retrieved from http://toxicslink.org/docs/Time-to-Reboot-2-Full-report.pdf accessed on 4 September 2019.

Toxics Link. 2016. *What India knows about e-waste*. New Delhi: Toxics Link. Retrieved from http://toxicslink.org/docs/What-India-knows-about-e-waste.pdf accessed on 4 September 2019.

Toxics Link. 2019a. *Time to reboot III e-waste rules: Assessing EPR compliance*. New Delhi: Toxics Link. Retrieved from http://toxicslink.org/docs/Time%20to%20Reboot%203.pdf accessed on 4 September 2019.

Toxics Link. 2019b. *Informal e-waste recycling in Delhi: Unfolding impact of two years of E-waste (Management) Rules 2016*. Delhi: Toxics Link. Retrieved from http://www.toxicslink.org/?q=content/informal-e-waste-recycling-delhi accessed on 2 February 2020.

Turaga, Rama Mohana R. 2019. 'Public policy for e-waste management in India: Issues and strategies'. *VIKALPA*, 44(3) 130–132. DOI: 10.1177/0256090919880655.

Turaga, Rama Mohana R., and Kalyan Bhaskar. 2019. 'Introduction: Colloquium – E-waste management in India: Issues and strategies', *VIKALPA*, 44(3) 127–129. DOI: 10.1177/0256090919880655.

UN ESCAP (United Nations Economic and Social Commission for Asia and the Pacific). 2012. *Fact sheet – Extended Producer Responsibility*. Retrieved from https://www.unescap.org/sites/default/files/25.%20FS-Extended-Producer-Responsibility.pdf accessed on 1 September 2019.

United Nations Environment Management Group (UNEMG). 2017. *United Nations System-wide response to tacking e-waste*. Geneva: United Nations. Retrieved from https://unemg.org/images/emgdocs/ewaste/E-Waste-EMG-FINAL.pdf accessed on 7 April 2020.

United Nations Environment Programme (UNEP). 2007. *E-waste Volume I: Inventory assessment manual*. Osaka/Shiga: United Nations Environmental Programme. Retrieved from http://greene.gov.in/wp-content/uploads/2018/01/E-waste-Vol-I-Inventory-Assessment-Manual.pdf accessed on 3 April 2020.

United Nations Environment Programme (UNEP). 2009. *Recycling – From e-waste to resources*. Berlin: UNEP & UNU. Retrieved from https://www.researchgate.net/publication/278849195 accessed on 20 March 2020.

United Nations Environment Programme (UNEP). 2010. *Assessing the Environmental Impacts of Consumption and Production: Priority Products and Materials*. United Nations Environment Programme. Retrieved from https://www.resourcepanel.org/reports/assessing-environmental-impacts-consumption-and-production accessed on 30 May 2020.

UNU/StEP Initiative. 2014. *One global definition of e-waste*. Solving the E-Waste Problem (Step) Initiative White Paper. UNU/StEP Initiative 2014. Retrieved from https://collections.unu.edu/eserv/UNU:6120/step_one_global_definition_amended.pdf accessed on 7 April 2020.

Walls, Margaret. 2003. *The role of economics in extended producer responsibility: Making policy choices and setting policy goals*. Discussion paper 03-11. Retrieved from https://media.rff.org/documents/RFF-DP-03-11.pdf accessed on 30 April 2020.

Waste 360. 'The benefits of a hub and spoke recycling system'. Retrieved from https://www.waste360.com/business/benefits-hub-and-spoke-recycling-system accessed on 2 August 2020.

Wath, Sushant B., P.S. Dutt, and T. Chakrabarti. 2011. 'E-waste scenario in India, its management and implications'. *Environmental Monitoring and Assessment*, 172:249–262. DOI:10.1007/s10661-010-1331-9.

Widmer, Rolf, Oswald-Krapf, Heidi, Sinha-Khetriwal, Deepali, Schnellmann, Max, and Heinz Böni. 2005. 'Global perspectives on e-waste'. *Environmental Impact Assessment Review*, 25(5): 436–458. DOI:10.1016/j.eiar.2005.04.001.

Wielenga, Kees. 2010. *Waste without frontiers: Global trends in generation and transboundary movements of hazardous wastes and other wastes*. Geneva: The Secretariat of the Basel Convention. Retrieved from http://www.basel.int/Portals/4/Basel%20Convention/docs/pub/ww-frontiers26Jan2010.pdf accessed on 8 April 2020.

Yadav, Shiv Shankar, and Asit Bandyopadhayay. 2015. 'The e-waste legislation and contemporary sustainability issues in India: A critical analysis'. *Asia-Pacific Journal of Management Research and Innovation*, 11(3): 245–250. DOI:10.1177/2319510x15588384.

Yadav, Sudesh, Yadav Satyamanyu, and Pawan Kumar. 2014. 'Metal toxicity assessment of mobile phone parts using Milli Q water'. *Waste Management*, 34: 1274–1278. DOI:10.1016/j.wasman.2014.02.024

YES Bank Ltd. And TERI-Business Council for Sustainable Development (BCSD). 2014. *E-waste management in India – The corporate imperative*, Mumbai: YES Bank and New Delhi: TERI-BCSD. Retrieved from http://cbs.teriin.org/pdf/researchreports/EWasteManagementReport.pdf accessed on 23 April 2020).

Yu, Jinglei, Eric Williams, and Meiting Ju. 2010. 'Analysis of material and energy consumption of mobile phones in China'. *Energy Policy*, 38: 4135–4141. doi:10.1016/j.enpol.2010.03.041.

Zeng, Xianlai, John Mathews, and Jinhui Li. 2018. 'Urban mining of e-waste is becoming more cost-effective than virgin mining'. *Environmental Science & Technology*, 52(8): 4835–4841. DOI:10.1021/acs.est.7b04909.

Acts and Rules

Environment Protection Act, 1986
Hazardous Waste (Management and Handling) Rules, 2003
Hazardous Waste (Management and Handling) Rules, 2008
Hazardous Waste (Management and Handling) Rules, 2011
E-waste Management Rules, 2011
E-waste Management Rules, 2016
E-waste Management (Amendment) Rules, 2018
WEEE Directive (2002/95/EC) of 27 January 2003
WEEE Directive 2003/108/EC of 8 December 2003
WEEE Directive 2012/19/EG of 4 July 2012

Legal Cases

K.N. Unnikrishnan vs. Cochin Port Trust & Ors. (2011)
M.C. Mehta Vs. Union of India & Ors. (2014)
Mahendra Pandey Vs. Union of India & Ors. (2017)
Shailesh Singh Vs. State of U.P. & Ors. (2018)
Madurai Farooq Ahmed vs. The Tamil Nadu Pollution Control Board (2019)

Websites

https://www.acs.org/content/acs/en/education/resources/highschool/chemmatters/past-issues/archive-2014-2015/smartphones.html
http://www.basel.int/Implementation/TechnicalAssistance/Partnerships/MPPI/Overview/tabid/3268/Default.aspx
http://www.basel.int/portals/4/basel%20convention/docs/meetings/cop/cop8/nairobideclaration.pdf
https://www.casemine.com/judgement/in/5b17d55b4a93267801004e7f
https://ec.europa.eu/environment/chemicals/reach/reach_en.htm
https://ec.europa.eu/environment/waste/weee/index_en.htm
https://ec.europa.eu/environment/waste/rohs_eee/index_en.htm
https://ec.europa.eu/environment/waste/rohs
https://echa.europa.eu/regulations/reach/understanding-reach
https://ehs.unu.edu/vice-rectorate/sustainable-cycles-scycle#overview
https://www.ellenmacarthurfoundation.org/circular-economy/concept/building-blocks
https://www.rohsguide.com/rohs-faq.htm
https://help.assentcompliance.com/hc/en-us/articles/360001203047-What-is-EU-RoHS-3-
https://rajyasabha.nic.in/rsnew/practice_procedure/book13.asp
https://unfccc.int/climate-action/momentum-for-change/lighthouse-activities/e-waste-from-toxic-to-green
https://unu.edu/projects/solving-the-e-waste-problem-step-initiative.html#outline
https://www.un.org/press/en/2004/unep204.doc.htm
http://www.step-initiative.org
https://www.waste360.com/business/benefits-hub-and-spoke-recycling-system (accessed on 2 August 2020)
www.attero.in
www.ban.org
www.archive.basel.int
www.ewasteindia.com
www.globalewaste.org
www.mercuryconvention.org
www.rohsguide.com
www.nsdcindia.org
www.pic.int
www.pops.int
www.sma.de
www.saicm.org
www.statista.com
www.swayam.gov.in
www.worldloop.org

INDEX

Aarhus Convention 26
Aarhus Protocol on Heavy Metals 26
access-to-waste 52
accountability 57, 63, 119, 170, 173–174
Advisory Services in Environmental Management (ASEM) 135
Africa 10–11, 13–18, 24–25, 28, 34, 71, 179; e-waste generation in 11; toxic waste flowing to 28
African Union 25
Agbogbloshie, Ghana 14, 80, 179
agenda 2030 15, 31–32, 150, 160
Ahmedabad Municipal Corporation (AMC) 172
Albania 17
aluminium 30, 72, 74–77, 81, 83, 87, 90, 102
Amendment Rules, 2018 109, 115–117, 119, 160
Andhra Pradesh 36, 123, 125, 136, 170
anthroposphere 97
antimony 41, 76, 83
APGAR score 14
appliances 1, 21–22, 35, 56, 70, 134; consumer 1; home 56; household 1, 22, 35, 134
Argentina 16–17, 27
Asia 10–15, 17–18, 34, 42, 80, 97, 135, 139; e-waste in 12; generation of 11–12
Assam 123, 125
ASSOCHAM-NEC 36
Atomic Energy Act, 1962 112
Attero Recycling Private Ltd 138, 140, 151
auditability 174
Australia 13, 17, 29, 37; e-waste generation in 13; National Television and Computer Recycling Scheme 13

awareness 6–7, 11, 20, 24, 30, 38, 41, 43, 50, 52, 56, 62, 64–66, 77–78, 114, 117–122, 125, 128–129, 133, 135–136, 139–140, 143, 145–147, 149–152, 155–160, 166–170, 172–173, 178–179; about use of chemicals 30; campaign 145; cost of 52; creation 120; electronics user 20; environmental 11, 64, 135; programmes 120, 125, 152, 157, 169; public 129, 157, 159; role of 24, 133, 149; social 135

Bamako Convention 25
Basel Action Network (BAN) 29, 89, 135
Basel Convention 7–8, 14, 24–25, 28–29, 33, 70, 109–110, 113, 128, 134–135, 139, 147; aims of 28; Article 1.1.a 14; Article 1.1.b 14; Article 6 28; Article 11 24; importance of 29 *see The Basel Convention on the Control of Transboundary Movements of Hazardous Wastes and their Disposal*
Basel Convention on e-Waste Management in Africa 25
Basel Convention on the Control of Transboundary Movements of Hazardous Wastes and their Disposal 7, 24
Basel Convention on the Control of Transboundary Movements of Hazardous Wastes and their Disposal (Basel Convention), The 7
Batteries (Management and Handling) Rules, 2001 112–113
Belgium 15, 55, 105
berylliosis 83

beryllium (Be) 4–5, 76, 78, 81, 83, 90
Bihar 125
bilateral agencies 151
bio-accumulation 5, 91
bio-accumulative 13, 69, 71, 82
biomass 97
biosphere 97
BIRD 35, 137
bismuth 89
BMZ 135
Bolivia 17
Bosnia 17
Boulding, Kenneth 97; *The Economics of the Coming Spaceship Earth* 97
brand environmental responsibility (BFR) 5, 13, 61, 64, 80, 83, 144, 167; ecosystem approach 64, 144, 166
Brazil 11, 17, 27, 37, 154
brominated flame retardants (BFRs) 4–5, 76
Bulgaria 17–18
Butyl benzyl phthalate (BBP) 23
buyback: program 56; scheme 147
by-products 5, 77, 81, 94

cadmium (Cd) 4–5, 20, 23, 27, 70, 73–74, 76, 78–81, 84, 89–90
California Electronic Waste Recycling Act, 2003 18
Cambodia 12, 17, 57
Cameroon 16–17
Canada 17, 29
capacity-building 136, 155, 157–158
carbon 16, 71–73, 75–76, 79, 89, 94, 100, 167, 175; emissions 100
carbon dioxide (CO_2) 13, 41, 72, 74–75, 94, 167; emissions of 13, 72
carbon footprints 16, 71, 73
carcinogenic 24, 69, 76, 83–84
Cartagena Decisions 28
cathode ray tube (CRT) 17, 24, 61, 74–76, 78, 80, 83–85, 111, 114, 177; environmental impacts of 74; regulations for recycling 17
cell phones 41, 61, 64–65, 70, 72–74, 81, 96, 122, 138; environmental impacts of a 73; health hazards of 81; manufacturing 73
CENELEC 176
Central America 27
Central American Integration System 27
Central Asia 11, 18
Central Institute of Plastics Engineering and Technology (CIPET) 105
Central Pollution Control Board (CPCB) 35, 90, 96, 109–111, 113–119, 121, 123–128, 136, 138, 140, 150, 158, 160, 167, 169–170, 176; duty of 125–126; performance of 119, 123, 125; as regulatory mechanisms 119
Centre for Materials for Electronics Technology (C-MET), Hyderabad 105, 126, 159, 173
Centre for Science and Environment (CSE) 90, 143, 169–170
ceramics 68, 77–78
Chandigarh 123, 125, 151
chemicals 1, 7–8, 21, 24–25, 29–30, 32, 34, 39, 68–69, 74–75, 79–83, 105; harmful 39; hazardous 24, 32, 79–80; life cycle 29; management 29; persistent 82; safety 29; substances 21; suspicious 21; use of 30
Chhattisgarh 153
children 14, 16, 35, 80, 85, 135, 140, 143–144, 172; impact on 16
Chile 17
China 11–12, 14–15, 17–18, 34, 37, 55, 57, 71, 80, 89, 135, 138, 179; Administration of the Recovery and Disposal of Discarded Electronic and Electrical Products 55
chlorinated Benzenes 89
chlorinated dioxins and furans (PCDD/Fs) 80
chlorine 79, 81–82, 84, 86
chlorofluorocarbons (CFCs) 4–5, 81–82
chromium (Cr) 4–5, 20, 23, 70, 73, 81, 84, 89–90; hexavalent 20, 23, 70, 84
CII 151
circular economy (CE) 2, 6–7, 16, 21, 30–31, 33, 37, 40–41, 57, 69, 93–102, 106, 108–109, 114, 144, 150, 159–160, 165–168, 171–174, 176, 180–181; challenges to 100; components of 100; conception of 97; concept of 97–98, 114, 181; model 99; opportunities for 100, 173; urban mining in 99
civil society 103, 112, 150–151, 158, 168, 178
civil society organisations (CSOs) 133, 145, 151, 155; role of 133
Cleaner Production Programme 50
Clean India Mission (Swachh Bharat) 38, 105, 133, 146, 150, 173
climate change 13, 70–71, 98
cobalt 41, 72, 76–77, 84, 101, 112
cobalt-60 tragedy 112
Cochin Port Trust 124, 127
collection: authorised centres 57; common centres 57

Index **201**

collection centres 55–57, 61–62, 64, 112, 114–115, 117, 119, 122, 125, 129, 160
Collective Producer Responsibility (CPR) 57–58
Colombia 17
committee on subordinate legislation 115
communication 1, 57, 95, 120, 155, 157, 169; revolution 1
communications sector 30
companies Act, 2013 116
compliance 7, 13, 16, 18, 20–21, 24–25, 27, 39–42, 49, 54–55, 57, 59–63, 65, 115–116, 118–121, 126–129, 147, 151–152, 156, 160, 165–166, 168–172, 180; legal 13, 16, 39–42, 49, 54, 57, 62, 120, 151, 160, 165–166, 168; mechanism 57; process 60; risks of 60–62; RoHS 24, 65, 116, 118–119, 126, 166, 170
Compound Annual Growth Rate (CAGR) 37
computers (PC) 1–2, 13, 15, 36, 70, 72, 74–75, 78, 82–83, 96, 102, 133, 135–139, 142, 147, 153, 171; environmental impacts of 74; games 2; peripherals 2
Conference of Plenipotentiaries in Basel, Switzerland 28
construction: sector 30; waste 4
Consume–Collect–Recover–Dispose 178
consumers: appliances 1; attitude of 152; behaviour 64, 147; bulk 37, 39–40, 114, 117–118, 155–158, 160, 167–169, 172–173, 180; business 20; domestic 20; goods 98; preferences 1; responsibilities of 37
consumption 6, 20, 32, 39, 49, 51, 53, 59, 70–74, 94, 98, 103–104, 126, 136, 148; pattern 136, 148
containers 1, 14–15, 55; mislabel 15; standardised 1
contamination 5, 14, 16, 80, 88–89, 93–94, 105, 112, 127, 167, 169, 171; chemical 80
COP8, 25, 28
COP10, 29
copper 5, 30, 41, 72–79, 81, 84–85, 89–90, 140
corporate sector 156
corruption 144
Costa Rica 17, 27
Council of the European Union 18
countermeasures against 16
crime 15; 'white collar' 15
critical raw materials (CRM) 94
cross-border movements 29
Customs Act 139, 147

Cyprus 12
Czech Republic 18

Dangerous Substances Directive 21
Darda, Vijay J. 110
decent work deficit 144
Delhi 36, 65, 89, 112, 125, 136, 138, 141–142, 152, 154, 158
depollution 53, 75, 180
Deposit Refund Scheme (DRS) 116–117, 119, 122
Design for Disassembly (DfD) 51, 176
design for environment (DfE) 108, 176
developed countries 6, 14–15, 134, 142, 147; e-waste generated in 11
developing countries 6, 11, 14–15, 42, 61–63, 88, 134–135, 154; EPR regulations in 63; e-waste generated in 11
development: economic 18, 62, 134; form of 1; index 3; sustainable 32, 42, 50–51, 93, 95, 97, 103, 176
devices 2, 9, 16, 22, 42, 64, 70, 77, 99, 101
dibutyl phthalate (DBP) 23
Digital India Mission 38, 105, 133, 146, 150, 152, 173
di-isobutyl phthalate (DIBP) 23
dioxins 69, 79, 81–82
dioxins and furans 87
di (2-ethylhexyl) phthalate (DEHP) 23
directive (EU) 2015/863 19, 22
disassembling 77, 179
dismantlers 64, 112, 114–119, 121, 123, 125, 142–143, 148, 151, 155, 158, 160–161, 167, 170–171, 180
dismantling 4–5, 35, 41, 69, 71, 75, 77–78, 88, 98, 101, 116–118, 125, 127, 144, 153, 155, 157, 160–161, 167, 170–171, 174–176, 178; deep-level 88; manual 69, 75, 88; systematic 98
disposal 2, 4–5, 7, 9, 13, 17–20, 24, 26–28, 30, 32–34, 36, 38–39, 49–53, 55–56, 59, 62, 68, 71, 74, 77, 79–80, 89, 93–94, 98–99, 102, 105–106, 108, 110–111, 113–114, 116–120, 124, 126–128, 134, 137, 141, 147, 150–152, 156, 166–167, 169, 172–173, 175–177, 179; assembly points 27; bans and restrictions 53; behaviour 36, 137; fee 52; fees 53, 56, 62; final 28, 30, 33, 49–52, 68, 71, 93, 106, 114, 176–177; methods of 20, 79; practices 30; processes 5; products 56; proper 5, 93, 124, 150; residue 99; safe 7, 27, 52, 134, 152, 175; system 5

DNA 14, 81, 84, 87; damage 14, 81
domestic courts 18
Draft E-waste Management Rules 149
dual model 57
dumping 11, 14, 18, 41, 69, 78, 89, 135;
 Durban Declaration 25; illegal 11, 41
dysprosium 73–74

East-Asia 18
e-bins 151
eco-design 57, 98
ecology 50, 97; industrial 50, 97
economic: benefits 6, 41, 105, 123, 145, 167, 181; boom 68; concerns 166, 173; development 18, 62, 134; growth 2, 5, 51, 94–95, 103, 110, 134, 175–176; markets 30; sustainability 39; viability 43, 95
economic growth in 51
economy 1–2, 6, 18, 30–31, 35, 38, 42, 57, 69–70, 93–95, 97–104, 106, 108–109, 135, 141, 144, 150–151, 154–155, 159, 165–166, 172, 174–176, 179–181; circular 2, 6, 30–31, 38, 57, 69, 93–94, 97–100, 102, 106, 108–109, 150, 165–166, 172, 174, 179–181; e-waste-based 94; formal 42, 108, 144, 151, 159, 166, 174–175; global 93; Indian 103; informal 35, 42, 144, 155, 165, 174–175; linear 98; local 18; restorative 30
ecosystem 5, 33, 35, 42, 180
Ecuador 17
education 6, 33–34, 62, 70, 102, 156
e-gadgets 114
e-giants 35
Egypt 11, 37, 154
electrical and electronic product (e-product) 2–4, 6, 39, 43, 52, 56, 60, 68, 70–72, 82, 114, 118, 129, 136, 148–149, 178
electrical and electronic sector 30
electrical and electronics equipment (EEE) 1, 3–4, 8–9, 16, 19–22, 24, 26, 32–33, 37–39, 41–42, 55–56, 61–62, 64–65, 69, 74, 77, 81–88, 94–95, 104–105, 108, 111–112, 114–119, 126, 136, 139, 147, 150, 156, 167, 170, 174; definition of 8; hazardous substances in, use of 20, 26; importance of 1; importers of 21, 55, 62; life cycle of 33; manufacturers and importers of 21, 55; manufacturing of 64, 112, 114, 116; product categories 9; production of 3, 32, 95; recycling of 20; repair of 16, 167; reuse of 16, 20, 167; waste 3
electronic devices 2, 16, 42, 70, 98; management of 16

Electronic Industries Association of India (ELCINA) 138, 147
electronics 1–2, 6, 14–15, 20, 22, 24, 56, 80, 88, 118, 134, 139, 152, 157–158, 174, 177; barcodes 1; gadgets 6; trading of 14; waste 2, 4, 8, 110–111, 128, 172
Electronics Corporation of India Limited (ECIL) 153
electronic waste (E-waste) 1–18, 20–21, 24–43, 49–50, 52–66, 68–72, 75–81, 88–90, 93–96, 98–102, 104–105, 108–129, 133–161, 165–181; administration of 18; adverse impact on health 66; approaches to 6; aspects of 16, 37, 105, 111, 129, 147, 167, 172; bins 151; cannibalised 77; categories of 9–10, 90, 108, 128; category 10; challenges 31; channelisation of 117, 119, 121, 155–156; characteristics of 43; classification of 166; rate 11–13, 18, 52; collection of 2, 6, 9–13, 15–16, 18–20, 24, 26, 30, 34–35, 37–40, 42–43, 49, 51–52, 54–57, 59–64, 75, 77, 88, 90, 98–102, 112–122, 125, 127, 129, 139–140, 143, 147–149, 151–153, 155–158, 160–161, 166–175, 177–178, 180; concept of 9; constituents of 96; contribution to global warming 14; cycles of 98; data on 2, 10, 14, 43, 125; definition of 3, 7–9, 15, 112–113; legal 7; disposal of 13, 17, 26–27, 110–111, 114, 116, 124, 126–127, 137, 147, 150, 152, 167, 172–173, 176–177; documented 10; production 18; domestic 17–18, 35, 39, 42, 112, 135; export and import of 14, 18, 36–37, 39, 42, 63, 135–136, 138–139, 147–148, 166, 171, 179; illegal 63, 136; monitoring 166, 171; flows of 5–6, 10, 13–15, 40, 61, 114, 154, 157, 180; drop in 11; estimation 39; quantity of 15, 116, 125; undocumented 5, 13; generation of 2–3, 6, 9–13, 15, 24, 30, 33–36, 39, 41, 43, 64, 114, 116–118, 122–123, 125, 136–138, 147–148, 150, 153, 179; domestic 137; generator of 6; global 10, 34, 76, 179; governance of 6; growth of 2, 32; handling 20, 110; hazardous 7, 66; hazards of 14, 78, 146, 157; household 36; illegal traffic of 28; impact 29, 180; importation of 27; imported 36–37, 39–40, 138–139, 146–148, 179; indicators 31; informal system 33; initiatives 33; inventorisation of 147, 152–153, 159, 176; issues 1, 28, 128; LCIA approach to 16; leakage of 39, 42, 62, 158, 168, 170–171, 180;

legislation/regulation/policy on 3, 8, 16, 108, 115, 133, 147, 169, 181; life cycle approach for tackling 31; limitation of statistics 3; management of 2, 4–7, 11–18, 20, 24–26, 29–33, 35, 37–42, 49–50, 52–53, 55–56, 58–59, 62–65, 70, 75, 90, 95, 101–102, 108–109, 111–113, 115–116, 118–119, 122–123, 125, 128–129, 133–134, 136, 141, 145, 147–148, 150–154, 156–161, 165–170, 172–175, 178–180; transboundary 14; mismanagement of 144; movements of 7–8, 14–16, 24, 27–28, 39, 70–71, 134, 179; transboundary 7–8, 14–16, 24, 27–28, 39, 70–71, 134, 179; pan-Indian initiatives for 133–134, 146; perception of 9; preparing inventory on 153; costs of 52; processing of 5, 52, 78, 81, 124, 145; procurement norms 35; quantity of 9–10, 12, 15, 116, 125, 134–135; raw materials in 13; recycled 12, 30; informal 14, 89–90, 139, 143, 154; recycling chain of 75, 98; recycling of 5–6, 10–11, 13–14, 16, 18, 27, 30, 33–34, 37, 54–56, 68, 75, 78, 80, 88–90, 95, 101, 112, 116, 118, 121–123, 129, 137, 139–140, 143–144, 146, 148, 152, 154, 157, 159–161, 166–168, 172, 174, 177, 179; reduction of 16, 20; residues 35, 171; reuse of 16; rules 65, 143; shipment of 34; shipping of 14; sources of 35, 37, 111; statistics 3, 9; storage of 116; structure and linkage of 149; tackling 1, 31; toxic 65; toxic companion of digital era 1–2; toxicity of 40, 65, 69; trade 15, 39, 137, 142, 179; trade chain 39, 142; informal 39; transboundary movements of 7, 15, 70, 134; treating 5–6, 35, 79, 88, 93, 129, 178; treatment 20, 111; treatment of 4, 41–42, 55, 70–71, 80, 90, 101, 124–125, 128, 134, 180; *see also* WEEE

Ellen Macarthur Foundation 93

employment 6, 33–35, 70, 94, 100, 102, 106, 144, 148, 154, 166–168, 173, 175; conditions of 35; indicators 148

end-of-life (EoL) solutions 2–4, 16, 20, 30–31, 33, 38–39, 42, 49–50, 52–53, 56–57, 64, 69, 71, 73, 77, 105, 112, 114, 117–119, 137, 157, 175–176; channelisation of 118; services 30; treatment 33, 73, 176

energy 1, 5, 16, 19, 39, 53, 59, 70–75, 93–94, 99, 101, 104–105, 156–157, 167, 175; generation 5; life cycle 74, 94; supply 1

engineering sector 30

entertainment 6

environment 1–2, 4–7, 13–14, 16–18, 21, 25, 28–33, 38, 40, 42, 49–52, 56, 60–61, 64, 66, 68–71, 75, 78–82, 88–89, 93–97, 100–101, 103, 105–106, 108–111, 113, 115–118, 120–121, 124, 127–129, 134, 136, 138, 143–149, 151–152, 154, 158–159, 165–167, 169, 171, 175–177, 179, 181; aspect of 16; toxic 70, 101; effects on 4, 70, 101; impact on 7, 28–30, 40, 61, 70–71, 80, 88, 101, 134, 144, 147, 152, 167; improved 40, 100; improvement in 2, 30, 50, 75, 100, 145, 176; protection of 60, 64, 95, 106, 124, 171, 175; safe 5–6, 14, 31, 50, 93–94, 108, 128, 148–149, 159, 175, 181; safe working 32

environmental: agreements 7, 18, 24–25; awareness 11, 64, 135; compensation 126; concerns 7, 13, 39, 70–71, 75, 140; considerations 52; costs 52–53; damage 6, 98; degradation 95, 102; governance 135; health 142, 181; costs 142, 181; impacts 4, 32, 41, 51, 54, 69–75, 95, 142, 152, 167; improvements 50–51; information 53; issues 109, 140; laws 109–111, 156; legislation 6; policy 27, 50–53, 109, 170; preventive strategies 50; problems 4, 33; protection 50, 64, 99, 134, 140, 149; protection policy 50; regulations 109, 157; risk assessment 180; risks 15, 25, 78, 180; sustainability 95

environmental agreements 7, 18, 24–25; multilateral 18

environmental Information System (ENVIS) 151

environmentally sound manner (ESM) 5, 28–29, 33, 42, 64, 70, 93, 101, 108, 111–112, 114–116, 118, 125, 153, 157, 174, 177

environmental policy 27, 50–53, 109, 170; Indian 109

environmental pollution 16, 35, 41, 106; countermeasures against 16

2005 Environmental Sustainability Index 135

Environment Management Group (EMG) 31

Environment Protection Act, 1986 (Act 1986/EPA, 1986) 109, 113, 115, 119, 127–128, 146

e-products 1, 4–6, 16, 24, 29, 33, 37, 61, 71, 75, 82, 93–94, 96, 108, 116, 129, 135,

138, 147, 149, 166, 172, 176–177; demand and supply of 94; demand for 37; disposal of 2; life-cycle of 4, 6, 33; life of 4, 149; lifespan of 3; production 39; stages of 94; users of 6
equipment 1–2, 8–10, 15, 22, 24, 36, 52, 56–57, 60, 62, 65, 69, 77, 85, 88, 98–99, 104, 114, 133, 142; cooling and freezing 15; electrical and electronic 1, 8–9, 22, 77, 104; importance of 1; electrical or electronic 8; information technology (IT) 2; large 9–10; medical 36; small 9–10; telecommunication 2, 9–10, 36; temperature exchange 9–10; video and audio 2
e-scrap 4, 9, 39, 152; dispose of 39
E-Stewards 176
EU Commission 95; legislation on waste 95
EU countries 7, 18, 57, 70, 134, 147, 169, 179
EU-India cooperation 106
EU-India summit 106
Europe 10–13, 17, 34, 51, 58, 80, 129, 145, 159; e-waste generation in 12; e-waste in 12, 129, 159
European Chemicals Agency (ECHA) 21
European Commission 51, 63, 106; *Packaging Waste Directive* 51
European Economic Area (EEA) 21
European Parliament 18, 22
European Union (EU) 7, 9, 11, 15, 17–22, 24, 26, 28–29, 37, 50, 57, 63, 70, 72, 94–95, 97–98, 103–104, 106, 134, 136, 138, 147, 169, 171, 179; environmental awareness in 11; e-waste 11; non-compliance of 18; laws 19; legislations 18–20; regulatory framework of 19; WEEE Directive in 134
European Waste Shipment Regulation (WSR) 28
EU Waste Framework Directive, 2008 26
e-waste disposal 13, 17, 26–27, 39, 56, 105, 108, 110–111, 114, 116, 119, 124, 126–127, 137, 147, 150, 152, 156, 167, 172–173, 176–177; Executive Order/guidelines for 173
e-waste export 135; implications of 135
e-waste management 2, 4–7, 11–18, 20, 24–26, 29–35, 37–42, 49–50, 52–53, 55–56, 58–59, 62–65, 70, 75, 90, 95, 101–102, 108–109, 111–113, 115–116, 118–119, 122–123, 125, 128–129, 133–134, 136, 141, 145, 147–148, 150–154, 156–161, 165–170, 172–175, 178–180; aspects of 15–16, 33, 37, 129, 147, 167, 172; challenges for 42, 53, 175; characteristics 11; cohesive thinking 38, 40; collaborations for 33; compliance costs for 62; components of 7, 112, 180; domestic 18; effective 2, 38, 59; importance of 6; jurisprudence of 128; law-driven 150; legislation or policy for 17; need for 6; opportunities for 173; policy issues for 148; practices 12–13, 63; informal 13; regulation of 25; regulatory framework for 64; thinking 7, 31, 38, 40, 165; treatment 4–5, 32, 39–42, 71, 80, 90, 124–125, 134, 166, 174, 180; trends of 15; UN initiatives for 31
e-waste Management (Amendment) Rules, 2018 37, 115
e-waste (Management and Handling) Rules, 2011 63–65, 90, 108, 112–116, 122–125, 133–134, 138, 146, 151, 154–156; limitations of 114
e-waste (management) Rules, 2016 37, 43, 55, 66, 90, 104, 108, 112, 115–117, 119–122, 124, 127–129, 134, 146, 152, 154–155, 157, 160, 167–168, 170, 173, 177–178, 181
e-waste recycling trust fund 27
e-waste roadmap 2030 for India: A compilation of thought pieces by sector experts 159
e-waste sector 18, 63, 115, 134–135, 144, 154–155, 159–161, 174; government control of 18; Indian 154, 160
export and import 14–16, 18, 21, 25, 28–29, 35, 37–39, 42, 63, 104, 108, 111–113, 117, 128, 135–139, 147–148, 166, 171, 179; ban of 25; e-waste 135; global 14; illegal 15, 18
extended producer responsibility (EPR) 2, 6–7, 13, 16, 20, 24, 27, 29–30, 34, 37–38, 41–43, 49–66, 95, 108–109, 111–123, 126, 128–129, 133–134, 144, 146, 148–149, 151–152, 155–156, 159–160, 165–170, 172, 176, 179, 181; acceptance and implementation of 30; aspects of 114, 121, 134; economic 134; categories of instruments 52; concept of 27, 50, 54, 111; definition of 50; development of 51, 58; economics of 149; effectiveness of 65, 115; enforcement of 60; as environmental strategy 51; evolution of 49–50; goals of 49, 53; impact of 63; implementation of 13, 30, 37, 49–50, 54–59, 63, 66, 121–122, 144, 148, 151–152, 169, 172;

challenges in 59, 63; initiatives for 66, 122; key considerations for 58; instruments 52–53; introduction of 50, 112, 134; legislation 54; multi-centric nature of 49; non-implementation of 126; performance of 66, 119; principle of 51, 53–54, 56, 114; objectives of 54; process to implement 54; programme 54; regulations 56, 63; as regulatory, enforcement 119–120; as regulatory mechanisms 119; scope of 116; transparency of 58; for waste management 52
extraction 30, 33, 35, 41, 73, 77–79, 89, 93–94, 97, 99, 103, 136, 138, 142, 158

Factories Act 1948 116
fibre-glass 76
fibre-optic cables 1
financial flows 35, 49
financial responsibilities 19, 52, 63
financial services 32; access to 32
First International Conference on Chemicals Management (ICCM1) 29
flame retardants 79, 84
fluorides 75
food chains 5
formal-informal integration 159
formal-informal partnership 31, 38, 144–151, 153–154, 160, 174, 179
formal-informal sector partnership 173
formalisation (registration, authorisation, and monitoring) 145, 148, 154–155, 159, 170
formal sector 144–145, 154
fossil, depletion 70
fuel 74, 97; use 16, 94

Gary, Davis 51; Producer Responsibility Principle 51
General Finance Rules (GFR) 173
German Ordinance on the Avoidance of Packaging Waste 51
Germany 12, 15, 34, 51, 55, 135
Ghana 11, 14, 17–18, 25, 27, 37, 71, 80, 179; Electronic Waste (Disposal and Recycling) Regulations 27
GIZ/GTZ 35, 81, 87, 120, 135–137, 147, 151, 154–155
glass 5, 68, 74–77, 81, 85, 88, 96, 102, 114, 135, 141, 147, 161, 171, 175
Global Environment Facility (GEF) 33
global e-waste monitor (GEM) 2, 9, 11, 13–14, 16, 30–31, 37, 53, 104, 138; GEM 2014 3, 9, 15, 138; GEM 2017 2–3, 9, 15,
31, 37, 53, 138; GEM 2020 2–3, 9, 11, 13–16, 30, 104
Global E-waste Statistics Partnership (GESP) 31–32
global warming 4, 13–14, 41, 71, 94; contribution of e-waste to 14
Goa 123, 160
Goa SPCB 160
gold 5, 41, 72–76, 78–79, 89–90, 96, 101, 142
goods 1, 15, 21, 35, 56, 96, 98, 134, 139, 152; consumer 98; electronic 35, 96, 152; industrial 21; second hand 15; white 56
governance and administration of 59
government agencies 116, 133, 136, 149–150, 160, 166, 172–173; coordination among 172; initiatives by 150
Government of India (GoI) 37, 41, 104–105, 108, 110–111, 113, 133, 146–147, 150–152, 159, 180; *Electronic Waste (Handling and Disposal) Bill, 2005* 110; *E-waste in India* 150; e-waste management by 159; *Guidelines for Environmentally Sound Management of E-Waste'* (Guidelines, 2008) 109–111, 113, 146; *Hazardous Material (Management, Handling and Transboundary Movement) Rules, 2007*, 110; *Hazardous Waste (Management, Handling & Transboundary) Rules* 110–111; *Hazardous Wastes (Management, Handling and Transboundary Movement) Rules, 2008 (Rules, 2008)* 110
Great Britain 12
green criminology 15
Green Customs Initiative (GCI) 28
greenhouse gas (GHG) 13–14, 69, 71, 73–74; emission of 13–14, 69, 71, 74
Greenpeace 80, 89, 141
green technology 38, 108, 173, 175
grievance redressal mechanism 173
gross Domestic Product (GDP) 41, 96, 103–104; growth of 103
guidelines 8, 16, 30, 33, 50, 60–61, 90, 111, 113, 116–117, 119–120, 159, 169, 173, 176, 178; operation management 50; regulating 16
guidelines for environmentally sound management of e-waste 90, 111, 113
Guidelines on implementation of E-waste (Management and Handling) Rules, 2011 125
Guiyu, China 14, 71, 179
Gujarat 36, 123, 140, 152, 160, 173
Gujarat Pollution Control Board (GPCB) 160

Haryana 123, 170
hazardous: components 41, 77; elements 7, 71; importation of 27; practices 40, 143
Hazardous and Other Waste (Management and Transboundary Movement) Rules, 2016 124
hazardous chemicals 24, 32, 79–80; use of 32
hazardous substances 4–5, 8, 20, 22, 24, 26, 32, 61, 78–79, 87, 111–113, 115–116, 126, 128, 144, 146, 148, 172, 175–176; use of 5, 20, 26, 32, 61, 112, 116, 126, 175–176
hazardous waste 4, 24, 27–28, 32–33, 42, 68, 109–113, 124, 127, 129, 149, 151, 169, 177; generation of 32; import of 112; ban on 112; management 25, 32, 129, 169; movements 24; transboundary movements of 24, 28
Hazardous Waste (Management and Handling) Rules (HWM Rules) 109–110, 112–113, 128
Hazardous Wastes (Management and Handling) Amendment Rules, 2003 113, 134
Hazardous Wastes (Management and Handling) Rules 2003, The 109
Hazardous Wastes (Management, Handling and Transboundary Movement) Rules, 2008 110, 113
hazards 21, 39, 53, 78, 81; health 5, 68, 81, 88, 90, 93, 115, 148, 175, 181; occupational 81
health 1–2, 4–7, 13–14, 16, 18, 21, 25–26, 28–34, 38–40, 42, 60–61, 66, 68–71, 76, 78–90, 93–94, 96, 98, 101, 108–109, 111, 115, 118, 124, 134, 136, 142, 145, 147–149, 151–152, 155, 158–159, 166–167, 175–177, 179, 181; concerns 5, 13, 68, 78; environmental 142, 181; costs 142, 181; impact on 7, 66, 69, 76, 98; occupational 14, 136; problems 4, 14, 33
healthcare 6
Heathrow Airport 2
Herzegovina 17
High Court of Kerala 124
High Court of Tamil Nadu 124
Himachal Pradesh 123, 125
Holwell, Dave 73
Hong Kong 12
human health 2, 4–6, 16, 21, 26, 28–33, 38–40, 42, 60–61, 70–71, 78–80, 82–89, 94, 101, 108, 124, 134, 148–149, 151, 159, 166–167, 175, 177, 179, 181; concerns 78; effects on 4; hazard 39; impact on 16, 28, 30, 32, 69, 71, 78,
82–88, 134, 167, 177; problems 33; protection of 21, 26, 108; risks to 6; threats to 5
Hungary 18
hydro chlorofluorocarbon (HCFCs) 4
ILO Guidelines on OSH Management Systems (ILO-OSH) 159
immune system 14, 76, 82, 86
importers 21, 27, 51, 55–56, 58, 62, 118–119, 142
incineration 20, 77, 79, 87
India 12, 14, 17, 30–31, 34–42, 50, 55, 57, 61, 64–65, 78, 80, 88–89, 93, 102–106, 108–113, 118–119, 123–129, 133–141, 144, 146–154, 157–159, 165–166, 169, 171, 173, 175–177, 179–181; circular economy in 102; EPR in 64; effectiveness of 65; implementation of 169; e-waste cohesive management in 37; e-waste flow and recycling in 40; e-waste in 35–37, 78, 109, 129, 136–137, 150, 159, 177; generation of 35–36, 136–137; imported 36–37; problem of 136; production of 137; projections for 37; e-waste management in 30–31, 38, 40, 42, 50, 64, 109, 134, 150, 158, 166, 179; legislation in 37; opportunities and challenges of 40–42; e-waste trade chain in 39; export-import policy 112; health hazards in 88; policy-making in 181; recycling facility in 123; regulatory framework of 108; regulatory regime for e-waste in 109; resource efficiency in 102; resource use in 102–103; *Solid Waste Management Act, 2008* 55; waste generation in 34
India-EU Resource Efficiency and Circular Economy Partnership 106, 179
Indian 109; environmental policy 109; e-waste sector 154, 160; informal sector 144; legislation 128
Indian Constitution: Twelfth Schedule 109
Indian Resource Panel (InRP) 103
indium 89, 101
Individual Producer Responsibility (IPR) 57–58
Indo-German-Swiss E-waste Initiative 135
Indonesia 12, 55
industrial ecology 50, 97
industry 1–2, 21, 55–59, 64, 81, 94, 96, 105, 111, 120–121, 126, 134–136, 140, 149–151, 156–158, 160, 176; associations 136; chemicals 21; electronics 2, 134; recycling 59, 140, 156; scrap 135, 140

Index **207**

informal sector 11, 13, 18, 30, 35, 38, 42, 54, 62–63, 65, 71, 78, 88, 90, 93, 105, 108, 114–115, 123, 129, 133, 139, 141–149, 152–155, 157–158, 161, 166–167, 170–172, 174–175, 177–179; formalisation of 145, 154; formalised 145; ill-equipped 129; Indian 144
information: environmental 53; instruments 53; technology 2; transformation of 1
information and communication technology (ICT) 34
information technology (IT) 2, 9–10, 22, 56, 87, 116, 134, 141, 150–151, 156, 170; equipment 2
infrastructure 6, 18, 31, 35, 38, 40, 43, 58–59, 61, 63–64, 88, 93–95, 101, 105, 120–122, 126, 140–141, 148–149, 153, 159, 161, 166, 170, 173–175, 177–180; inadequate 35; recycling 43, 63–64, 93, 105, 122, 141, 161, 175, 180
inhalation 79, 81, 83, 86
innovation 2, 21, 42, 59, 121, 166, 173, 179; technical 2
Institute for Global Environmental Strategies 49
institutions 1, 39–40, 49, 54, 103, 116, 124, 136, 139, 150–151, 154, 160, 168–169, 172, 175, 178; international 103
intellectual property 95; security 95
international chemicals management 29
international conventions 24, 108, 128
International Finance Corporation (IFC) 151, 158–159; e-waste programme 158
International Labour Organisation (ILO) 4, 6, 15, 35, 73, 93, 98, 139, 143–144, 148, 150, 159, 175; approaches to e-waste 6
international legislative frameworks 18
international obligations 28
international policy framework 29
International Resource Panel (IRP) 95
International Solid Waste Association (ISWA) 50, 53–54, 58, 63, 166
International Telecommunication Union (ITU) 33, 119
internet 1
investment 6, 13, 62, 95, 154, 166, 174, 178; optimisation 62; security 95
iPhone 73, 81
Ireland 15, 55
IRGSSA 136
iron 30, 74–77, 87, 96
Israel 12
Italy 12, 55
ITES 156

Jamaica 11
Jammu & Kashmir 123
Japan 12, 17, 29, 34, 37, 56–57; *Home Appliance Recycling Law* 56; *Law for the Promotion of Effective Utilization of Resources* 56; WEEE management regulation 56
Jharkhand 123
job 2, 6, 32, 35, 41–42, 57, 96, 104, 144–145, 165, 167, 174–175; creation 2, 6, 32, 144–145, 174–175
jurisprudence 109, 128, 151, 165–166

kabaadiwala 39–40, 65, 152, 157
Karnataka 36, 123
Karo Sambhav Pvt. Ltd 158–159
Kawakami, Tsuyoshi 159
Kenya 11, 17, 179
Kerala 66, 122, 124
knowledge 1, 29, 65, 94, 133, 135, 139, 145–146, 149–150, 179; sharing of 1, 34
K. N. Unnikrishnan vs. Cochin Port Trust & Ors 124, 127
Korea, Republic of 14, 17, 29, 37, 56–57
Korforidua 80
Kuwait 12
Kyrgyzstan 12

labour 1, 6, 32, 35, 42, 88, 93, 95, 99, 106, 120, 137, 141, 144, 148, 155, 167; cost of 88, 95, 141; market policies 6; rights 32; semi-skilled 35; skilled/trained 95; social security for 35; wages 35
landfilling 53, 70, 79, 101, 175
landfills 2, 4, 11, 16–17, 20, 42, 69–70, 77, 79–81, 88, 101–102, 111, 134, 141–142, 148, 171, 175; bans of scrap 16; state-of-the-art 80
laptops 74
Latin America 15, 17, 24, 27
leachates 77–79
lead (Pb) 4–5, 16, 20, 23, 27, 33, 37, 41, 53–54, 59, 62, 69–70, 72–76, 78–81, 85, 89–90, 102, 104–105, 113–115, 128, 140–141, 144, 151, 166, 171–172, 177, 180; fumes 80
legislation/regulation/policy 1, 3, 6–8, 11–13, 16–22, 24–31, 33–35, 37–39, 43, 49–64, 68, 71, 80, 90, 95, 97, 100, 103, 108–113, 115, 121–122, 126, 128–129, 133–134, 136, 138–139, 141, 144–150, 152, 154–159, 165–166, 170–171, 173, 175–176, 179–181; administrative 16;

architecture of 165–166; companion 20; enforcement of 179; environmental 6, 27, 50–53, 109, 157, 170; environmental protection 50; EPR 54, 56, 63; EU 19; on e-waste 108; fiscal 144; framework 16; implementation of 43; Indian 113, 128; instruments 49–51, 53–54, 60, 62, 121; international 134, 149; labour 144; labour market 6; macroeconomic 144; measures 50, 53–54; national 3, 11–13, 19, 58; principle 27, 50–51, 53; recommendations 6; risk management 144; sectoral 144; social 144, 158; social protection 144; status of e-waste related 16; structural 144
legislation/regulatory 7, 10, 16, 18, 20, 24, 29, 70, 110, 133, 147; EU 18, 20; frameworks 7, 18; international 18; policy 16
Lenovo 65
Libreville Declaration 25
life cycle 4, 19, 29, 31, 33, 41, 50–53, 62, 70–72, 74, 93–94, 97–98, 175; costs 51; energy 74, 94; environmental improvements 50–51; product 52–53, 62
Life Cycle Impact Assessment (LCIA) 2, 16, 38, 70–71
light emitting diodes (LEDs) 83, 85
Lindhqvist, Thomas 50–51, 169
linear economy model 98–99
liquid crystal display (LCD) 24, 74, 85
lithium 81, 85, 101
livelihood 2, 42, 167; opportunities 2
logistics 1, 30, 38–39, 42, 100, 114, 140–141, 149, 177, 180; reverse 30, 149
London Guidelines for the Exchange of Information on Chemicals in International Trade (London Guidelines) 29
LPG 75

Macedonia 17
Madagascar 17
Madhya Pradesh 36, 123
Madurai Farooq Ahmed vs. The Tamil Nadu Pollution Control Board 124, 127
magnesium 72, 87
Maharashtra 36, 87, 110, 114, 123, 136–137
Maharashtra Pollution Control Board (MPCB) 137, 170
Mahendra Pandey Vs. Union of India & Ors 126, 128
Make in India Mission 38, 105, 146, 150, 173
Malaysia 56; Draft Regulation on Recycling and Disposal of EEE 56; *Solid Waste and Public Cleansing Management Act, 2007* 56

management 1–2, 4–7, 9, 11–20, 24–35, 37–43, 49–50, 52–56, 58–60, 62–65, 70, 75, 90, 95, 97–98, 101–102, 104, 108–113, 115–116, 118–119, 121–123, 125, 128–129, 133–134, 136, 141, 144–145, 147–154, 156–161, 165–170, 172–175, 178–180; e-waste 2, 4–7, 11–18, 20, 24–26, 29–33, 35, 37–42, 49–50, 52–53, 55–56, 58–59, 62–65, 70, 75, 90, 95, 101–102, 108–109, 111–113, 115–116, 118–119, 122–123, 125, 128–129, 133–134, 136, 141, 145, 147–148, 150–154, 156–161, 165–170, 172–175, 178–180; practices 1, 12–13, 25, 63, 145; risk 144; waste 2, 5–7, 9, 11–20, 24–25, 30–35, 37–42, 49–50, 52–53, 56, 58–59, 62–64, 70, 75, 95, 97–98, 101–102, 108–112, 115–116, 118–119, 122–123, 125, 128–129, 133–134, 136, 141, 145, 147–148, 150–154, 156–161, 165–170, 172–175, 178–180
manganese 74, 89
manufacturers 21, 35, 39, 49–51, 53–55, 60–61, 115–116, 119, 135–136, 140–141, 157
Manufacturers Association of Information Technology (MAIT) 135, 147
manufacturing 4, 30, 43, 64, 72–75, 77, 94, 112, 114, 116, 152; process 30
markets 6, 13–14, 19–21, 30, 35, 39–40, 42, 52, 55–57, 65, 74, 77, 95, 101–102, 118, 122–123, 126, 135, 137, 139–140, 142–143, 146–147, 149, 153–154, 156, 158, 161, 166–167, 170–171, 173–175, 178–181; economic 30; EU 19, 21; internal 14; refurbishment 35, 137, 149; second hand 65
MARPOL 124, 127–128
massive open online courses (MOOC) 152
material flow analysis (MFA) 38–39
materials 3–4, 7–8, 13–14, 23, 30–33, 35, 37–43, 51–54, 57, 59–62, 64, 69–73, 76–77, 81, 84, 87–88, 93–106, 108, 114–115, 117, 122, 129, 137, 139–145, 148–149, 151, 153, 155, 158, 166, 168–169, 171, 174–178, 180–181; abiotic 103; balancing 39; biodegradable 98; biotic 103; circulation of 99; complex 101; consumption 32; domestic 32; critical 94; demand for 104; filler 77; global use 37; hazardous 77, 81, 100; homogeneous 23; intrinsic value 61, 76; metallic 4; nonhazardous 77;

non-metallic 4; non-recyclable 77; petroleum-based 4; primary 97; product 98; recoverable and reusable 71; recovered 35, 38, 95, 99, 102, 114, 139, 141, 171, 175, 177–178; recovery of 30, 39–40, 42, 69, 77, 94, 105–106, 114, 135, 140, 143, 174; secondary 3, 30–31, 35, 39, 43, 53–54, 62, 105, 108, 115, 122, 144, 148–149, 153, 166, 171, 174, 176–178, 180–181; virgin 7, 93–94
M.C. Mehta Vs. Union of India & Ors 124, 126, 128
Melanesia 17
Mercosur Policy 27
mercury (Hg) 4–5, 13, 20, 23, 29, 69–70, 73–74, 78–81, 85, 89–90, 116–117, 119, 127, 167; deposition of 13; emissions of 69; inorganic 13
metals 4–5, 33, 39, 41, 61, 68–69, 71–81, 83–84, 86, 88–90, 94, 96–97, 99–102, 105–106, 114, 124, 127, 135–136, 138–143, 147, 158, 161, 167, 169, 171, 180; base 5, 75; copper 5, 30, 41, 72–79, 81, 84–85, 89–90, 102, 140; critical 101–102; demand for 99; gold 5, 41, 72–76, 78–79, 89–90, 96, 101–102, 105, 142; hazardous 73; heavy 78–79, 88, 124, 127; leaching effects of 69; platinum 5, 41, 74–75, 94, 101, 105; precious 5, 75–76, 100–102, 105, 140, 147; primary 74; recovered 102; recoveries 33; selenium 5, 74; silver 5, 41, 72–73, 75–76, 86, 89–90, 96, 101–102, 105; toxic 80, 83; zinc 5, 74, 81, 84, 86, 89–90, 140
Metal Scrap Trade Corporation (MSTC) 39, 169, 180
methanol 77
Mexico 17, 37
Micronesia 17
micro-organisms 5
Micro, Small and Medium Enterprises Development Act, 2006 112
Microsoft 65, 154
Minamata Convention on Mercury 29
minerals 4, 33, 74, 97, 103–104; deposits 33; non-metal 97; non-metallic 103; strategic 33
mining 7, 31, 33, 41, 70, 72, 74–75, 94, 97, 99–104; virgin 99
Ministry of Electronics and Information Technology (MeitY) 11, 37, 41–42, 104–105, 114, 150, 152, 159, 165, 172–173; *E-waste awareness for bulk consumers* 150

Ministry of Science & Technology 173
Mobile Phone Partnership Initiative (MPPI) 28
mobile phones 15, 35, 37, 61, 64, 73, 96, 133, 137, 139, 144, 152
MoEF 90, 96, 110–111, 125–126, 135–136
MoEFCC 115, 118, 123, 125, 127–128, 159, 170, 172, 176; performance of 123
Moldova 17–18
Montenegro 17
Montreal Protocol 29
Morocco 11
multi-lateral environmental agreements (MEA) 24–25, 28–29
municipal corporations 171
municipal solid waste (MSW) 2, 5, 79, 102, 110–111, 113, 124; management 5
Municipal Solid Wastes (Management & Handling) Rules, 2000 (MSW Rules) 110–111, 113
mutagenic 24, 69, 71
mutual trust-based partnership 59

Nairobi Declaration 28
Namibia 11
National Environmental Policy, 2006 (NEP) 113, 145, 149, 159
National Green Tribunal (NGT) 109, 124, 126–128, 170
National Institution for Transforming India (NITI) Aayog 11, 37, 41–42, 95, 97, 103–105, 114, 159, 165, 173, 176
National Policy on Electronics, 2012 159
National Skill Development Corporation (NSDC) 150, 159, 175
natural resources 39, 95, 97; conservation of 100; degradation of 95; demand for 95; restorative capacity of 98
neodymium 73–74
Netherlands 15
neuro-development 14
New Zealand 13, 17
NGO 136, 147, 155, 157–158, 173
nickel 72, 74–77, 86
Nigeria 11, 14–18, 37, 179; person-in-the port 14; 'person-in-the port' project in 14
Nokia 61, 64, 144
non-compliance 18, 21, 115, 119, 165
non-government agencies 150, 160
non-hazardous substances 5, 172
non-metals 141
North America 11, 15, 17–18, 34
Northern Europe 12
Norway 3, 12

obsolescence 2, 42, 137–138
Oceania 10–13, 17, 34; e-waste generation in 12
Odisha 66, 122–123, 170
OECD Council Decision 28
open-air burning 5, 25, 78–80, 89
organised sector 36
Organization for Economic Co-operation and Development (OECD) 28, 52, 59, 138; defined EPR 52
original equipment manufacturers (OEM) 60, 62, 181
ozone layer 71, 82

PACE 2, 4, 11, 41, 74, 96, 98
Pacific Island 13
Pacific Island countries and territories (PICTs) 13
packaging 51–52, 59, 73–74, 93; waste 51–52
Pakistan 14, 89, 135, 138
palladium 41, 72–75, 101
Panama 17
Pan India Awareness Programme (PIAP) 152
Paraguay 27
Parliamentary Standing Committee 103
Parliamentary Standing Committee on Science and Technology, Environment and Forests 110
Partnership Measuring ICT for Development 32
PCB 41, 68, 70, 75–80, 101–102
Persistent organic pollutants (POPs) 68, 81, 167, 180
Peru 17
PGM 72
pharmaceuticals 49
Philippines, the 12, 14, 56; ecological solid waste management act of 2000 56
phosphorus 4–5, 75
plastics 4–5, 68, 71, 74, 76–84, 86, 88–89, 96, 102, 105, 135, 140–141, 147, 161, 171, 175–176; BFR 5, 80
Poland 18, 55
pollutants 4, 7, 24, 39, 68–69, 80–82, 89–90, 94, 112, 148; chemical 80; organic 4, 68, 81
'polluter pays' principle 50–51, 109
pollution 7, 16, 35, 37, 39, 41, 70–71, 77, 79, 89, 94, 101, 105–106, 113, 124, 127–128, 135, 144–145, 156, 169; assessment of 169; environmental 16, 35, 41, 106; marine 124, 127–128

Pollution Control Committee (PCC) 109, 121, 125
pollution control devices 101
polyaromatic hydrocarbons (PAHs) 4, 180
poly brominated biphenyl (PBB) 21, 23, 70, 83
poly brominated diphenyl ethers (PBDEs) 5, 21, 23, 70, 76, 80–83, 89
poly chlorinated biphenyl 4
polychlorinated biphenylsa 82
polychlorinated dibenzo-p-dioxin furans (PCDD/Fs) 5
polychlorinated namphalenes (PCNs) 89
Polynesia 17
poly vinyl chloride (PVC) 4–5, 69, 76, 79, 81–82, 84–85, 87, 139
portable electronic devices 2
poverty 18, 135, 144, 176
precautionary principle 50, 109
pre-processing 75, 77, 88, 100–101
private sector 18, 103
processing 5, 52, 55, 57, 61, 75, 77–78, 81, 88–89, 95, 100–101, 112, 117, 123–125, 127, 129, 139–140, 145, 147, 158, 167, 180
producer responsibility organisation (PRO) 37, 39–40, 43, 50, 55–59, 62–63, 115–121, 134, 146, 155, 157–159, 166, 168–170, 173–174, 180; challenges faced by 63; concept of 63; functioning 134; performance of 63; role of 50, 57–58; scope of 57
producers 2–3, 13, 16, 19–21, 24, 26–27, 37, 41–43, 49–50, 52–65, 112, 114–123, 126, 134–136, 144, 146, 149, 152–158, 160, 166–168, 170, 172, 177, 179–181; economic burden of 54; legal compliance by 168; roles and responsibilities of 64–65, 112, 114, 116
product design 19–20, 30, 41, 49, 52, 61–62, 98, 108, 114, 148, 156, 176; improvement in 176
production 3, 6, 18, 20–21, 26, 32–33, 39, 41, 49–51, 53, 59–60, 70, 72–75, 94–95, 97–98, 104, 108, 133, 135–137, 140, 148, 165, 175–176; chain 98; closed-loop 94; costs 94; EEE 95
products: categories 9, 59, 90; design 19–20, 30, 41, 49, 52, 61–62, 98, 108, 114, 148, 156, 176; development of 5; discarded 4, 122; electronic 15, 19, 26, 56, 102; environmental design of 54; EoL of 16; flows 49; life cycle of 19, 50, 52–53, 62;

materials 98; recycling of 30, 49, 152; reusability of 98; usability of 4
Profitable Environment Management (PREMA) 136
Punjab 36, 123, 125
Punjab Pollution Control Board 125

Qatar 12
quality of air and water 169
quality of life 2, 5, 124, 143, 149

Rajasthan 123
rare earth elements 4, 94
raw materials 4, 13, 30–33, 37, 73, 93–94, 98–100, 102–104, 142–143, 181; acquisition of 33; demand 32; embedded 99; extraction and production of 73; extraction of 33, 93; primary 103; secondary 30, 100, 104
recovery 4–7, 16–20, 24, 26, 28, 30, 35, 38–40, 42–43, 49, 52–55, 57, 61–62, 69, 75–77, 88–89, 93–97, 100–102, 104–106, 108, 111, 113–115, 117, 121–122, 129, 135, 140–145, 147–149, 153, 161, 166–168, 172–174, 176–178, 180; costs 101; efficient 30; materials 39, 69, 77, 94, 106, 135, 140; processes 76; resources 4–7, 16, 24, 28, 30, 35, 39, 49, 54, 61–62, 75, 88, 93, 95–97, 100, 104, 106, 108, 121, 140, 144–145, 148–149, 161, 166–167, 172–173, 176–178, 180
recyclability 52, 99–100
recycle 5, 9, 18–19, 24, 30–31, 56, 99, 110–111, 143, 166, 171, 174, 176
recyclers 3, 13, 39–40, 42, 55, 58, 61–62, 64–65, 88, 90, 99, 112–121, 123, 125, 135–137, 140, 142–146, 151–158, 160–161, 167–168, 170–172, 177–178, 180–181; formal 13, 39, 140, 144–146, 153–154, 158, 181; informal 39–40, 88, 136, 140, 146, 154, 158, 180; investment conditions for 13
recycling 2, 4–6, 9–11, 13–14, 16–20, 24, 26–27, 30–35, 37–43, 49–57, 59–65, 68–71, 73–78, 80, 88–90, 93–95, 97–105, 108, 111–116, 118–119, 121–123, 125, 127–129, 133–149, 151–161, 165–168, 170–181; activities 2, 18, 149, 175, 178; capacity 35, 122–123, 140, 160, 180; chemical 77; culture 165–166, 178–179, 181; economics of 61, 145, 149, 153, 177; efficiency 101; e-waste 11, 14, 18, 27, 56, 68, 78, 80, 88–90, 95, 123, 129, 139–140, 143–144, 146, 154, 157, 159, 179;

facilities 80, 103, 123, 125, 129, 149, 157, 178; financial burden of 18; formal 11, 104, 123, 140, 152–153, 177, 181; illegal 115; improper 5; industry 59, 140, 156; informal 11, 78, 80, 88, 140, 154, 177; infrastructure for 18, 43, 63–64, 88, 93, 105, 122, 141, 161, 175, 177, 180; methods 88, 141; methods of 5, 65; obligations 57; operations 14, 78, 88; physical 77; problems of 33; processes of 43, 69, 76–77, 89, 101, 103, 105, 118, 129, 142, 177–178; formal 105; related issues 122; rudimentary methods 5, 71, 88, 90; safe 19, 152; society 179, 181; substandard 14; sustainable 2, 5; technique and technology 26, 35, 70, 93, 98, 100–101, 141; trade 40, 143
recycling chain 75, 95, 98, 101, 145, 149, 154; efficiency of 101
recycling sector 40–41, 129, 140, 143
refining 75, 77, 100, 117; processes 77
refrigerators and freezers 96
refurbish 4–5, 7, 30–31, 39–41, 114, 166, 174
refurbishers 115–116, 119, 151, 167, 174
refurbishing 3, 18, 117, 149, 166–167, 173
refurbishment 4, 35, 41, 57, 116, 137, 149; market 35, 137, 149
Regional E-waste Monitor: East and Southeast Asia 12
Registration, Evaluation, Authorisation, and Restrictions of Chemical Substances (REACH) 7, 17, 19, 21, 24, 26; processes of 21
regulatory: bodies 66, 109, 120, 122–124, 128, 149, 156, 160, 165–166, 169, 172; frameworks 6–8, 18–19, 29–30, 37, 42, 50, 53, 57, 64, 71, 108, 110, 134, 138, 141, 144, 151, 174, 176, 178–179; norms 15; provisions 70, 144, 159
release, realise, responsibility (3Rs) 6
remanufacturing 30, 57, 98, 100
renovation 30
repair 2–7, 16, 30–33, 41–42, 98–99, 108, 114, 129, 135, 149, 156, 158, 165–167, 173–174; options 6; processes 4
repairing 18, 42
repair, refurbish, resource recovery (3Rs) 5
repair, reuse, refurbish, responsibly disposed, recycle and resource recovery (6Rs) 5, 30, 38, 166, 172, 178
report 33
reprotoxic 24, 71
residues 18, 35, 77, 79, 89, 93, 99, 118, 141,

147, 171, 174, 177; recycling and disposal of 177
resins 68, 76–77; oil-based 77
resource efficiency (RE) 2, 6–7, 30–31, 37, 40, 59, 68, 93–95, 97, 100, 102–106, 108, 114, 133, 148, 150, 159–160, 165–166, 171, 173, 177, 180
resources 1–2, 4–7, 16, 24–25, 28, 30, 35, 38–39, 41, 43, 49, 54, 57, 59–62, 68, 70–71, 73–76, 79, 88, 93–104, 106, 108, 114, 121, 133, 140, 144–145, 148–150, 155, 158–161, 165–167, 170–173, 175–178, 180–181; adequate and predictable 25; availability 43; continuum 103; critical 41, 94; use and reuse 94; depletion 93, 95; efficiency 2, 6, 59, 68–69, 93–94, 97, 100, 102–104, 108, 114, 133, 146, 148, 150, 159–160, 165–166, 173, 177, 180; groundwater 79; lack of 25; loops 30; monetary 1; natural 2, 5, 70, 95, 98, 100, 103, 167, 175; problem to 6; recover 30, 104; recoverable 70, 101; recovery 4–7, 16, 24, 28, 30, 35, 39, 49, 54, 61–62, 75, 88, 93, 95–97, 104, 106, 108, 121, 140, 144–145, 148–149, 161, 166–167, 172–173, 176–178, 180; recovery and reuse 4; recovery of 96, 100, 177; re-using 30; scarcity of 38, 94; supply chain 94; supply constraints 95; use of 2, 5, 38, 71, 93–95, 97, 102–103, 108, 175; optimal and efficient 2, 5; virgin 94
respiratory ailments 78
responsibility: economic 51; informative 51; physical 51–52
responsible recycling (R2) 176
restricted substances 20–21, 24
Restriction on Hazardous Substances (RoHS) Directive 7, 17, 19–24, 26, 65, 70, 112, 116, 118–121, 126, 148, 157, 166, 170, 175, 180; compliance 24, 65, 116, 118–119, 126, 166, 170; reduction in 148; RoHS1, 22–23; RoHS2, 19, 21–23; RoHS3, 19, 21–23
reuse 3–5, 7, 9, 15–20, 24, 30–33, 39, 49, 53–54, 74, 88, 93–94, 98–99, 111, 114, 135, 137, 143, 147–149, 165–167, 175–176; optimal 30; preparation for 9
reuse, recycling, recovery (3Rs) 5–6, 19, 30, 149
Ricoh 65
rights: labour 32; to repair 2
Rotterdam Convention on the Prior Informed Consent Procedure for Certain Hazardous Chemicals and Pesticides in International Trade 7, 24
Russia 18, 80
Rwanda 11, 17
satellite TV 1
scrap 4, 9, 16, 39–40, 135, 138–140, 142–143, 147–148, 152–153, 169, 180; industry 135, 140
scrapping 5
SDG 32–33, 38, 150, 158–159, 166; indicators 32
seal-of-approval 53
Second International Conference on Chemicals Management (ICCM2) 29
security 1, 15, 35, 95, 104, 156, 175; implications 15; intellectual property 95; investment 95; social 35, 175; systems 1
Serbia 17
Shailesh Singh Vs. State of U.P. & Ors 127
shared model 57
silica 74, 78
silicon 76, 87
silicon Valley Toxics Coalition (SVTC) 135
silver 5, 41, 72–73, 75–76, 90, 96, 101
Singapore 12, 17, 56–57; legislation for e-waste management 56; National Environment Agency 56; National Voluntary Partnership Programme 56
skills upgradation 145
Slovenia 17
SMEs 147, 153–154
social: benefits 6; organizations 6; security 35, 175
society 1, 50, 64, 94, 98, 103, 112, 126, 141, 150–151, 158, 165–166, 168, 178–179, 181; environmental goals of 50; modern 1
Solid Waste Management Act, 2008 55–56
solid waste management (SWM) 109, 128, 154
Solving the E-waste Problem (StEP) initiative 8–9, 31, 33; White Paper 8–9
South Africa 11, 16–17
South America 17, 34
South Asia 18
South Korea 17, 29, 56–57; EPR in Recycling Law 2003 56
South Pacific 24, 27
Spain 14–15, 55
Sri Lanka 16–17
standardisation 33, 60, 160–161, 176, 180
stannum 89
State Administration of Taxation of China 55

Index

state pollution control boards (SPCB) 37, 109–110, 114–115, 117–119, 121–125, 128, 140, 150, 156, 158, 160, 167, 169–172, 180–181; performance of 123, 170
steel 72, 81, 86
stibium 89
Stockholm Convention on Persistent Organic Pollutants 7, 24
Strategic Approach to International Chemicals Management (SAICM) 7, 18, 29
Strategy on REs in EEE sector 37
Strategy on resource efficiency in electrical and electronic equipment sector 104
Strategy paper on resource efficiency, GoI, The 104
Sub-Sahara 34
subsidy 52, 55–56, 99; utilisation 55
Substances of Very High Concern (SVHC) 21
sulphur 74, 86
supply chain 1, 21, 30, 39–40, 52, 54, 69, 94, 143, 165, 168; global 1, 165; reverse 30, 52, 54, 168
sustainability 29–30, 32–33, 39, 50, 95–96, 103, 122, 135, 143, 157, 161, 177–181; economic 39; environmental 95
Sustainable Cycles (SCYCLE) programme 31
sustainable development 32, 42, 50–51, 93, 95, 97, 103, 176; principles of 50
sustainable development goals 31
Swachh Bharat 38, 105, 146
SWAYAM 150, 175, 178
Sweden 12, 50, 55
Swiss Federal Laboratories for Materials Testing and Research/Swiss Federal Institute for Materials Science and Technology (EMPA) 135–136, 147
Swiss State Secretariat for Economic Affairs (SECO) 135
Switzerland 12, 28, 136
Synthetic Precipitation Leaching Procedures (SPLP) 70

Taiwan, Province of China 12, 17, 56; waste disposal act 56
take-back 16–17, 20, 26, 50, 52–53, 55–57, 60–61, 64, 114, 117–119, 122, 133, 135, 144, 151, 156; campaigns 64, 133, 144; policies 156; policy 61; system 55, 57, 60, 64, 114, 117–119, 135, 144
Tamil Nadu 36, 66, 122–125, 127, 136
Tamil Nadu High Court 124
tax 6, 52–53, 55, 134, 145; administration 55; material 52–53; regime 6; structure 134; upstream combination 52
TBBPA 76, 83
Technical Guidelines on Environmentally Sound E-Waste Management for Collectors, Collection Centers, Transporters, Treatment Facilities, and Final Disposal 179
technical, innovations 2
technological: advancement 1; developments 61
technology 1–4, 6–7, 30, 35, 37–39, 41–42, 60–61, 68, 70, 77, 79, 88–89, 93–95, 98, 100–101, 104–106, 108, 110–111, 113, 123, 126, 129, 136–137, 140–141, 145, 147–150, 154, 156, 158–159, 161, 166–167, 170, 173, 175–178, 180; affordable 7; development 6; digital 1; growth of 2; hazardous 79; indigenous 105; inefficient 35; information 2; innovative 88, 100; obsoleteness of 4; pre-processing 88; informal 88; sophisticated 101
Telangana 66, 122–123, 153
telecommunication 2, 9–10, 36; equipment 2, 9–10, 36
telephones 2, 85, 153
television (TV) 13, 15, 24, 75, 96, 136–138, 177
terbium 73–74
TERI-BCSD 72, 156
TERI report 151
textile sector 49
Thailand 56; National Integrated Strategy for the Management of WEEE 56
thallium 89
tin 41, 74, 76, 78–79, 89
toxic: additives 4; substances 25, 29, 79; waste 4, 28, 65
toxicity 2, 4, 16, 31, 39–40, 52, 65, 68–71, 78, 80, 82–90, 94, 101, 141, 146, 148, 167, 171; types of 16
Toxicity Characterisation Leaching Procedure (TCLP) 70
Toxics Link 35, 41, 65, 76, 78–79, 87, 89–90, 115, 121–122, 133, 139–140, 147–148, 151–152, 156, 172; report 172
toxins 39, 68–70, 78, 80, 88–89, 94, 101, 134, 140–141, 147–148
trade 14–15, 26, 28, 38–40, 96, 100, 104, 111, 133, 137, 139, 141–143, 145, 149, 152, 165, 174–176, 179; global 14, 96, 165; illegal 15, 26; internal 14; recycling

40, 143; regional 14; value chain 40, 111, 137, 141–142, 179; stages of 142
trade chain 38–39, 133, 141–143, 149, 174–175; e-waste 39, 142
trainings 33, 145–146, 155
transboundary movements 7–8, 14–16, 24–25, 27–28, 39, 42, 70–71, 110, 134, 147, 179; control of 25, 147; data on 14; hazardous wastes 147; issue of 14; unregulated 71
transparency 57–58, 63, 118–119, 143, 155–156, 170, 173–174
transportation 1, 33, 35, 37, 42, 54, 56, 61–63, 73–74, 88, 99, 116–118, 156, 168, 171, 174, 176
transporters 119
treaties 18–19
treatment 4–7, 19–20, 24, 26, 32–33, 38–43, 49, 54–56, 62–63, 70–71, 73–74, 76–80, 90, 101–102, 111, 113, 117–118, 124–125, 128–129, 134, 166, 174, 176, 179–180; mechanical 78; methods 78
TSR Subramanyam Committee 103
Turkey 12

Uganda 17
UK 15, 17
Ukraine 18
UNEMG 33
UNEP 28, 70, 88, 95–96, 136; manual 137
UNICEF 33
UNIDO 33
United Nations Environment Management Group (UNEMG) 1, 33–34, 73–74
United Nations Environment Programme (UNEP) 8, 28, 50, 68, 70, 74, 88, 94–96, 98, 101–102, 136–138; *Assessing the environmental impacts of consumption and production: Priority products and materials* 70; *Inventory Assessment Manual* 8; *Recycling–from e-waste to resources* 95
United Nations (UN) 1–2, 9, 31, 33–34, 52, 59, 68; collaborations and partnerships by 33; initiatives by 31, 33; types of 33; initiatives for e-waste management 31
United Nations (UN) initiatives 31, 34
United Nations University (UNU) 8–9, 31, 33, 128
United States: Electronics Action Plan 17; Sustainable Materials Management (SMM) 17
United States Environment Protection Agency 17

United States of America (USA) 2, 10–11, 13, 15–17, 29, 34, 37, 87, 135, 138, 147, 171; e-waste generation in 11, 15; National Strategy for Electronics Stewardship framework 17; Resource Conservation and Recovery Act 17; Sustainable Materials Management (SMM) 17
UNU-ViE SCYCLE 31
urban local bodies (ULBs) 171–173, 180
urban mining 7, 31, 99–100, 102–104; costs of 99–100; organised 99
urban poor 40, 143
urban solid waste 32
Uruguay 17, 27
Uttarakhand 123, 151
Uttar Pradesh 36, 90, 123–125, 127, 143, 160
Uttar Pradesh Pollution Control Board (UPPCB) 124, 127

vaporization 80
Vietnam 12, 17, 56–57; Draft Regulations 56
voluntary consensus sustainability standard (VCSS) 157, 161, 180

Waigani Convention 27
washing machine 1, 96
waste 1–21, 24–43, 49–66, 68–81, 87–90, 93–105, 108–129, 133–161, 165–181; bio-medical 4; commercial 56; in environmentally friendly manner of 2; complex 4; construction 4; continuum 103; definition of 8; disposal of 2, 5, 18, 24, 98; electronic 2, 4, 8, 110–111, 128, 172; generation 2–3, 6, 9–13, 19, 24, 28, 30, 32, 34–36, 39, 41, 43, 51, 125, 136–138, 147–148, 150, 179; hazardous 4, 14, 24–25, 27–28, 32–33, 42, 68, 109–113, 124, 127, 129, 147, 149, 151, 169, 177; hierarchy 18, 24; illegal activity 15; liquid 4; management 2, 5–7, 9, 11–20, 24–25, 30–35, 37–42, 49–50, 52–53, 56, 58–59, 62–64, 70, 75, 95, 97–98, 101–102, 108–112, 115–116, 118–119, 122–123, 125, 128–129, 133–134, 136, 141, 145, 147–148, 150–154, 156–161, 165–170, 172–175, 178–180; minimisation of 2, 5; mix 15; movements of 24; municipal 2, 5, 79, 102; packaging 51–52; preparation for reuse 19; prevention of 19; radioactive 27; residential 56; residual 11, 98; shipping of

24; solid 2, 4–5, 32, 56, 79, 102, 109, 127, 154, 172; toxic 4, 28, 65; transboundary movement of 7–8, 14–16, 24, 27–28, 39, 42, 70–71, 134, 179; treatment of 32; types of 169
waste disposal 39, 56, 79, 102, 105, 108, 119–120, 152, 156, 173; methods of 79
Waste Electrical and Electronic Equipment (WEEE) 4–5, 7–9, 14–15, 17, 19–20, 24, 26, 29, 35, 39–42, 55–58, 68, 82, 90, 100, 102, 113–114, 129, 133–137, 149, 154, 178; categories of 8, 19; composition of 68; disposal of 5; import of 15; management of 5, 154; treatment of 5
Waste Extraction Test (WET) 70
waste management 2, 5–7, 9, 11–20, 24–25, 30–35, 37–42, 49–50, 52–53, 56, 58–59, 62–64, 70, 75, 95, 97–98, 101–102, 108–112, 115–116, 118–119, 122–123, 125, 128–129, 133–134, 136, 141, 145, 147–148, 150–154, 156–161, 165–170, 172–175, 178–180; categories 9; curative 13; EPR for 52; framework of 5–6; hierarchy 5; legislation 25; strategy 98, 118; transfer of 53; types of 49
WEEE assessment study 137

WEEE Directives 7–9, 17, 19–20, 24, 26, 42, 58, 129, 134–135, 178; Directive 67/548/EEC 21; Directive 2002/95/EC 22; Directive 2011/65 EU 22; Directive 2011/65 / EU 22; Directive 2015/863 21; implementation of 26
WEEELabex 176
West Bengal 36, 123
Western Africa 18
Western Asia 12
Western Europe 12
workers 5–7, 14, 16, 18, 29, 42, 69, 78–81, 89, 93, 96, 118–119, 142–145, 148, 150, 152, 154–155, 158–159, 161, 172–176, 179, 181; conditions of 14; exposed 5, 69; impact on 16; informal 144, 155, 158; protection of 29, 94; recycling 18, 80; rights 148–149, 155; violation of 149; working conditions 7, 93, 148, 150, 175
World Bank Group 151
World Economic Forum (WEF) 2, 4, 11, 74, 96, 98; report 2

Zambia 16–17

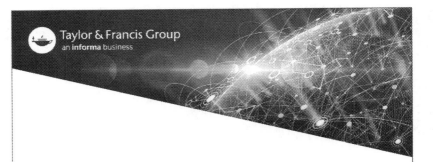

Printed in the United States
by Baker & Taylor Publisher Services